MOTHER OF THE REDEEMER

MOTHER OF THE REDEEMER

Aspects of Doctrine and Devotion

Lectures of Maynooth Union Summer School

EDITED BY

KEVIN McNAMARA

Professor of Dogmatic Theology, St. Patrick's College, Maynooth

SHEED & WARD, INC. — NEW YORK

1960

Library of Congress Catalog Card Number: 60-7308

𝔑𝔦𝔥𝔦𝔩 𝔒𝔟𝔰𝔱𝔞𝔱:
                    EDUARDUS GALLEN,
                              Censor Theol. Deput.

𝔍𝔪𝔭𝔯𝔦𝔪𝔦 𝔓𝔬𝔱𝔢𝔰𝔱:
              ✠ IOANNES CAROLUS,
                         Archiep. Dublinen.,
                                    Hiberniæ Primas.

        Dublini, *die 1a Maii, anno* 1959.

                          M. H. Gill & Son Ltd., Dublin, 1959.

        Manufactured in the United States of America

CONTENTS

INTRODUCTION

This book contains the text of twelve lectures delivered to a
group of priests attending a Summer School in Mariology held
by the Maynooth Union at St. Patrick's College, Maynooth,
from 29 June to 3 July, 1958. The course of lectures was
planned in honour of the Lourdes Centenary Year, and it is
with the intention of providing a more permanent memorial of
this occasion, as well as in the hope of benefiting a wider audience, that the lectures are now being made available in book
form. Apart from the addition of footnotes and bibliographical material and the elimination, in so far as this was possible, of
overlapping, the lectures are here presented with very little
change from their original form.

The object of the course was to enable priests to revise and
bring up to date their knowledge of a part of theology which has
developed rapidly in recent decades. The emphasis throughout
was on presenting a solid theological basis for the unique rôle
accorded to Our Blessed Lady in Catholic belief. In carrying
out this task the lecturers were conscious of the pastoral pre-
occupations of the majority of their hearers and made it their
aim, in so far as an adequate treatment of the subject-matter
permitted, to avoid the more abstract reaches of theological discussion and the intricacies of exegetical controversy. It will be
readily understood, however, that any serious consideration of
the Old Testament teaching on Our Lady would have been
quite impossible without a close and patient exegesis of the
relevant texts; while the discussions evoked by recent specula-
tions concerning the meaning of Our Lady's virginity in childbirth seemed to demand that on this point also, in so far as
was possible within the limits of a single lecture, the evidence
should be carefully sifted with a view to evaluating the true
significance of the relevant patristic statements and ecclesiastical
documents. Elsewhere the discussion generally moves along
broader lines, though the temptation to over-simplify or to do

less than justice to the demands of strict theological method is
resisted throughout. The rival views on the main controverted
points are carefully and fairly presented and adequate reasons
given wherever a writer has, even tentatively, expressed a
preference in disputed matters.

Given the circumstances of its origin, it will scarcely be
necessary to remark that this volume is not intended to fill the
part of a handbook or formal treatise of Mariology. Notwithstanding the wide range of mariological topics covered in the
lectures, the reader who desires to study the inner structure and
organization of the theological treatise *De Beata Maria Virgine,*
and to place this treatise correctly within the general frame-
work of theology, will find it necessary to supplement the
knowledge gained in these pages by having recourse to a
modern mariological textbook or encyclopaedia. Fortunately
such a work, measuring up to the highest standards of present-
day mariological writing, is now being made available in English under the general editorship of Juniper B. Carol, O.F.M.
The second volume of this work *(Mariology,* Milwaukee, 1957)
contains an excellent survey of these introductory questions by
the distinguished Jesuit theologian, Cyril Vollert.

The reader who has already some acquaintance with Mariology will have little difficulty, however, in perceiving in the
present volume indications of the main characteristic trends in
mariological studies in recent times. Throughout the lectures
Our Lady and her privileges are presented in the closest relationship to the Person of her divine Son. This is in complete
accord with the reaction against an isolated and practically
independent Mariology which has been so prominent a feature
of the work of twentieth century mariologists and is continuing
to have far-reaching effects on the shape and content of the
treatise on Our Lady. This treatise is today becoming ever
more successfully integrated with other departments of theology, in sharp contrast to the jejune and scarcely scientific
Mariology which was so much in vogue in the eighteenth and
up to the concluding decades of the nineteenth century. In
that period progress was measured chiefly in terms of new
honours and titles vindicated for the Mother of God; and
while it would be altogether wrong to decry such activity or to

suggest that it has not an important and abiding place in the programme of the mariologist, it was all too commonly carried on at the periphery of the theological synthesis and by the application of general laws or axioms which were not flexibly enough interpreted to allow for God's sovereign freedom in fashioning Mary's destiny.

Today, however, Mary's place by the side of her Son at the centre of God's redemptive plan is being ever more thoroughly vindicated, with a consequent enrichment not merely of Mariology but of theology as a whole. The inner life of the Trinity, to each of whose Persons Mary is united by an intimate and special relationship; the meaning of redemption, especially in what concerns human co-operation in God's saving plan; God's loving concern for the human race as shown forth in a new way in her who is the Mother and Associate of the divine Redeemer and the spiritual Mother of His Mystical Body; the Church of Christ as co-operating in and reflecting the spiritual maternity of Our Lady, and as moving towards a destiny which is already anticipated in an eminent degree by the Immaculate Virgin assumed into heaven; the meaning of maternity and the place of woman in the divine plan of creation and salvation—these are some of the important theological questions on which new light is being thrown by contemporary studies in Mariology. While the following chapters provide formal treatment of only one or two of these questions, the portrait of Mary which they present is sketched against the background of this general scheme of ideas, thus gaining considerably in perspective and in clarity of outline.

A few concluding remarks may not be out of place on recent discussions concerning "the fundamental principle of Mariology." Many mariologists today, concerned with the task of constructing a more scientific Mariology, are seeking to formulate some fundamental thesis concerning Our Lady from which the whole series of Marian doctrines can be deduced, or round which, at least, it can be systematically organized. The divine maternity, Mary as the New Eve, as Mother of the Whole Christ, as the most perfectly redeemed of all human kind, as image or type of the Church: these are but some of the proposals advanced to solve this problem. Keen discussion of the question is likely to continue, but if one may judge by results so far nothing is likely to emerge from the debate which will call for any departure from the traditional idea that Mary's divine motherhood forms the ultimate foundation of all her privileges and the key to an understanding of her many-sided rôle in the economy of salvation. Mary is the Mother of Christ, and Christ is God—hence her unparalleled gifts of grace and unique dignity among God's creatures.

This does not mean, however, that all Mary's privileges can be rigorously deduced from her divine maternity considered as an abstract relationship, that is to say, apart from the strong light which is thrown on it by the redemptive mission of her Son and the part which she herself was called to play in that mission in the eternal and free designs of the Creator. Revelation assures us that Mary, as Mother of the Redeemer, was to enter fully into the redemptive purposes of her Son; that her divine motherhood, in the concrete, is a redemptive motherhood, bringing in its train a whole series of consequences intimately associated with the various aspects of her Son's victory over sin through his Passion and bodily Resurrection. It is the function of the theologian, guided by the divinely-enlightened and infallible Magisterium, to reflect upon the vocation of the Mother of God as presented to us in its entirety in the revealed deposit; to ponder, analyze and correlate the many facets of her destiny and discover their evidences in Scripture and Tradition; to develop his reflections along the lines of progress marked out in advance by the Magisterium, and—chief among his tasks—to show how the doctrines proposed by the Church for the belief of the faithful are contained in the original deposit. In carrying out this task he must be on his guard lest, by relying on a kind of reasoning that is insufficiently attuned to divine revelation, he be led astray by abstract and *a priori* considerations of what is necessary or fitting. He must make it his concern to be guided at every stage by the inner logic of the revealed message, by the consistent and harmonious pattern of the divine plan concerning Mary, communicated to men in the revelation of Christ. In this way, as he deepens his understanding of God's decrees eternally predestining Mary and her mission, he will attain with each new insight a more adequate notion of the divine maternity; he will see how all other graces and privileges of Mary have been decreed by God in consideration of this her primary dignity and fundamental ministry. While he may not hope to deduce from it the entire Marian synthesis, he can with good reason accept it as the fundamental principle of Mariology, as the point which polarizes all his reflections and, by that very fact, guarantees to the various propositions established by him cohesion, unity and order.

It only remains for me to express my warm thanks to those of my colleagues in St. Patrick's College, Maynooth, who shared in the labour of reading the proofs, and to those students of the College who helped with the typing and with the preparation of the Index of Persons.

KEVIN McNAMARA.

Our Lady in the Old Testament—I

By P. G. Duncker, O.P.

IT will cause no surprise that a Summer School devoted to the study of Our Lady should open with a discussion of the teaching on Our Lady in sacred Scripture. The Scriptures are one of the twin sources of divine Revelation and, inasmuch as they are directly the Word of God, the more important source. Since, however, the Old Testament contains very little about Our Lady, it may be asked why two lectures are devoted to it, while only one is allotted to the New Testament, and to each of the particular mariological themes to be treated in the course. The answer is that the few Old Testament texts concerning Our Lady have been the object of so much discussion that it would be impossible to give a fair idea of the present state of the question concerning them in a single lecture. And I am grateful to the committee in charge of the Summer School for allowing me to divide the matter over two lectures.

In this lecture I intend to explain modern exegesis of Gen. iii:15.

We certainly cannot expect non-Catholic authors to give very much support to a Marian interpretation of this text. In a very recent article Cazelles mentions works of various writers on the subject, all of whom restrict the interpretation of our verse to a desperate struggle between men and serpents, or, at most, between man and evil; and he cites only one Protestant author who finds a messianic reference in the text.[1] However, there are still quite a number of Protestants, chiefly of the traditional " orthodox " variety—in my own native country of Holland, for example—who strongly defend the messianism of Gen. iii:15. But none of them admits in it any reference to Our Lady.

[1] H. Cazelles, " Genèse iii:15. Exegèse contemporaine," in: *La Nouvelle Ève (Bulletin de la Société Française d'Études Mariales)*, 2 (1957), 91-93. He reviews the more important publications on the subject from 1950 onwards.

Turning to Catholic interpretations of Gen. iii:15, we may assert that theologians and exegetes, generally speaking, agree that some reference to Our Lady is to be found in the text.   This is particularly true of the recent studies of the problem that have appeared in the wake of the definition of the dogma of the Assumption and of the Marian Year.

Though there is no official declaration *ex cathedra*, it is the common teaching of the Church that in Gen. iii:15 the complete victory of Our Lady over the devil is announced: in this sense the text receives the name *Protoevangelium*. Recently it has been very forcibly argued that this teaching is proposed in the Bull *Ineffabilis Deus* of 1854.

In the final session of the Mariological Congress held in Rome in 1954, Father Bea maintained:

(1) That Pius IX intended to use Gen. iii:15 and Lk. ii:28 as proper, conclusive scriptural arguments, because the Fathers of the Church and the ecclesiastical doctors intended to teach (*docuerunt*) the mariological sense of both texts;

(2) That the Pope not only referred to this doctrine of Tradition explaining Scripture, but also himself *nomine proprio* declared that the most holy Virgin has crushed the head of the serpent;

(3) That we are here faced with an authentic christological and mariological, though not solemnly defined and infallible interpretation of Gen. iii:15 proposed by the *Magisterium ordinarium Ecclesiae* and demanding the assent of the faithful;

(4) That such a papal declaration has its own proper authority, since the Church " is by divine decree the interpreter and custodian of sacred Scripture, the depository of Tradition living within her; she is the gateway to salvation, herself a source from which she may derive the truth, under the protection and guidance of the Holy Spirit."[2]

However, even though the teaching of the Church demands that we take account of the mariological meaning of Gen.

[2] A. Bea, S.J., " Bulla *Ineffabilis Deus* et Hermeneutica Biblica," in *Virgo Immaculata, Acta Congressus Mariologici-Mariani Romae Anno MCMLIV Celebrati*, 3, *De Immaculata Conceptione in Sacra Scriptura*, Rome, 1955, 2 ff. For the text quoted cf. pp. 7, 8.

iii:15, it is still an open question in what way Our Lady is mentioned. For, as Father Bea too admits, the Pope in his Bull has in no way indicated the precise biblical sense in which a reference to Mary is to be found in our text. [3]

The various mariological interpretations of Gen. iii:15 nowadays proposed can be summarized as follows: Our Lady is directly intended in the literal sense; Our Lady is indirectly intended according to the so-called *sensus plenior*, being either understood together with Eve, or included with Christ in the seed of the woman; Eve is to be regarded as the "type" of Mary. [4] Since, however, both the *sensus plenior* and the *sensus typicus* presuppose the literal sense, it is this latter that we propose to examine in the light of modern publications.

Gen. iii:15 is part of the Yahweh Elohim's judgement on the serpent. We must take for granted here that this serpent represents the evil spirit, the demonic power, in later pages of the Bible called Shatan (adversary), which in the Septuagint is translated by *diabolos*, whence the Latin *diabolus* and our "devil." All Catholics unanimously hold this interpretation and a number of non-Catholics agree with us on the point.

In the first part of the verse the serpent is addressed; the second part has the expression " seed of the serpent "; in the third part the serpent is again spoken of. " Seed of the serpent " is a mere figure of speech and the devil is meant. The evil spirit, a demonic power, has no seed as our sacred author knew full well; he merely uses this expression, as Rigaux rightly, I think, observed, to have a counterpart to the expression " seed of the woman." [5] There is practically no distinction between the serpent and the seed; both represent the same evil spirit, demonic power, the devil. [6]

---

[3] Loc. cit., 10.

[4] These various interpretations are best expounded by V. J. Bertelli, " L'Interpretazione mariologica del Protovangelo negli esegeti e teologi dopo la Bulla *Ineffabilis Deus*," *Marianum*, 13 (1951), 257-291, 369-395. A summary of the opinions of 166 authors from 1859 till 1948.

[5] B. Rigaux, O.F.M., " La Femme et son lignage dans Genèse iii:14-15," *Revue Biblique*, 61 (1954), 340.

[6] The opinion, proposed by some authors, that the wicked, sometimes called " sons of the devil " (cf. Jo. viii:44; Acts xiii:10; also Mt. iii:17, xxiii:33), are the seed of the serpent, must be rejected on account of the context, which supposes the opposition between man and the demonic power, and also because the wicked are to be considered rather the victims of the devil.

To this is first opposed the woman and then the seed of the woman, and a third time again the seed of the woman.

This last assertion cannot seriously be called in question. The Hebrew *hu'*, a masculine pronoun, is properly speaking a personal pronoun, but very often used as a demonstrative one. In the context it refers to the masculine noun *zera'*, meaning seed. The Septuagint renders this word by the neuter *sperma* but the pronoun by *autos* (masculine) which is not grammatically correct; we should expect *auto* (neuter). The Vulgate has *ipsa* which is certainly wrong; though in the new critical Vulgate edition *ipsa* remains, since the editors thought it St. Jerome's original reading.[7]

There is question in our text of enmity between the serpent on the one hand and, first the woman, then the seed of the woman on the other; in the final clause of the sentence both the seed of the woman and the serpent are said to do something, the one with regard to the head of the serpent, and the other with regard to the heel of the seed of the woman. I deliberately rendered the meaning of the last part of our text in such a vague way because a difficulty has to be solved before we are able to give the exact reading, if this be at all possible.

It may suffice here to say this: the difficulty concerns the exact reading of the Hebrew verb *shuf*, which, according to the Massoretic text occurs twice in this part of the sentence, each time in a different form. In the Septuagint to these two forms of the Hebrew *shuf* correspond two forms of the Greek verb *tēreo* (to observe, to lie in wait). In the Douay version, however, which through the Latin Vulgate goes back to the Hebrew text, we find first, " to crush," then " to lie in wait." How is this to be explained? According to the use of the verb *shuf* in the Hebrew text of Job ix:17—in Ps. cxxxix:11, the sole other passage in which the verb occurs in the Hebrew Bible, it has to be corrected to another one—and in comparison with other semitic languages, the proper meaning of the verb *shuf* seems to be " to crush," so that we would have to translate: " it (the seed of the woman) shall crush thy head,

[7] Cf. H. Quentin, *Biblia Sacra iuxta Latinam Vulgatam Editionem*; *Genesis*, Rome, 1926, 151; idem, *Essai de critique textuelle*, Paris, 1926, 113.

and thou shalt crush its heel." This, of course would be rather difficult for a serpent to do, so that the phrase means that the serpent is trying to wound the seed of the woman at its heel, even gravely and mortally. However, it is possible that two different verbs *shuf* are intended, the one meaning " to crush," the other a later simplified form of the Hebrew verb *sha'af, shafaf* meaning " to snap " or " to snatch at " and, consequently, " to lie in wait." [8]

After all this one will readily admit that it is difficult to give an exact rendering of both verbs in Gen. iii:15. Yet, this exact rendering is not absolutely necessary in order to grasp the real meaning of the sentence. The position of the seed of the woman is undoubtedly much more favourable than that of the serpent; for, even if the serpent would have some success in its attempt to reach the heel of the seed of the woman in order to wound the seed mortally, yet before it can do so the seed of the woman aiming at the head of the serpent will be able to crush it.

The construction of the sentence confirms this: first of the seed of the woman it is said that it will crush or try to crush the head of the serpent; then of the serpent that it will snatch at the heel of the seed of the woman; hence the seed of the woman is presented as on the attack and the serpent as on the defence. The evidence for this is still stronger if we understand the Hebrew *waw*, which unites the two members of the phrase, as having adversative value: the seed of the woman will crush or try to crush the head of the serpent but, to defend itself, the serpent will aim at its heel. Hence the position of the two combatants supposes and insinuates the superiority of the seed of the woman, and, consequently, its final success. This is, moreover, strongly corroborated by the context. Our phrase is part of one of the three sentences of judgement passed on the three actors of the drama of the Garden of Eden. Each of them is found and declared guilty, and punished. But there would be no real punishment of the serpent if the seed of the woman did not finally defeat it. In addition, it is to be noted, as many have already pointed

[8] Cf. Koehler-Baumgartner, *Lexicon in Veteris Testamenti Libros*, Leiden, 1953; also P. Dhorme, *Le Livre de Job*, Paris, 1926, 123.

out, that the punishment in the three condemnatory sentences is executed, not only by God, but also by the victim of the culprit: man by the land that for his sake is cursed; the woman by her husband, who will now dominate over her; and, consequently, the serpent by the seed of the woman, who, seduced by it, will now defeat it. In Gen. iii:15 there is no question of punishment of the woman, but by means of her seed she takes revenge on the serpent for having seduced her.[9]

So far we have seen that the enmity put by God between the serpent and the woman, between its seed and hers, will end in a final victory of the seed of the woman as a punishment for the serpent. But the chief points have still to be dealt with: who are the woman and the seed of the woman?

If we look at the context, there seems to be question all through of one and the same woman, later, in Gen. iii:20, called Eve. She is the one given to man as his helpmate, and primarily as his wife to procreate with him the human race. She is seduced by the serpent, and seduces in her turn her husband. Together they try to hide themselves from God, but He calls them from their hiding-place. Summoned by God to give an account, man puts the blame on the woman, and she on the serpent. Hence, when God judges and condemns the serpent, putting enmity between it and the woman, one would readily expect that the same woman is intended, all the more so since the Hebrew word *ha'ishshah* has the definite article, which usually refers to what has already been spoken of. A great many Catholic authors, therefore, maintain that there must be surely question of Eve in Gen. iii:15, and that it would be a defiance of the most elementary rules of exegesis to exclude her.[10]

Presupposing that Eve is the woman intended, one would be induced to consider the seed of the woman in the second member of our text as the human race, mankind, for: (1) seed taken metaphorically as posterity, offspring, issue, is commonly

---

[9] Cf. Rigaux, loc. cit., 338.

[10] Cf. Rigaux, loc. cit., 344, referring to A. Robert, " La Sainte Vierge dans l'Ancien Testament," *Maria* (ed. du Manoir), 1, Paris, 1949, 35.

used in the collective sense: (2) in the text "seed of the woman" stands in parallelism with "seed of the serpent," which latter phrase suggests a collectivity of evil spirits, though, as a figure of speech, it merely represents the demonic power; (3) a few verses later (Gen. iii:20) the woman is called Eve, precisely because mother of all the living. If, however, seed of the woman in the second part of the text is to be understood as Eve's posterity, the human race, mankind, it seems only logical to give it the same meaning in the third and last part, where the pronoun used undoubtedly refers to the seed of the woman.

Yet, against this seemingly obvious interpretation of the woman and her seed some serious criticism can be made.

We said that seed as posterity, offspring, issue, is commonly used in the collective sense, but it occurs also, and rather frequently, in the Old Testament to designate an individual; we have already a very striking example in Gen. iv:26, where Eve, having given birth to another son, called his name Seth, saying: "God hath given me another seed, for Abel whom Cain slew." And it may be noted too that in this and in all the other examples that can be offered, seed is always meant to be a son, never a daughter.[11]

Now, in the last part of Gen. iii:15, the seed of the woman is not opposed to the seed of the serpent, but, as in the beginning of the sentence, to the serpent itself as an individual. According to the law of parallelism the seed of the woman as an individual would surely fit in better; the individual serpent would then be defeated by an individual (masculine) opponent belonging to the human race. The masculine *autos* of the Septuagint, though grammatically wrong, favours this individual interpretation, at least for the time the Greek translation was made, the third century B.C., and may well be the expression of much older Jewish tradition. Finally, the whole narrative of Paradise and the fall of man is, also by many Catholics, attributed to the Yahwistic tradition, which from the state of oral transmission was put down in writing about the ninth century B.C. At that time the

[11] Cf. J. Coppens, "Le Protoevangile. Un nouvel essai d'exégèse," *Ephem. Theol. Lov.*, 26 (1950), 16, 17.

promises given by God to Abraham, Isaac, and Jacob, speaking of a blessing in which all the nations of the world would participate, and likewise the prophecies of Jacob and Balaam, pointing to a future ruler, were surely well known. The Yahwistic author writing down such oral traditions when composing Gen. ii and iii, where he very profoundly explains the problem of evil in the world, and understands that Satan, the superhuman cause and instigator of it, will eventually be defeated by the seed of the woman he seduced, very likely intended this seed to be that of the future ruler, attaching thus an individual and messianic sense to it. This consideration, which I have briefly outlined, is amply developed and strongly urged by Coppens, and still more by Rigaux who comes to these conclusions: (1) the serpent is the demon; (2) the seed of the woman denotes the Messias; (3) the enmity terminates with the crushing, i.e. with the expulsion of the demon and the establishment of all God's rights in the eschatological future.[12]

With regard to the woman herself we observed that she should be Eve, the woman who is spoken of in the context, and to whom the definite article attached to the Hebrew word seems to point, since the definite article usually refers to a person or thing already dealt with. But it must be remembered that in Hebrew the definite article has a much wider use.[13] It may e.g. mark a species or class of things or persons and a good example is offered in Eccles. vii:2: " I have found a woman (with the article) more bitter than death."

To this use of the article Coppens has lately called attention. Referring to Gen. ii:23-4, where the woman given by God as a helpmate to man is called *ishshah* because taken out of *ish* (man), and man (*ish*) is said to leave his father and mother in order to cleave to his wife (*ishto*), he observes that in the latter sentence there is surely no question of Adam and Eve, but a general rule applying to every man and woman contracting a marriage; whereas in the former sentence a general pronouncement is made concerning not only Eve, but every

---

[12] Rigaux, loc. cit., 340-343.
[13] Cf. e.g. Gesenius-Kautzsch, *Hebräische Grammatik*, 27th ed., Leipzig, 1902, par. 126, and P. Jouon, S.J., *Grammaire de l'Hébreu biblique*, Rome, 1923, par. 137.

woman, since they are all called *ishshah*, as the constant usage in the biblical Hebrew clearly proves. As in those sentences, so also in Gen. iii:15, woman in general would be intended, the whole female sex. And to those objecting that in Gen. ii:23-4 the definite article is not used, Coppens replies that a species or class of persons or things occurs in Hebrew either with the definite article or without it; and that the article before " woman " in Gen. iii:15 could even be so understood as to determine the woman in general, the female sex, spoken of in Gen. ii:23-4. He further points out that *ha'ishshah* has this general meaning, not in the strictly narrative sections of Gen. ii and iii, but merely and precisely in those three texts (Gen. ii:23, 24; iii:15), each of them a kind of oracle; and he concludes by contending that the sacred author, though designating with the woman of Gen. iii:15 the whole female sex, all women, yet had particularly in view some of them, by way of antonomasia or excellence:

> . . . undoubtedly (he had in mind) Eve, the woman of the narrative, with whom the enmity had originated; also—and especially—in view of the accent put in the last stichus on the posterity, on the final combat and victory, the Woman called to give birth to the Victor . . . The Mother of the Saviour would thus appear as viewed not formally, but indirectly; she is connoted, and this not in the seed nor in Eve, but as mother of the seed in the term *'ishshah*, comprising the whole female sex. [14]

Rigaux agrees with this opinion only up to a certain point. He rejects Coppens's interpretation of the woman in Gen. iii:15 as representing all women, of whom some are more particularly intended and Mary principally, though according to the *sensus litteralis plenior*. But Rigaux admits that Gen. ii:23, 24 does not designate Eve *tout court*, but every woman; we must even say that right through Gen. ii and iii both Adam and Eve, though considered as individuals, at the same time represent the whole human race, every man and woman, not merely by being their first parents, but still more because

---

[14] Coppens, loc. cit., 26-32; the texts quoted are on p. 31 and p. 30.

every human being experiences their concupiscence and shame, their sin and alienation from God, their pains and sufferings:

> If thus "the woman" can take a wider sense than Eve-individual, the term appears to be well chosen to give to Eve denoted by "the woman" a value and a rôle that surpass Eve wife of Adam and first sinner. Eve defeated shall one day be victorious.

For we surely have to consider Gen. iii:15 as an oracle. Together with the following verses 16-19 it is singled out from the context by rhythmic prose; and just as the punishment of the woman in v. 16 and of the man in vv. 17-19 is for all times, so the enmity with the devil does not terminate with Eve, but is projected into the future pointing to the final victory of the Messias. Moreover, according to the Yahwistic tradition of Genesis, women like Sara, Rebecca, Rachel, in the biblical history of salvation and redemption, have been associated with men, chiefs of families or tribes, who themselves are pictured with the significance and importance of their descendants and groups. It would in no way be surprising, therefore, but rather to be expected that the sacred author, in keeping with that tradition, when writing about Eve in Gen. iii:15, should think of her principally in relation to the future Messias,

> as representing, in the struggle against him who has introduced evil into the world, that supreme force of God availing himself of her who has introduced disobedience, in order to link her up with the author of salvation,

viz. as the mother giving birth to Him; for

> Eve, who in Gen. iii:15 appears only in view of the posterity, is carried into the future precisely by the destiny of her descendant.

And Rigaux concludes:

> Summing up, if in Gen. iii:14-15 we have an eschatological and messianic oracle of a unique spiritual value by the loftiness of its conception and the force of its denouement; if, on the

other hand, the woman must be joined to man in the struggle and victory unto redemption as she is united to man in sin and fall unto abasement, then we cannot demand a clearer indication authorizing us to connect the Messias with that woman who will be for him woman in the rôle of mother, and to perceive in this first hymn of divine victory the primary glimmer of a revelation that goes on specifying itself. [15]

According to Rigaux Gen. iii:15 designates Mary in the strict literal sense. [16]

I am very much aware that I have not done full justice to Rigaux's interpretation of Gen. iii:15; one should oneself read his whole article. If I have tried in this paper to propose precisely his ideas on the matter in hand, and also those advanced by Coppens, it is because they both have approached our much-debated subject from a new, more scientific and modern point of view, offering observations and arguments that previously had hardly ever been touched upon [17] and had never been developed so extensively and cogently.

A Catholic exegete must surely be guided by the other source of divine Revelation, viz. sacred Tradition, and by the authentic declarations of the *Magisterium Ecclesiae*; consequently, the common teaching of the Church on Gen. iii:15 obliges him to take account of its messianic and mariological sense. But by this he is not dispensed from examining a biblical passage in a properly scientific way, since the Holy Scriptures are composed by sacred authors who, apart from divine inspiration, wrote like all the profane authors: according to their own mentality, outlook and ability, with all their human, intellectual and literary qualities, subject to and influenced by the ideas, views, and conceptions common to their own surroundings and current among the people of their own time and nation.

" Philology and literary criticism, text and context, are the working instruments of an exegete," Rigaux rightly

---

[15] Rigaux, loc. cit., 343-348; the texts quoted are on p. 346, p. 347, and p. 348.
[16] Loc. cit., 326-338.
[17] Rigaux, loc. cit., 329, n. 1, refers to A. M. Dubarle, *Les Sages d'Israel* (Lectio Divina, 1) Paris, 1946, 9-13, and to J. Guitton, *Le Développement des idées dans l'Ancien Testament*, Aix-en-Provence, 1947, 111-130.

observes, adding that theologians unanimously and exegetes to a great extent have too much isolated Gen. iii:15.[18]

Both Coppens and Rigaux follow the theory proposed by de Vaux [19] that old traditions about Paradise and the Fall of man were put down into writing towards the ninth century B.C. But these traditions certainly did not go back to the time man appeared on the earth, some 100,000 years before ! Nor can it reasonably be maintained that, apart from the great religious truths and facts undoubtedly contained in Gen. ii and iii, all the particulars about Adam and Eve—their names, their way of living and acting, the whole description of Paradise with the names of the trees and the rivers, etc.— have been revealed by God. It is the sacred author who composed the narrative, who made God pronounce the judgement in Gen. iii:15. And a diligent enquiry about this author, about the Yahwistic tradition of which he was an exponent, about the national and religious ideas and aspirations of his time and of the people he lived among, and whom he primarily wrote for, brought Coppens and Rigaux to the understanding of Gen. iii:15 as explained above. Their great merit is to have endeavoured to show that a strictly scientific, viz. philological and literary-critical study of the text and its context will lead to a messianic and mariological interpretation of Gen. iii:15, inasmuch as the sacred author himself intended both the Messias and his Mother, though as yet in a vague way, surely not realizing that he was pointing to Our Lord and Our Lady, a fact which only later revelation made known.

Of course their interpretation stands or falls with their outlook on the author and his time. Difficulties remain, which only further study can solve; but these scholars seem to be on the right track.

[18] Rigaux, loc. cit., 328.
[19] R. de Vaux, O.P., *La Sainte Bible*, Jerusalem, 1956, 3-8.

Our Lady in the Old Testament—II

By P. G. Duncker, O.P.

OUR second lecture will deal with the other Old Testament passages concerning Our Lady. The first of them is Isaias vii:14 about the " virgin " conceiving and bearing a child to whom she shall give the name Emmanuel. Quite a number of non-Catholic authors admit the messianic character of this text, and even in a certain way the virginity of the child's mother, though they do not acknowledge any relation to the Blessed Virgin.

All Catholics agree that according to the common teaching of the Church there must be some reference to Our Lord and Our Lady in our text, either in the literal or typical sense, as a pontifical document of the year 1779, condemning I. L. Isenbiehl's attempt at a new explanation of Is. vii:14, has expressly declared.[1]

The literature on the subject is immense.[2] Let us here examine the text according to the more recent publications that throw some light on the matter.

First a few words on the historical context. In the year 734 B.C. Syria and Israel were preparing to invade Juda. The latter did not want to join with them against the common enemy Assyria; they planned, therefore, to overthrow the Davidic dynasty, to dethrone its king Achaz, and to substitute one of their friends, the son of a certain Tabeel, on whose support they could depend. Isaias received an order from Yahweh to take his son Shear-Yashub—a symbolic name, meaning " a remnant shall return "—and meet Achaz (like his

---

[1] Cf. *Enchiridion Biblicum*, 3rd ed., no. 74.

[2] Apart from the various commentaries there are a great number of articles on the subject of which a list up to 1951 is drawn up by J. Coppens, " La Prophétie de la '*Almah*, Is. vii:14-17", in *Ephem. Theol. Lov.*, 20 (1952), 648-650. More recent publications will be noted in the course of this paper. The latest commentary on Isaias is: Angelo Penna, Can. Reg. Lat., *Isaia* (La Sacra Bibbia—Garofalo) Torino-Roma, 1958.

people very much in fear) at a place south of Jerusalem, where the king was inspecting a water-supply with a view to an eventual siege. The prophet had to assure Achaz not to be afraid, that Syria and Israel were at the end of their power and would not succeed in their plan to overthrow the Davidic dynasty: " Thus saith the Lord: it shall not ensue, it shall not be." Isaias knew too well Nathan's prophecy (2 Sam. vii:10-16), to which he twice alludes (Is. xxxvii:35; xxxviii:5): " that David's dynasty would be established for ever before Yahweh." But the king had to believe, have faith in Yahweh, otherwise he would not be able to save the dynasty from disaster (Is. vii:3-9).

This first prophecy is, in the text, directly followed by a second (from v. 10 onwards); however, some time may have elapsed before it was pronounced, as seems to be suggested by the introductory formula, " And Yahweh spoke again to Achaz," and by the fact that it was addressed to the house of David, which rather supposes the king to be in his palace, and surrounded by his family and court.

Achaz had appeared not to be inclined to put his trust in Yahweh; he preferred to follow his own political views, viz. to invoke the aid of Assyria against Syria and Israel (2 Kings xvi:7), not realizing that he was thus preparing for the common enemy the way to his own country, Juda. So Isaias, profoundly conscious of his divine mission and firmly convinced that Yahweh would never allow the Davidic dynasty to be overthrown, went once more to Achaz for a second and final attempt to make him confide in Yahweh and give up his disastrous policy. Knowing that Yahweh would surely help the king out of his difficulties, if only he would have faith in his God, who was ready to give him whatever pledge he desired of divine assistance, the prophet solemnly conjured him: " Ask thee a sign from Yahweh, thy God, be it in the Sheol below, or in the heavens above." [3]

The Hebrew 'oth, just as the English " sign," has several meanings. According to the context, which supposes the previous prophecy, in our verse it undoubtedly means a divine

---

[3] For similar signs cf. Ex. iv:1-9; Judg. vi:36-40; Is. xxxviii:7, 8.

token: whatever Achaz himself would prefer and select out of the whole realm of creation, even something portentous, a prodigy, a miracle, to convince him that God Himself had spoken through His prophet and to assure him of Yahweh's protection against Syria and Israel, so that they would not overrun his country, would not dethrone him and overthrow his dynasty.

But the king, already determined to appeal to Assyria, excused himself: he will not ask for a sign, he does not want to tempt Yahweh. Whereupon Isaias, reading Achaz aright and knowing that his policy was supported by his family and court, with holy indignation apostrophizes all of them: "Hear ye therefore, house of David: is it not enough for you to weary men (Isaias refers to their attitude towards himself), that you must weary my God as well? (i.e. the God in whom Isaias believed, in whose name he spoke, rejected by them, no longer their God). Therefore, Yahweh himself will give you (in the plural, for the whole house of David, the Davidic dynasty is meant) a sign: " Behold a virgin shall conceive, and shall bring forth a son, and his name shall be called Emmanuel," as the text is rendered by the Douay version according to the Latin Vulgate.

The Hebrew 'almah is very likely from the stem 'lm = to be strong, vigorous, and means a marriageable girl, as the corresponding masculine 'elem denotes a marriageable lad. This is confirmed by the other examples of the word 'almah in the Old Testament;[4] there is no proof that it means a young married woman. Such a girl would, as a rule, be a virgin; and in Gen. xxiv:43 Abraham's servant Eliezer called Rebecca a 'almah, who in v.36 of the same narrative was said to be a betulah. This latter word means only virgin; whereas the former, having a wider sense, normally though not necessarily includes virginity. Neither does the Greek parthenos of the Septuagint translating the Hebrew 'almah necessarily mean virgin, since this word can also have the

---

[4] The texts are Gen. xxiv: 43; Ex. ii:8; Ps. lxviii:26; Prov. xxx:19; Cant. i: 3, vi:8; also Ps. xlvi:1 and 1 Chron. xv:20. As to the last two texts cf. Coppens, loc. cit., 656 f. Prov. xxx:19 seems to refer to the natural inclination of a young man towards a young woman whom he wants as his wife; cf. Gen. ii:24.

wider sense of *'almah*, as has recently been pointed out.[5] Isaias would have used the word *'almah*, because *betulah* excludes the idea of childbearing.

However, lately attention has been called to the fact that the notion of prodigious, divine, even virginal births of a child that would usher in a new era of bliss and prosperity was known, not only in the hellenistic world, but earlier among the Phoenicians, with whom the neighbouring Israelites had already had relations. In particular, it has been pointed out that in the Ugaritic poem of the goddess Nikkal the sentence occurs: " the *galmatu* shall bear a son," that *galmatu* corresponds to the Hebrew *'almah*, and that as parallel to *galmatu* is found *betulat* (virgin). Since the Ugaritic literature could easily have been known to Isaias, and also to the people, at least to the more cultured of those to whom he was speaking, the idea of a virginal birth would not have been too extravagant to the prophet's hearers.[6]

Coppens following Mowinckel's suggestion that *galmatu* originally might have meant a noble marriageable girl, a royal princess, thinks it possible that the Hebrew *'almah* may also have acquired the same meaning.[7]

An English Jesuit, E. Burrows, has proposed the possibility that Isaias, knowing the Ugaritic texts, stripped them of their mythological elements and applied them to certain eschatological and messianic ideas already known in his time from the blessings of Jacob (Gen. xlix:1-27). These, he contends, refer to the signs of the zodiac. Juda, compared to a lion, would be represented by the zodiacal sign of the same name. And in the well known messianic text of the blessing concerning Juda that speaks of the sceptre that will not be taken away from Juda until etc., the difficult *shiloh*, a *crux interpretum*, is understood by Burrows as designating Shela, head of one of Juda's clans, the clan from which David descends, and consequently as designating the ideal king to come; this clan, and particularly the ideal king, would be indicated by the zodiacal sign,

---

[5] G. Delling, " Parthenos " in *Theologisches Wörterbuch zum Neuen Testament*, begründet von Gerhard Kittel, Band 5 (Gerhard Friedrich), 831.

[6] Cf. Coppens in *Ephem. Theol. Lov.*, 1952, 668 ff., who deals with this question and gives ample literature.

[7] Coppens, loc. cit., 670.

Virgin. Hence, when Isaias spoke of the virgin bearing a son, his audience would at once have understood that he meant the Messias.[8]

There is, surely, a great deal uncertain, hypothetical, fantastic in all this, though it may contain certain elements of truth. A recent non-Catholic author, J. Stamm, has severely criticized another modern writer, E. Hammershaimb, who tried to show Isaias's dependence on Ugaritic texts such as these.[9]

Personally I am convinced that Isaias's oracle is to be explained in a much simpler way, as I hope to demonstrate in the course of this paper.

Continuing our examination of the text, I must further observe that, though 'almah is marked with the definite article, one could just as well translate " a girl " as " the girl," since on the one hand no other woman is mentioned in the context, and, on the other, one particular woman was certainly well determined in the mind of the prophet, and also evident to his hearers in some sense, as we shall see.

Of the 'almah it is said that she shall conceive and bring forth a son. The Hebrew text has a feminine adjective harah i.e. pregnant, and a feminine participle joledeth i.e. bearing. One could, therefore, strictly speaking translate: Behold the (or: a) girl is pregnant and bearing a son. However, there was surely no question of childbearing at the moment Isaias spoke; and the grammatical construction, especially after " behold " (hinneh) is a quite common one to express a future, either an immediate or a more distant one.

It is further said that she will call his name Emmanuel. The Hebrew weqarath, though unusual, can easily be explained as an older form of the third person feminine. The Vulgate, and also the Syriac version, translate: " shall be called," which supposes a slightly different consonantic Hebrew verb, as in the Qumran text.[10] The Septuagint has: " thou (Achaz) shalt call," to be explained by the same con-

---

[8] E. Burrows, The Oracles of Jacob and Balaam, London, 1938; cf. also Coppens, loc. cit., 670 f.

[9] J. Stamm, " Die Immanuel-Weissagung, ein Gespräch mit E. Hammershaimb," Vetus Testamentum, 4 (1954), 20-33; E. Hammershaimb, " The Immanuel Sign,"

[10] Cf. the latest edition of the Hebrew Bible.

sonantic verb, but with a different vowel-punctuation. However, the reading of the Massoretic text must be maintained, for Isaias apparently used a typical formula, by which wonderful childbirths were usually announced. So we find exactly the same wording in Gen. xvi:11, where the Angel of Yahweh says to Hagar: " Behold thou shalt conceive and bear a son and call his name Ismael "; again in Judg. xiii:7, where the Angel of Elohim says to Manue's wife: " Behold, thou shall conceive and bear a son," and in v. 24 it is she who calls him Samson; also in 1 Sam. ii:10 Anna herself calls her son Samuel, " because," she said, " I have asked him from Yahweh." In each of these texts it is the mother who gives the name to her child; the father, though quite clear from the context, remains in the background, for the accent lies on the special, wonderful intervention on the part of God Himself. Now, since with the very same words used for these wonderful childbirths, surely known to his hearers, Isaias announced that the 'almah was going to conceive and bear a son and give it a name, he undoubtedly wanted to bring home, and all certainly understood, that the childbirth he too was speaking about would be principally due to Yahweh's personal intervention. Neither is a father mentioned here; he is not even in any way indicated in the context, and the mother is called 'almah precisely to insist all the more that by God's intervention the child would be born.

Emmanuel, the name given to the child, is a symbolic name, meaning " God with us," and particularly apt to denote Yahweh's unfailing protection and assistance; for at the great moments of Israel's history God has often expressly assured His people that He is with them, also giving a sign of his divine assistance. It is so when Moses has to bring out the people from Egypt (Ex. iii:12), and when Gedeon is ordered to deliver Israel from the Madianites (Judg. vi:11-14, 36-40). The sensational victory of Gedeon is in fact twice recalled by Isaias, foretelling the downfall of Assyria, Juda's great enemy (Is. ix:4, x:26). Also to David Yahweh had several times promised to be with him (1 Sam. xvi:18; xviii:2, 14; xx:13; 1 Kings i:37 etc.).

From the explanation so far given of Is. vii:14 I venture to draw the following conclusions:

(1) The sign announced by Isaias to the house of David is the child to be born from a marriageable girl, normally a virgin, by the special intervention of Yahewh Himself and to be named Emmanuel as a pledge of divine protection; a sign, as the names of Isaias and his sons were " signs and tokens in Israel from Yahweh Sebaoth who dwells on the Mount Sion " (Is. viii:18).

(2) The name Emmanuel had to make it clear to the Davidic dynasty that Yahweh remained with it, that he would maintain it as he had promised by Nathan's prophecy, and not permit it to be overthrown by Syria and Israel.

(3) The child must, therefore, be a descendant of the Davidic dynasty, a king after God's heart, whose faith in Yahweh will be in striking contrast to Achaz's unbelief, and whose reign will show him worthy of the name Emmanuel.

These conclusions drawn from the text itself and the fore-going context I find confirmed by the sequel of the oracle and by what is further said about Emmanuel.

In chapter 8, a parallel to chapter 7 with similar oracles, not directed to the king and the house of David, but to the people, Emmanuel is twice expressly mentioned. Having announced the speedy deliverance from Syria and Israel, this time by giving the symbolic name of his second son: Mahar-Shalal-Hash-Baz (i.e. soon booty, shortly spoil), soon to be born as a sign of it, but knowing that the people also, like the king in chapter 7, refuse to put their trust in Yahweh, Isaias foretells the Assyrian invasions of Juda, which he considers to be the land of Emmanuel. A warning is added for the nations that their plan against Juda will not succeed—either a prediction of Sennacherib's unsuccessful campaign in 701 (Is. xxxvi:1) or of the final defeat of all Juda's enemies in a further future—" because," as the text says, " God is with us," an evident allusion to the name Emmanuel (Is. viii:1-10). The most obvious explanation of these two texts concerning Emmanuel is that he is looked upon as the king of Juda, and that for his sake Juda will finally be delivered from its enemies, precisely because he is the ideal king to be raised up by Yahweh himself.

Supposing, however, that Emmanuel is meant to be a descendant of the Davidic dynasty, it follows that the 'almah cannot possibly be Isaias's wife or some other common woman, as many have maintained. But if a future king is meant, why not Ezechias, Achaz's son, a very pious and excellent monarch, the antithesis of his father, much praised in the sacred writings? His mother, Abiyya, daughter of Zachary (2 Kings xviii:2), perhaps the same as the one whom Isaias took as a witness (Is. viii:2), would then be the 'almah.

However, apart from the difficulty already mentioned with regard to this word, of which there is no indication that it was ever used for a married woman, one wonders why the prophet called the queen 'almah. Steinmann, one of the few Catholic authors who contend that Isaias must have meant Ezechias, supposes that Abiyya had just entered the royal harem as a wife of second rank.[11] But if so (and this would have to be proved), she could, as wife, no longer be called 'almah. And if the prophet merely foresaw that she was going to be taken as a wife, since the grammatical structure is to be explained rather as a future, how did he know that she was going to bear a son? Why did Achaz call him Ezechias, if the name announced by the prophet and given by Abiyya is Emmanuel? There is also a serious chronological difficulty, for, unless one emends the texts, one will have to admit that Ezechias was born before Isaias pronounced his oracle; and to change the twenty-five years said to be his age when he began his reign (2 Kings xviii:2) into fifteen to fit the thesis one wants to prove is very arbitrary.

To understand that Emmanuel is a descendant of the royal Davidic dynasty and at the same time to know who he is, we must look at a wider context. In chapter 9, after the partial deportation of Israel by Sennacherib in his campaign of 732, the prophet affirms that Israel will be restored, for: " A child is born to us, a son given to us (prophetic perfect).

[11] J. Steinmann, *Le Prophète Isaie, sa vie, son oeuvre et son temps* (Lectio Divina, 5), Paris, 1950, 90, n. 11.

Authority shall be on his shoulder, and his name called: Wonder-counsellor, Divine-hero, Father forever, Prince of peace (names denoting the principal qualities a true monarch ought to have, and recalling those of the great kings of the Davidic dynasty, of its heroic founder and the wise Solomon, but possessed by the one here announced in the highest degree).[12] His is great authority, and there is no end of peace, upon the throne of David and over his kingdom; to establish it and sustain it in righteousness and justice henceforth forever." (Is. ix:5-6). In chapter 11 Isaias again announces the coming ruler of a re-established Juda: " There shall come forth a shoot from the stock of Jesse (another, a new David, from what was left of the Judean royal dynasty, compared to the trunk of a tree hewn down, cf. Is. x:33, 34), and a sapling shall sprout out of its root. And the spirit of Yahweh shall rest upon him: the spirit of wisdom and understanding, the spirit of counsel and might, the spirit of the knowledge and fear of Yahweh " (Is. xi:1-3). Again the future king is presented with the main attributes of an ideal ruler, here culminating in the fear and knowledge of Yahweh, by which he will be just, impartial, protecting the poor and punishing the wicked, in direct contrast to the present king Achaz as to many of the past who were rebellious to Yahweh and oppressors of the people. His reign will be one of wonderful harmony among the inhabitants of Sion, described by the idyllic picture of wild beasts grazing quietly together with domesticated animals, so that a boy can tend them, " for the land shall be filled with the knowledge of Yahweh." (Is. xi:1-9).[13]

There can be no serious doubt that these two oracles concern the same person and that he is the same Emmanuel of Is. vii:14; moreover, that these two have also to be linked up with Nathan's prophecy about the establishment of the

---

[12] According to the grammatical construction there seems to be question of four names; and in relation to the other names the version " Divine-hero " seems preferable to " God Mighty "; cf. E. Kissane, The Book of Isaiah, 1, Dublin, 1941, 112. I have often, gratefully, used his translations of the Hebrew texts.

[13] This explanation of Is. xi:6-9 is to be preferred to the more common one that Isaias here refers to a paradisiacal peace of the messianic times; cf. Kissane, loc. cit., 143.

Davidic dynasty for ever before Yahweh (2 Sam. vii:16). Steinmann contends that in them too Ezechias is primarily intended by the prophet, but he admits with regard to the first:

> The nature of the young prince is so excellent and infallible, the power Yahweh endows him with so extensive, that he must have something superhuman,[14]

and as to the second:

> No temporal prince could fulfil the programme of a government so perfect as traced by Isaias.[15]

Indeed what is said in those two oracles about the descendant of the Davidic dynasty surpasses all we know of Ezechias and his reign.   Hence the sense is not, as Steinmann proposes, that Ezechias is the *typus Messiae*, or that through Ezechias the Messias is meant,[16] but that the ideal king to come and to be expected is solely and directly intended by Isaias. The same is true of Is. vii:14, which can be rightly understood only in connection with and in the light of the two others; and the explanation given is confirmed as we shall see in Micheas v:1-3.

However, the verses following on Isaias vii:14 and continuing the oracle seem to connect the birth of Emmanuel with the historical events of Isaias's time; and how could he possibly be a sign for the house of David, if, in reality, he was to be born more than seven centuries later?

Before answering this seemingly grave and serious objection, I must first say something about these verses, of which vv. 15 and 16, especially, unfortunately swarm with difficulties.

As to v. 15: (1) What is meant by the butter (a kind of sourish milk, corresponding to the modern *leben* in Palestine) and honey the Emmanuel will have to eat? The expression is commonly understood in a figurative sense; but does it denote a state of prosperity (think of the " land that floweth with milk and honey," e.g. Ex. iii:8, 17), or a state of misery, since the expression again occurs in a context where there

14 Steinmann, loc. cit., 126.
15 Steinmann, loc. cit., 170.
16 Steinmann, loc. cit., 89, n. 3; 92.

is manifestly question of great distress (Is. vii:21, 22),[17] or a kind of heavenly, divine food, in which sense it is to be found in oriental literature? (2) How is the Hebrew *leda'to* to be rendered: butter and honey the child shall eat in order that he may know, or: until he knows, or: when he will know to refuse the evil and to choose the good? Three translations, each of them defended by various authors. (3) Have the words, " to know to refuse the evil and to choose the good " here their usual meaning, viz. to have come to the age of reason; or do they, perhaps, mean a higher knowledge by which the person in question will be able to distinguish as a mature man, or even to govern wisely?[18] (4) Some consider the whole verse to be a gloss. (5) Brunec recently contended that the boy in v. 15 is Shear-Yashub.[19]

With regard to v. 16 we observe that the introductory words, " for before the child shall know to refuse the evil and to choose the good," are followed by a sentence which is rather awkward grammatically, and difficult to translate, as may be seen from the Douay version: " the land which thou abhorrest shall be forsaken of the face of two kings." What does this mean? Leaving the Massoretic text intact, one would have to translate: " the land whose two kings thou art afraid of shall be deserted "; but (1) Syria and Israel are two different kingdoms, so one could hardly speak of their land; (2) the Hebrew word *'adamah* is never used elsewhere in a political sense, but to designate the cultivated land; (3) it is disputed whether the desertion of Syria and Israel (cf. viii:1-4) is meant, or Juda is referred to, since from v. 17 onwards the devastation of this country is undoubtedly dealt with (cf. Is. viii:5-8). To solve these difficulties some authors strike out the whole verse, others only the second part, viz. " whose two kings thou art afraid of "; some

[17] Mgr. E. Kissane, " Butter and Honey shall he Eat," recently defended this opinion; cf. *L'Ancien Testament et l'Orient, études présentées aux VIes journées bibliques de Louvain* (11-13 septembre 1954) in *Orientalia et Biblica Lovaniensia*, 1, Louvain, 1957, 169-173.

[18] As to this last opinion cf. E. Power, S.J., " The Emmanuel Prophecy of Isaias," *Ir. Eccl. Rec.*, (70) 1948, 299-301; also Coppens, " La Prophétie de la '*Almah*,' 658, 663.

[19] M. Brunec, " De Sensu ' Signi ' in Is. vii:14," *Verbum Domini*, 33 (1955), 257-266, 321-330; 34 (1956), 16-29. The other opinions on verse 15, like those on v. 16, are mentioned in the various commentaries, which often refer to special publications.

translate: " the land on whose behalf thou fearest two kings,"
a rendering that surely must be rejected; others again divide
the text after the word " land," connecting the rest with
the following verse, in this way: " before the child shall
know to refuse the evil and choose the good, the land (of
Juda) shall be deserted (by Syria and Israel). Whereas thou
art in fear before the two kings, Yahweh will bring upon
thee . . . " Many authors, however, retain the Massoretic
text as it stands, whence they take the land to be deserted,
not as that of Juda, but of Syria and Israel together.

The pericope vv. 17-25 on the whole is clear; it evidently
announces the devastation of Juda; there is but one difference
of opinion: whether this devastation is to be ascribed to the
Assyrians alone or to them and the Egyptians together. Of
course, those who consider the eating of butter and honey a
symbol of prosperity are bound to reject vv. 21 and 22 as
an interpolation into a context of misery.

An ingenious and risky attempt to explain everything
smoothly is the one proposed by Feuillet; he changes the
order of the verses in this way: 14a, 16 (Juda's deliverance
from Syria and Israel; the sign is then the boy Shear-Jasub);
17-20 and 23-25 (devastation of Juda); 14b, 15, 21, 22
(messianic prophecy of final salvation).[20]

I have only summarized briefly the various difficulties of
the verses following Is. vii:14, with the manifold attempts to
solve them. Where the texts are so much disputed, it seems
hopeless to argue from them one way or another. Yet,
notwithstanding so much uncertainty, some points seem to
me quite clear.

As we explained Is. vii:14, the child to be born from the
'almah by Yahweh's personal intervention and called Emmanuel
was a sign of Yahweh's continual faithful protection: the
Davidic dynasty would remain " as established forever before
Yahweh," according to Nathan's prophecy, and would not,
therefore, be overthrown by Syria and Israel. If then it is
said that before Emmanuel will be able to refuse the evil
and choose the good the land will be deserted, this land

[20] A. Feuillet, " Le Signe proposé à Achaz et l'Emmanuel," *Recherches de Science Religieuse*, 30 (1940), 129-151.

must be, in spite of the alleged difficulties, that of Syria and Israel together; the danger to the dynasty came at the moment from them. Now Syria was completely destroyed by Assyria's king Tiglath-Phalassar III during his campaign of 732, and Israel at the same time partially destroyed and for the rest overrun, till it ceased to exist in 722. Hence, if Emmanuel is supposed to be born shortly after Isaias's prophecy in 734, Syria and Israel could well be said to have been deserted before he was able to refuse the evil and choose the good.

In this case there seems to be an evident link between the the birth of Emmanuel and the desertion of Syria and Israel. However, we have already observed that the same disaster of Syria and Israel is foretold by the parallel oracle of Is. viii:1-4 in more or less the same way, and, as is commonly admitted, shortly after the oracle of Emmanuel. In that parallel oracle we read: " before the child (Mahar-Shalal-Hash-Baz, Isaias's second son, recently born to him of his wife) shall be able to say ' my father ' and ' my mother,' the riches of Damascus (Syria's capital) and the spoil of Samaria (capital of Israel) shall be carried away before the king of Assyria." Here we have a clear, manifest sign that could be verified in a few years' time, connecting in a very real and concrete way the birth of Isaias's second son with Juda's delivery from Syria and Israel. In the prophecy of Emmanuel the connection between his birth and the fact must be admitted, but as an ideal one, as Lagrange [21] already suggested and Tournay [22] recently proposed. By his prophetic insight into things Isaias was convinced that, according to Nathan's prophecy, Yahweh would raise up an ideal ruler from the Davidic dynasty, and he awaited him so eagerly that he imagined him already born and announced him in relation to Juda's deliverance from Syria and Israel. Yet, at the same time he did not know when that ruler would in fact come; he was even conscious that it would not happen in the proximate future

[21] M. J. Lagrange, O.P., " Le Vierge et l'Emmanuel," *Revue Biblique*, 1 (1892), 484 f.

[22] R. Tournay, O.P., " L'Emmanuel et sa Vierge-Mère," *Revue Thomiste*, 55 (1955), 254 f.

and realized that Juda had to be punished first, as he also foretold (Is. vii:17-25; viii:5-8). When shortly afterwards Isaias announced the more concrete, clearer sign of his own second son (Is. viii:1-4), Emmanuel was still in his mind; for Juda was for him the land of Emmanuel (Is. viii:8) and it will finally be saved on account of him (Is. viii:10). Also in the other two oracles mentioned he understood the Emmanuel he had in mind as coming in a later future.

That by the sign of Emmanuel was intended the survival of the Davidic dynasty, but by means of an ideal king who would be raised up by Yahewh's special intervention and would therefore be the very opposite of the present king, Achaz with his house must surely have realized; but it would have meant little to them, since they had lost all faith in Yahweh. However, it remained a grave warning for his successors, and must have greatly consoled those who still believed in Yahweh, those who were open to the prophet's teaching, his disciples, of whom Isaias declared: " the testimony is bound up, the teaching sealed in my disciples " (Is. viii:16). They saw in it, as in the other Isaian oracles, a confirmation of their messianic hopes, eagerly awaiting their fulfilment with Isaias himself: " And I will wait for Yahweh, who hides his face from the house of Jacob, and I will hope in him " (Is. viii:17).

Apart from the hopeful and consoling aspect, the principal one, the Emmanuel prophecy also included a grave warning, as we already said, and a severe threat, inasmuch as the announcement of a serious disaster to come upon Juda was linked up with it (Is. xvii:17-25; cf. viii:5-8). This was to be expected as a punishment for so much unbelief and contempt of Yahweh on the part of Achaz and his house; and this was, moreover, quite in accordance with Nathan's prophecy, for " if he (David's seed, the king) did wrong, Yahweh would chastise him after the manner of men " (2 Sam. vii:14). Achaz had to understand that the land that he was trying to serve according to his own political views without any trust in Yahweh would be devastated, and, to begin with, on his account, and by the very same military power, Assyria, whose aid he had wrongheadedly invoked.

In conclusion, if by Emmanuel Isaias intended the ideal king to be raised up by Yahweh, the Messias, Christus, Our Lord, then by the 'almah, his mother, he meant Mary, Our Lady. Since, however the prophet had very likely no special revelation about the human-divine character of Emmanuel, which only the New Testament made clearly known to us, it is not necessary to suppose a similar revelation with regard to the virginity of the 'almah at the moment of conceiving her child. As Kissane says: " He (Isaias) was probably not aware of the full import of the revelation of which he was the medium." [23] The term 'almah is used to stress even more than in the other examples of wonderful childbirths Yahweh's personal intervention, so that the child to be born is principally due to him; but at the same time Isaias chose the word under divine inspiration, and God intended by it the Blessed Virgin, and consequently the virginal birth of her Son, both signified in the oracle according to the sensus plenior.

We can be brief with the remaining Old Testament texts concerning Our Lady.

In Micheas v:1-3 Yahweh announced that from the clan Ephrath (Ephrath is originally a clan, cf. 1 Chron. ii:19, xxiv: 50, living in the region of Bethlehem, and was later used to indicate that city, cf. Gen. xxxvi:19, xlviii:17; Jos. xv:19; Ruth iv:11; here Bethlehem seems to be a gloss, already inserted into the text before the Septuagint version), though the smallest or the least important of the clans of Juda, shall come forth the one who will be his ruler in Israel, and whose origins are from long ago, from the times of old (probably referring to the time of David, the great descendant of the clan Ephrath, perhaps even to the very beginnings of the clan itself). There can be no doubt that here is meant the ideal king, the new David, Isaias's Emmanuel, the Messias.

And if Yahweh abandons Juda (an allusion to the Assyrian invasion in 701, or even to the Babylonian exile), it will only be " until the time that she that travaileth hath brought forth." There are quite a number of authors (among them for example Coppens) who contend that by the " woman in

[23] Kissane, The Book of Isaiah, vol. 1, 89.

travail " the clan Ephrath with its city Bethlehem is meant;[24]
but the old interpretation that we here have an evident
allusion to the 'almah of Is. vii:14, on which Micheas depends,
is surely to be preferred. Here also there is nothing said about
a father. Just as in Is. viii:8 Juda will be saved because of
Emmanuel, so here, for the sake of the new David intended,
his brethren are said to return. It is also predicted that he
will tend them as a shepherd by the strength of Yahweh
and His power, and that he will extend his might to the
extremities of the world: words that recall what is said of
Emmanuel in Is. ix:5-6 and xi:1-9. Steinmann admits that

> this infant Messias far surpasses Ezechias and shall fulfil the
> most wonderful promises of the past.[25]

Micheas v:1-3 is thus certainly a prophecy concerning Our
Lady together with Our Lord; though neither was this
prophet aware of the full meaning of the revelation he was
transmitting.

Jeremias xxxi:22, the famous " femina circumdabit virum,"
should be resolutely dismissed as a messianic and mariological
text. It was for the first time understood as such by St.
Jerome [26] (followed by a number of ancient writers, not,
however, by the Fathers), who explained the Hebrew text
as meaning that the Virgin (Mary) compassed (in her womb)
the Man (Christ). But this translation is quite impossible,
since the Hebrew noun neqebah, denoting the female sex as
such, is most unfitting to designate a virgin, and the Hebrew
form tesobeb (from sabab) can hardly be used in the sense
given to it by St. Jerome. The interpretation has now been
generally abandoned, though not long ago Closen contended
that the words according to the sensus plenior could be
understood of Our Lady protecting the Mystical Body of
Christ.[27]

[24] Cf. Coppens, in Ephem. Theol. Lov., 672, who refers to other authors; he also
mentions E. Burrows (cf. supra p. 17, n. 8) who finds a confirmation of his theory
expounded on p. 16, taking Ephrath to be Shela's clan.
[25] Steinmann, Le Prophète Isaie, 268.
[26] PL 24, 914 f.
[27] G. E. Closen, S.J., " Femina Circumdabit Virum," Verbum Domini, 16 (1936),
295-304.

A great many explanations have been offered, but most authors think that the text is corrupt; the Septuagint has already something quite different. Of the explanations that are not based on a correction of the text, two are more common. To understand these we must first know the reading of the whole of verse 22: " How long wilt thou tarry, rebellious daughter (Israel refusing to return to Yahweh)? for Yahweh has created a new thing on the earth : a woman shall compass a man."

The first of the two more common explanations is: " a woman (Israel) shall look for a man (Yahweh) "; surely a new thing that Israel, always so rebellious, will now of herself return to Yahweh.

The other explanation is as follows: " A woman surrounds (with care) a man," and the novelty is to be seen in the fact that if Israel will only return to the land it shall find the country so quiet and peaceful that not men, as is usual, will protect women, but now women can protect men."

However, all authors admit that they only give their interpretation for want of a better one.[28]

Recently Ziener pointed out that the new creation spoken of is to be found in the vv. 23-26, which many consider a later interpolation: Yahweh shall completely transform the situation of Juda's cities, so that again there will be found in them prosperity and justice. If this interpretation is right, and it seems quite plausible, the words " a woman will compass a man " become superfluous; and Ziener ingeniously shows that they have been inserted into the text by dittography, and should simply be expunged.[29]

Finally we have only to add that various other texts taken from the prophetical and sapiential books and the psalms, often applied by the Fathers and in the Liturgy to Our Lady, are not mariological texts in the strict biblical sense, but mere accommodations of the Bible text; though they have a certain value because of the use the Church made of them.

---

[28] The latest commentary on Jeremias is: B. Wambacq, O. Praem., *Jeremias, Klagliedern, Baruch, Brief van Jeremias* (De Boeken van het Oude Testament), Roermond-Maaseik, 1957.

[29] G. Ziener, " Femina Circumdabit Virum, Jer. xxxi:22," *Biblische Zeitschrift* (Neue Folge), 1 (1957), 282 f.

Our Lady in the New Testament

BY CONLETH KEARNS, O.P.

THE subject-matter of this conference is not the very wide one which the title, taken as it stands, would indicate. The aim is rather to deal with the subject of " Our Lady in the New Testament *according to recent Catholic exegesis.*" Exegesis is an integral part of theology, and the development of Marian theology, so characteristic of the Church's intellectual and spiritual life today, includes a corresponding movement in the field of Catholic exegesis. There are certain trends of research, reflection and discussion amongst exegetes which are bringing to light new aspects and new depths in even the most familiar Marian texts of Sacred Scripture. Taking the decade 1948-57 as a sufficient length of time within which to note some main features of this trend, I should like here to attempt two things. First, to survey very briefly some characteristic procedures and results of Catholic mariological exegesis over the period in question; and secondly, to illustrate some of these a little more in detail as they are concerned with some aspects of the Gospel story of the Annunciation in particular. It is chiefly in connection with this latter point that the restricted bibliography given below may be found useful.[1]

---

[1] Audet, Jean-Paul, O.P., " L'Annonce à Marie " in *Rev. Bibl.*, 63 (1956), 346-374.
Braun, F. M., O.P., *La Mère des Fidèles*, 2nd ed., Tournai-Paris, 1954.
Bonnetain, P., "Immaculée Conception" in *Dictionnaire de la Bible, Supplement*, 4, Paris, 1949, 233 ff., especially 254-270.
Ceroke, Christian P., O.Carm., "Luke i:34 and Mary's Virginity" in *Cath. Bibl. Quart.*, 19 (1957), 329-342.
Ceuppens, P. F., O.P., *Theologia Biblica*, 4, De Mariologia Biblica, ed. Ima, Romae, 1948, ed. 2da, Romae, 1951.
Gaechter, Paul, S.J., *Maria im Erdenleben: neutestamentliche Marienstudien*, zweite Auflage, Innsbruck, 1954.
Laurentin, René, *Queen of Heaven: A Short Treatise on Marian Theology*, translated from the French by Gordon Smith, Dublin, 1956. (The French original is entitled *Court Traité de théologie mariale*, 2nd ed., Paris, 1956).
Id. *Structure et théologie de Luc I-II* (Études Bibliques), Paris, 1957.

I

RECENT MARIOLOGICAL EXEGESIS OF THE NEW TESTAMENT

The scope of recent work. The great biblical encyclicals and other recent directives of the Holy See have repeatedly stressed the importance, for Catholic exegetes, of keeping purely philological and historico-literary learning in their subsidiary place, and of devoting their main efforts to bringing out the doctrinal and spiritual values of the inspired word. Representative of many similar exhortations is that of Pius XII in the Encyclical *Divino Afflante Spiritu*:

> Let Catholic interpreters be specially careful not to confine their exposition—as unfortunately happens in some commentaries — to matters concerning history, archaeology, philology, and similar sciences. These should indeed be given their proper place so far as they may be of assistance to the work of interpretation; but commentators must have as their chief object to show what is the theological doctrine touching faith and morals of each book and text, so that their commentary may not only assist teachers of theology in expounding and corroborating the dogmas of faith, but also be useful to priests in their work of explaining Christian doctrine to the people, and help all the faithful to lead a holy and Christian life.[2]

The response of Catholic biblical scholarship to these incentives has been widespread and significant. Not only

Lyonnet, Stanislaus, S.J., *Le Récit de l'Annonciation et la maternité divine de la Sainte Vierge*, Rome, 1956 (tiré à part de *l'Ami du Clergé* du 10 Janvier, 1956: Conférence donnée à l'Institut Biblique Pontifical, Rome, le 10 Janvier, 1954).
Osty, E., P.S.S., *L'Évangile selon Saint Luc* (Bible de Jérusalem), 2de édition revue, Paris, 1953.
Schmid, Josef, *Das Evangelium nach Lukas* (Regensburger Neues Testament), dritte Auflage, Regensburg, 1956.

[2] Pope Pius XII, Encyc. *Divino Afflante*, Eng. trans., C.T.S., no. 29 f.; see also ibid. no. 55 f.; and see Leo XIII, *Providentissimus Deus, Enchiridion Biblicum*, ed. 2da, Romae, 1954, nos. 105, 107, 114; Benedict XV, *Spiritus Paraclitus, E.B.*, nos. 482-485; Pius XII, *Humani Generis*, Eng. trans., C.T.S., no. 21; Pontifical Biblical Commission, Instruction *De Scriptura Sacra Recte Docenda* (May, 1950) *E.B.*, nos. 598, 601.

has the subject of biblical theology been tackled in a systematic way,[3] but commentators on particular books and passages have been stressing more and more the divine content of the inspired word which forms the object of their studies. This tendency, naturally, is reflected in the exegesis of the mariological passages of Scripture as well as elsewhere. Father Ceuppens in the Preface to his *Mariologia Biblica* (the fourth volume of his *Theologia Biblica* referred to above) indicates as a main object of his exegetical work on Our Lady " ut Ipsa magis magisque cognoscatur, intensius ametur, ferventius honoretur." The title of Laurentin's work on the Infancy Story of St. Luke is, significantly, " Structure *et théologie* de Luc. 1-2." Father Gaechter in the Foreword to his *Mary in her Earthly Life* points out that two of the studies it contains extend beyond the purely exegetico-critical field into the theological. The sub-title of Father Braun's *La Mère des Fidèles* is " Essai de *théologie* johannique." [4] One satisfactory result of this trend of exegesis is that it brings out with great clearness how deeply and how securely the spreading tree of Catholic Mariology is rooted in the revelation of the Scriptures. As Laurentin aptly points out:

> In the sixteenth century Protestants and Catholics were too ready to agree about the supposed " silence of Scripture " concerning the Virgin: a pretext for the former to reject mariology altogether, and for the latter to develop a para-scriptural Mariology. It is time to explode this obstinate and pernicious slogan. It is already losing force, since for some time now Protestants have been rediscovering Mary *through* Scripture, while Catholics are rediscovering her *in* Scripture.[5]

Methods of recent work. The exegetical methods employed

[3] See e.g. Heinisch, *Theology of the Old Testament*, Eng. trans. by Rev. William G. Heidt, O.S.B., revised ed., Collegeville, Minnesota, 1958; P. van Imschoot, *Théologie de l'Ancien Testament*, Tomes 1, 2, Paris, 1954, 1956; P. F. Ceuppens, O.P., *Theologia Biblica*, 4 vols., 2nd ed., Rome, 1949-1951; Max Meinertz, *Theologie des Neuen Testaments*, 2 vols., Bonn, 1950; J. Bonsirven, S.J., *Théologie du Nouveau Testament*, Paris, 1951.

[4] See his reference to " le souci, aujourd'hui croissant, d'enraciner la théologie, singulièrement la théologie mariale, dans la Sainte Écriture " (op. cit., 23), and to the necessity " de revenir à une interprétation théologique des textes bibliques " (ibid., 11).

[5] Laurentin, *Queen of Heaven*, 37; see also Braun, op. cit., 189-192.

by the commentators in question involve nothing really new. There is, however, a new *emphasis* on certain procedures of established exegetical technique. First, as regards the New Testament at any rate, more attention than formerly is paid to the *personality* of the human author, his predilections, his literary qualities and mannerisms. These and other suchlike elements, it is now more and more realized, are integral to his presentation of the facts and doctrines which form his subject-matter. For example it is nowadays a commonplace that a literary artist like St. Luke makes use of the very order and disposition of his narrative (to which he himself draws particular attention, Luke i : 3) to bring out subtly but unmistakably the doctrinal inwardness of many of the facts and sayings which he records. This is a point to which we shall return below. Secondly, the principle that the New Testament is the " fulfilment " of the Old is today being used with more discrimination and insight, and at the same time with greater frequency and fruitfulness than formerly. Correspondences between the two Testaments are proving to be both more subtle and more pervasive than had previously been realized. Intimately connected with this acute awareness of the Old Testament background of so much of the New Testament there is, thirdly, the new importance attached to what has come to be known as " typology." This is a subject which is still to some extent in debate amongst exegetes. Exaggerations and uncertainties have not yet been eliminated. But it is being more and more admitted that certain New Testament writers—sometimes even by the very vocabulary and turn of phrase which they make use of—often put forward the personalities or events of which they write as divinely-designed fulfilments of certain of God's dealings with Israel as recorded in the Old Testament. This theory involves certain elements additional to the familiar concept of the " typical " sense of the Old Testament. It insists, for example, that the principle of " typology " is not validly applicable unless the Old Testament term of comparison, besides a general resemblance to the New Testament one, contains also the beginnings of a fulfilment of it. The second must be the historical and providential continuation and completion of the first. [6] A striking application of the principle to the story of the Annunciation will be noted below.

Some results of recent work. The methods we are speaking of have thrown at least some new light on all the Marian passages of the New Testament. (1) *The Annunciation*: see below. (2) *The Visitation* (Lk. i: 39-56): amongst the points now more convincingly brought out, especially by a fresh study both of the Angel's dialogue with Our Lady and of her *Magnificat*, is the fact that her fullness of grace included a personal familiarity with the messianic prophecies and pre-figurings of the Old Testament, and with its deeper spiritual teachings in general. This knowledge of hers is shown to have been rooted in her prayerful and reflective familiarity with the sacred text itself. [7] Another fact now recognized is that St. Luke here proposes Our Lady to us as the personification of the group that formed the fine flower of Israelite spirituality in later Old Testament times, namely " the poor " or " the humble." [8] (3) *The Presentation in the Temple*: here, among other points, the tendency now is to stress the close connection between St. Luke's account of Our Lady's association with the Passion of her Son (Simeon's prophecy, Lk. ii:34, 35) and St. John's account of Our Lady on Calvary (Jn. xix:25-27). The whole question of the doctrinal affinity between these two Gospels is being nowadays opened up along new lines, with Our Lady emerging as one of the significant links between them. [9] (4) *In St. John's Gospel*: the evangelist's way of presenting his facts, and his stress on certain keywords used

---

[6] See e.g. Dom Charlier, O.S.B., *The Christian Approach to the Bible*, 270-72. A fundamental work in connection with " typology" is Jean Daniélou, S.J., *Sacramentum Futuri: études sur les origines de la typologie biblique*, Paris, 1950; for a bibliography of the subject see J. Coppens, *Les Harmonies des deux Testaments: essai sur les divers sens des Écritures . . .*, Paris, 1949.

[7] " Every sentence in this Canticle (*Magnificat*) is an echo of some passage of the Bible . . . Here we see Mary so steeped in the word of God that she borrows from it its very expressions. Little wonder, then, that God replies to her in like terms. To the Virgin nourished on the Scriptues, the divine messenger himself speaks the language of the Scriptures." (Laurentin, *Queen of Heaven*, 21, 22).

[8] The theme of " the poor " etc. is treated by A. Gelin in *Les Pauvres de Yahvé* (Témoins de Dieu, Paris, 2nd ed., 1955). " Avec la Vierge du *Magnificat*," he says, " la lignée arrive à un sommet; avec Jésus à sa perfection " (op. cit., 10). See also *Le Dieu des pauvres*, 1, 2 (Cahiers Bibliques " Évangile "), Paris, 1955; and, as regards our Lady, Laurentin, *Queen of Heaven*, 19, n. 5.

[9] See e.g. Braun, op. cit., 27-30; Laurentin, *Queen of Heaven*, 28-30.

by Our Lord (e.g. the term " woman " in Jn. ii:4 and xix:26),
are seen to give fresh significance, with Old Testament
undertones, to his accounts of Our Lady at Cana and on
Calvary.[10] This in turn links up with (5) *the reference in
Apoc. xii:1-6 to "the Woman clothed with the sun"*: here Père
Braun, especially, has traced out a chain of " typology " whose
links are Eve—the Woman of Gen. iii:15, 16—the Woman
of Cana and of Calvary—the Woman clothed with the sun—
the People of God—Our Lady as the type of the Church.[11]

II

THE ANNUNCIATION IN RECENT EXEGESIS

Recent exegetical discussions of this fundamental mariological passage (Lk. i: 26-28) seem to centre mainly in
two questions: (1) Did Our Lady know clearly from the
beginning that her Son was divine? (2) Does Our Lady's
question " How shall that be, for I know not man? " really
imply a purpose on her part to remain perpetually a virgin?
Here, we must confine ourselves to the former question, as
it is not possible to treat both within the limits of our paper.[12]

The question as to whether Our Lady knew from the
beginning the divinity of her Son has come to the fore in
exegetical and theological discussions in recent years. Among
other places it was debated at some length in the pages of the
Irish Ecclesiastical Record over the years 1945-47, where diver-
gent views were put forward by Fr. Hugh Pope, O.P., Fr.

---

[10] The main part of Père Braun's work is devoted to this theme; see also Laurentin,
Queen of Heaven, 30-33.

[11] Op. cit., 131-176; Laurentin, *Queen of Heaven*, 33-37. On the other side,
however, arguing that this " Woman " does not represent our Lady, see e.g. Ceuppens,
op. cit., 2nd ed., 207-209.

[12] As to our Lady's question " How shall that be . . . ? " the normal line followed
by Catholic interpreters from patristic times onwards has been that it does not make
sense except on the basis of a *votum* or *propositum* on our Lady's part of perpetually
remaining a virgin. In antiquity only the Pseudo-Athanasius is found to interpret
it otherwise (*Sermo in Annuntiationem Deiparae*, 8, amongst the works of St. Athanasius,
Migne, *PG* 28, 927). He is followed, in the 16th century, by Cardinal Cajetan, O.P.
(*in Luc.* h. l.). Modern Catholic commentators who depart from the usual line are
Landersdorfer, O.S.B., in *Biblische Zeitung*, 7 (1909), 70 ff.; Haugg, *Das erste biblische
Marienwort*, Stuttgart, 1938; Gaechter, S.J., op. cit., 94, 95 (agreeing with Haugg);

Edmund Sutcliffe, S.J., and Fr. Peter, O.F.M.Cap. It is instructive for our present purpose to compare the lines followed in that earlier discussion with that taken by the slightly later exegetical movement we are now describing. (1) The earlier discussions, while taking St. Luke's account of the Annunciation as their starting-point, drew many of their arguments also from a much wider field, including especially the views of the Fathers and the conclusions of systematic theology. The movement we are describing, on the contrary, is a purely exegetical one. It aims at penetrating the sense conveyed by the inspired passage itself, using for this purpose all, and only, the resources afforded by text, context, and parallel places of the Old and New Testament. (2) It makes much, especially, of the outlook, scope, method, and other characteristics of the inspired author of the narrative itself. St. Luke's personality, religious and artistic, his aim, his way of arranging his material and other literary procedures of his, as well as the deliberately doctrinal stamp which he imprints on his subject-matter as he reports it, are in the forefront of recent exegetical discussions. The earlier ones are largely silent about this. (3) The principles of " typology," not then worked out or applied so securely as they have been since, do not figure to any notable extent in the earlier discussions; they pervade the later ones. Father Peter, O.F.M. Cap., indeed, penetratingly drew attention at some length to the significance of St. Luke's use, in his presentation of the event, of the verb *episkiazein* (" to overshadow," v. 35), with its pregnant allusion to the Pillar of Cloud in Ex. xl:32-36 and elsewhere.[13] That is a notable link between the earlier discussions and the later ones. But at the time the richness of this vein, afterwards to be exploited to such good effect by Lyonnet, Laurentin and others, had not yet been brought out.

Schmid, op. cit., 42, 43 (Haugg's view; Boismard, O.P., in a review of Schmid's work, also approves this view, *Rev. Bibl.*, 63 (1956), 603 f.); Audet, O.P., art. cit., *Rev. Bibl.*, 63 (1956), 365-372. See critiques of Landersdorfer in Lagrange, *Luc*, xxx, and Ceuppens, op. cit., 69; for critiques of Haugg see Ceuppens, ibid., 71-73, and Ceroke, art. cit., 338 f., 341; for critiques of Audet see Ceroke, ibid., passim, and Laurentin, *Structure*, 178, n. 3.

[13] *Ir. Eccl. Rec.*, 67 (1954, i), 150; 69 (1947), 119, 120. In his support Fr. Peter cites Schaefer and Scheeben, as well as the poetry of Robert Hawker.

Some of the characteristics of St. Luke's outlook and method of presentation, helpful in discovering what *he* wishes to convey to us in this passage are: (1) His consciousness of the gradualness of God's revelation. That revelation, he brings out, grows constantly throughout the Old Testament; it reaches a climax in the present passage. (2) His way of bringing home to the reflecting reader that in the present passage itself there is a gradualness in the manner in which this fullness of revelation is worked up to. (3) The way he subtly stresses significant words and expressions and accentuates implicit allusions connected with Old Testament prophecies and pre-figurings, so as to bring out their fulfilment in the present passage. In this his use of the principles of " typology " is to be observed especially. In particular, as to his principle of gradualness, the following three stages of the Angel's message are to be noted.

(1) To begin with, it is self-evident that the message asserts that Mary's Son is to be the promised Messias of Old Testament prophecy. Verse 31, " Behold thou shalt conceive in thy womb and shalt bring forth a son and thou shalt call his name Jesus" is an echo of the messianic prophecy of Is. vii:14b, " Behold the virgin shall conceive and bear a son, and shall call his name Emmanuel " (Hebrew text, Mgr. Kissane's trans.). Verses 32, 33 are also full of allusions to Old Testament messianic prophecy (see below). And besides this Lyonnet and others have noted in the expressions " Rejoice . . . the Lord is with thee " (v. 28) and " Fear not, Mary " (v. 3), reminiscences of messianic passages in the Minor Prophets.[14]

(2) But in the messianic prophecies here alluded to, especially in vv. 32, 33, there is a further depth to be noted. Here we find deliberate echoes and indeed some elaborations of three of the most significant Old Testament prophecies concerning the messianic King: 2 Sam. vii: 12-16, Dan. vii:13, 14, and Is. ix:6, 7. The first of these is the oracle of the prophet Nathan to David, the tap-root of the Davidic

---

[14] Soph. iii: 14-17; Joel ii:21-27; Zach. ix:9-10; for details see Lyonnet, op. cit., 10; Laurentin, *Structure*, 64-73; Ceuppens, op. cit., 61.

messianism of the Old Testament. It speaks of the everlasting
kingdom or kingship which is to be granted to the offspring
of David, with a throne that " shall be firm for ever." [15]
The term " an everlasting kingship " might well, in a broad
sense, be verified of a whole dynasty or succession of purely
human kings. But to say of a single individual that he, as
Messias, is to have " an everlasting kingdom " or " an eternal
kingship " is to break out of the narrow circle of Old Testament messianic concepts and to imply that the Messias spoken
of belongs to a transcendent or superhuman order. And this
is precisely what the Angel does.[16] He does the same regarding
Daniel's prophecy of the " Son of Man." There we read: " Lo,
one like a son of man came with the clouds of heaven, and
he came even to the Ancient of days, and they presented him
before him. And he gave him power, and glory, and a kingdom: and all peoples, tribes and tongues shall serve him:
his power is an everlasting power that shall not be taken away:
and *his kingdom that shall not be destroyed* " (Dan. vii:13, 14).
In its original context the figure of the " Son of Man," like
those of the Lioness, the Bear, the Leopard, and the Fourth
Beast in the preceding part of the vision, fluctuates between
the collective and the individual sense (Dan. vii:3-8). As those
" four beasts " represent at one moment individual kings—
Nabuchodonosor, Cyrus, Alexander, and Antiochus Epiphanes
—and at another moment the peoples over whom those kings
ruled, so too the Son of Man seems at one moment to represent
a future individual king, and at another " the people of the
saints of the Most High " (v. 27). The Angel applies the
prophecy to an individual, the Son of Mary: " Of his reign

---

[15] 2 Sam. vii:16. The allusion in v. 13 to an individual son of David for whom the
Lord " shall establish the throne of his kingdom for ever " is regarded as an interpolation by many textual critics; see Ceuppens, *De Prophetiis Messianicis*, Romae,
1935, 119.

[16] " C'est ouvrir une porte sur le surnaturel, car ce qui est infini dans un sens sort
des conditions des choses humaines " (Lagrange, *Luc*, h. l.); Ceuppens elaborates
" Angelus nunc annuntiat quod vaticinium Nathan, in persona quadam determinata,
in filio Mariae nascituro, in Messia plenam suam adimpletionem habebit: (1) Filius
Mariae erit de domo David, nam *sedebit super thronum David patris sui*; quae verba
naturam humanam Filii Mariae respiciunt; (2) *regnabit in domo Iacob in aeternum, et
regni eius non erit finis*; haec verba non amplius de dynastia David, sed de persona
Messiae praedicantur : Messias regnabit in aeternum, regnum eius erit absque fine.
Qua ultima propositione sumus iam in ordine supernaturali " (op. cit., 67, 68).

there shall be no end" (Lk. i:33). The third prophecy referred to, that of Isaias, also speaks of the Messias as exercising his royal authority " upon the throne of David, and over his kingdom; to establish it and sustain it in justice and righteousness henceforth forever " (Is. ix:6, Mgr. Kissane's trans.). This again the Angel predicates of Mary's Son: " The Lord God shall give unto him the throne of David his father; and he shall reign in the house of Jacob for ever, and of his reign there shall be no end " (Lk. i:32, 33). Moreover in the same prophecy of Isaias here alluded to the Messias is described in the mysterious terms " Divine-hero, Father for ever " (Is. ix:5, same trans.)—again an invitation to break out of the purely human order of messianic concepts and rise up to the superhuman. The Angel's words, fusing the prophecy in which these mysterious terms occur with the two preceding ones, certainly do place Mary's Son in that mysterious, super-human and transcendent order.

(3) But do they not rise to something still more sublime and at the same time more specific? For answer we turn to the climax of the message: " The Holy Ghost shall come upon thee, and the power of the Most High shall overshadow thee, and for this very reason that which is to be born shall be holy, it shall be called the Son of God " (v. 35, after Lagrange's rendering of the Greek). The word " overshadow " is weighty with meaning here. It is the same verb (*episkiazein*) which is used in the Septuagint translation of Ex. xl:32-36. In that passage, and in many similar ones in the Old Testament, the Pillar of Cloud *overshadows* the Tabernacle, or the Temple, as a visible sign of the invisible Presence of the Divinity Itself within the Holy of Holies, upon the Ark of the Covenant (see Ex., loc. cit.; Num. ix:15-23; Lev. xvi:2; 3 Kings viii:6-11; 2 Par. v:13, 14 etc.). The two complementary elements of this divine manifestation should be noted. They are (1) the overshadowing Cloud, representing the God of Heaven, transcendently *above* mankind; and (2) the " Glory " or Presence *within* the building, representing God Himself, present to His People, dwelling in their midst. That Presence was at the same time a figure, a promise, and the beginning of the fulfilment of His more wondrous Presence still in

after years, when "the Word was made flesh and dwelt amongst us." [17] The application of this to Our Lady is clear. The Power of God shall overshadow her; the Divinity itself shall take up its Presence within her. She is to be a living Tabernacle or Temple, a Holy of Holies within which God Himself shall dwell in the midst of His People. She is the true Ark of the Covenant.

With this exegesis of the first part of v. 35, the second part (whose exact construction and rendering has puzzled commentators) becomes clear: "For this very reason, that which is to be born shall be holy, it shall be called the Son of God." That these last words "the Son of God" are to be taken in all their fullness of meaning and in no mere messianico-human sense is now clear, in the light of all that precedes.

One confirmation of this exegesis is found in the fact that the whole narrative of the Visitation which immediately follows (Luke i:39-45, 56) is full of subtle echoes of the story of David's transfer of the Ark of the Covenant to Jerusalem, in 2 Sam. vi:2-11.[18] Another and more obvious confirmation is found in St. Luke's own account of the Transfiguration, Luke ix:28-36.[19] In that passage, (1) the Apostles see Our Lord's " glory (doxan) " (v. 32); (2) the Cloud " overshadows " them (episkiazein, the same Greek verb as in Luke i:35 and

---

[17] John i:14, where exegetes see an intentional connection between the Greek verb skēnoun, to dwell, and the corresponding Hebrew shakan; as well as a further connection with the word "glory" which follows. A recent commentator on St. John writes: " It has been thought that the word skēnoun was chosen here with special reference to the word doxa, which follows. It recalls, in sound and meaning, the Hebrew shakan, which means ' to dwell '; the verb is used of the dwelling of God with Israel (e.g. Ex. xxv:8; xxix:46; Zach. ii:14), and a derived noun shechinah was used (though not in the Old Testament) as a periphrasis for the name of God himself. Further, the bright cloud settled down (shakan) upon the Tabernacle (Ex. xxiv:16; xl:35), and since this cloud was the visible manifestation of the presence of God . . . the abiding presence of God suggested his glory (kabod, doxa; see below) " (C. K. Barrett, Gospel according to St. John, London, 1956, 138). We have here, clearly, an instance of what was referred to above, the hidden but unmistakable affinity between the Gospel of St. John and that of St. Luke, with their respective " Mariologies " as one of the vital bonds between them.

[18] For the details see Lyonnet, op. cit., 15, n.2; Laurentin, Structure, 79-81.

[19] See Laurentin, Structure, 76. It is puzzling, however, to find Laurentin writing at this point: " Sans doute le mot gloire employé en Ex. xl:35 n'est-il pas repris dans le récit de la Transfiguration, ni par Luc (ix:34) ni par les synoptiques (Mt. xvii:1-8; Mc. ix:2-8)." Not, indeed, in ix:34, but in ix:32 St. Luke significantly departs from the phraseology of Mt. and Mk. and writes of Peter, James, and John: " eidon tēn doxan autou, they saw his glory." The resemblance to John i:14 is striking: " etheasametha tēn doxan autou, we saw his glory." Cf. 2 Pet. i:17.

in the Septuagint of Ex. xl:33); (3) the Father expressly declares the divine Sonship of Christ: " this is my chosen Son; hear him " (v. 35, critical Greek text).

Conclusions. (1) The divinity of Mary's Son is revealed in this passage. It is not revealed abruptly, nor in abstract terms; but gradually, and in organic and " typological " dependence on foreshadowings of the Incarnation already contained in the Old Testament.

(2) Revealed in this gradual and concrete way, it is assimilated by Our Lady in a corresponding way: gradually, and in concrete terms which are rooted in the Old Testament. There is no sudden blinding flash of complete illumination. St. Luke's narrative shows us two things: (a) on God's side, a gradual revelation in concrete terms; (b) on Our Lady's side, a reflective and prayerful mind, a sensitive responsiveness to all God's dealings with her People and with herself personally, an awareness of the spiritual inwardness of the most profound passages of the Old Testament.

(3) For the full significance of all the Angel said to come home finally to Our Lady, St. Luke's telling of the story shows us that two further elements were needed and duly supplied. The first was the unfolding *in historical fact* of the implications of the Incarnation here announced. All that followed from the primordial fact and doctrine of the Incarnation—such as the Visitation, the Birth in Bethlehem, the Presentation, the Finding in the Temple—helped to make clearer its divine dimensions. The second was Our Lady's own reflective and prayerful response, over a period of time, to that primordial revelation and its subsequent unfolding. To this response St. Luke himself deliberately draws our attention at intervals in what followed: " Mary kept treasuring up all these things, pondering them in her heart." " His mother kept treasuring all those things in her heart " (Luke ii:19, 51).

Our Lady in the Patristic Age

By P. G. Duncker, O.P.

IT is surely not easy to give in one lecture a fair idea of
Our Lady in the patristic age. It will necessarily have to
be a general picture, and I shall try to draw this in such a
way that one can see in it the main features by which the
Blessed Virgin presented herself to the Fathers as time
went on.

Because of the more recent marvellous increase of devotion
to Our Lady, which on the one hand has induced the Church
to pronounce itself more definitely on various points of
Marian doctrine and, on the other, is also itself partly the
result of these ecclesiastical declarations, an ever richer
literature has lately been produced, exalting, explaining,
defining many privileges of the Mother of God. And I want
here to confess my debt to the principal more scientific
publications mentioned in the notes to this paper.[1]

Laurentin entitles his brief survey on Our Lady through
the ages: " La découverte de Marie dans les temps."[2] This
is indeed the impression one gets after having studied the
place the Blessed Virgin occupied in the patristic age; she
had to be and was, little by little, discovered. Of course
she was always there as the virginal Mother of Jesus, as she
had already been announced to some degree in the Old Testament and as she clearly appeared from the New. But how
discreetly and unpretendingly! As soon as Christ sets out for
his public mission his Mother retires, to reappear only at the
supreme moment, when her Child dies on the Cross for the
redemption of mankind. Ever more numerous are the authors
who see in the word " woman," addressed by the Son to his

---

[1] The study I am most indebted to is that published by G. Jouassard, "Marie
à travers la patristique, maternité divine, virginité, sainteté," in *Maria* (ed. du
Manoir), 1, Paris, 1949, 69-157.

[2] R. Laurentin, "La Vierge Marie," in *Initiation théologique*, 4, Paris, 1954, 241-73.

Mother both in Cana and on Calvary, an allusion to her as the new Eve and the proclamation of her spiritual maternity.

With similar discretion Our Lady is presented in the first centuries, as far as one can judge from the texts that have come to us. And yet, they already contain the essentials of what can be said of her. Apart from the New Testament testimonies, of which Father Kearns has already spoken, of the apostolic age we know only that her virginal conception of Christ was commonly held. But the second century already offers us a few texts of the greatest importance. In St. Justin's *Dialogue with Trypho* the Virgin Mary is compared with Eve, still virgin, untouched, who, having accepted the word of the serpent, brought forth disobedience and death; whereas Mary, having received with faith and joy the announcement that the Spirit of the Lord would come upon her and the virtue of the Most High overshadow her, and that therefore the One to be born from her would be holy, the Son of God, answered: " Thy will be done." [3] Still stronger and more significant is the testimony St. Irenaeus gave in his *Adversus Haereses* and *Demonstratio*: Eve, having a husband, but still virgin, disobedient, is the cause of death for the whole human race; Mary, to whom a husband was already appointed, yet virgin, obedient, became the cause of salvation for all mankind.[4] And arguing against Tatian, who did not believe that Adam and Eve after their fall were restored to grace, St. Irenaeus wrote:

> It was just and necessary that Adam should be restored in Christ, in order that the mortal be absorbed and engulfed by immortality; (also) that Eve should be restored in Mary, in order that, a Virgin becoming the advocate of a virgin, the disobedience of a virgin be wiped out and abolished by her obedience as Virgin.[5]

In these second century texts Our Lady is thus already designated as: the new Eve, Virgin, holy, Mother of God, co-operatrix of Our Lord in the salvation of mankind,

[3] PG 6, 712.
[4] Adv. Haer., 3, 22, 4, PG 7, 958 f.
[5] Patrologia Orientalis, 12, 772 f.

mediatrix as advocate interceding for Eve; the following ages will only bring out these Marian prerogatives more clearly and develop them.

The idea of Mary as a contrasting parallel to Eve crops up again in the works of many Fathers and ecclesiastical writers: Tertullian, Origen, St. Gregory Nazianzen, St. Gregory of Nyssa, St. Cyril of Jerusalem, St. Epiphanius, St. John Chrysostom, St. Ambrose, St. Jerome, St. Augustine and others down to St. John Damascene.[6] Often they do not present much more than was already said by St. Irenaeus, but the meaning of the parallel becomes clearer and is deepened. From the first it had contained the theme of " recirculation " or " recapitulation," as it is called: what was begun with Adam and Eve has taken a new commencement with Christ and Mary. So St. Gregory Nazianzen points out that we now have " the birth (of Christ) instead of creation, the Virgin in the place of the woman (Eve), Bethlehem for Eden, the manger for Paradise." [7] But the most important contribution to the unfolding of the parallel was made by St. Epiphanius, who very often comes back to it. It would be too long to cite here all his texts concerning it, and it may suffice to give the synthesis of his doctrine in the words of A. Müller:

> The Virgin Eve is the prototype of the Virgin Mary; this is to be seen at once in her title " Mother of the living " and in the promise of the *Protoevangelium*; both are for the first time fully realized in Mary. Whereas Eve has brought death the Son of Mary has been life, the conqueror of the Serpent. He is also the only first-born of whom it can rightly be said that he has opened the maternal womb. The word about Adam and Eve that Paul applied to Christ and the Church holds good for Mary and Christ. Joined to Mary Christ has formed himself

[6] Cf. G. Jouassard, " La Nouvelle Ève chez les Pères Anténicéens" in *La Nouvelle Ève (Bulletin de la Société Française d'Études Mariales)*, 1, 1954, 35-54; B. Capelle, O.S.B., " La Thème de la Nouvelle Ève chez les anciens docteurs latins," ibid., 55-76; Th. Camelot, O.P., " Marie, la Nouvelle Ève, dans la patristique grecque, du Concile de Nicée à saint Jean Damascène," ibid., 157-72; cf. also R. Laurentin, " L'Interprétation de la Genèse iii:15 dans la tradition jusqu'au début du XIIIe siècle," ibid., 77-154.

[7] *Oratio* 2, 24, PG 35, 433.

a body, and from its side has come forth the Church in the mystery of water and blood.[8]

The parallel " Eve-Church " is also a very frequent one in the writings of the Fathers, and Eve is likewise compared to other women such as Sara, Mary Magdalene, the women at Jesus' tomb; but the main parallel has always been for them " Eve-Mary."

That Our Lady, as Virgin, conceived her divine Son has never been doubted in the patristic age; but the truth about her corporal integrity at the moment of her childbearing (*virginitas in partu*) and about her never having had any other children than Jesus (*virginitas post partum*) was only gradually made clear and accepted by all.

This double virginity of Mary was much insisted upon in the apocryphal writings e.g. the so-called *Protoevangelium* of James; but we are not too sure which of the elements composing them go back to the second century. Moreover, the apocrypha with their so patently legendary and fantastic features are by no means the right source from which to gain a just idea about Our Lord and Our Lady, though not everything is *a priori* to be considered false. It is even quite likely that antipathy towards these writings among the more level-headed, together with the fear of rising heresies such as those of the Docetists and Marcionites, induced the Fathers to be rather discreet and even a little hesitant about the virginal prerogatives of Our Lady.

Tertullian firmly holds the virginal conception of Jesus; [9] yet in his polemical writings he seems to present the birth of Our Lord as quite normal [10] and maintains that the " brethren of the Lord " were Mary's children.[11] Clement of Alexandria defended both Mary's virginity *in partu* and *post partum*, though he had to admit that several—and these were not necessarily all heretics, for he never stigmatizes them as such—did not accept the former.[12] Whether one

---

[8] A. Müller, *Ecclesia-Maria. Die Einheit Marias und der Kirche*, Freiburg (Schweiz), 1951, 144; cf. Camelot, loc. cit., 160-63.

[9] *De Praescriptione*, 13 and 36, PL 2, 31, 60.

[10] *Adv. Marcionem*, 3, 11, PL 2, 363 f.

[11] Cf. e.g. *De Carne Christi*, 7, PL 2, 811-814.

[12] *Stromata*, 7, 16, PG 9, 529-32.

of them was Origen, his own successor at the Alexandrian
School, cannot be proved with certainty from authentic texts;
but Jouassard is rather inclined to take that view.[13] With
the more ascetical circles of his time Origen maintained
Mary's virginity *post partum*, as he himself expressly declares;
which statement, however, again implies that in other circles
people thought differently.[14] Eusebius is very well aware of
the hesitations about Mary's perpetual virginity, though
personally he holds that she had no other sons.[15] St. Athanasius is on the whole very reticent about the Blessed Virgin, yet
in a Coptic text ascribed to him he defends the same opinion
against those who recognized the brethren of the Lord as her
children; we do not know what he thought of her virginity
in partu.[16] Something similar is to be said of St. Ephraem,
at least according to his authentic writings; no more than
Athanasius does he seem to regard the subject in question as
a matter of faith.[17] That Mary had other sons was publicly
preached by Eunomius in the presence of Eudoxius, bishop
of Constantinople; they both were Arians, but they regarded
Our Lady as the holy Virgin on account of her virginity *in
partu*.[18] A certain author whom one identifies with St.
Basil wrote against that sermon; he thinks it absolutely
impossible that Mary ever had other children, but adds
that faith is not touched by it, since her virginity up to
the Incarnation only is required; after that time " it is not
of great importance as to that mystery." He also knows
that there are many *philochristoi* who think as he does, and
prefers to adhere to their view, calling them the " well-
thinking." [19] St. Epiphanius is the first to describe as heretical
the view that Mary had children besides Jesus,[20] and largely
through his authority the number of its supporters continually
dwindled. Stronger hesitation remained on Mary's virginity

[13] " Marie à travers la patristique," 78-82.
[14] *Comm. in Mattheum*, 10, 17, PG 13, 876 f.
[15] *Admonitio ad Apol. S. Pamphili pro Origene*, PG 17, 554; *Comm. in Ps.* 68, 9,
PG 23, 937-40.
[16] Cf. L. Th. Lefort, " S. Athanase, ' Sur la virginite,' " *Le Muséon*, 42 (1929),
197-275; Jouassard, " Marie à travers la patristique," 87.
[17] Cf. Jouassard, loc. cit., 87 f.
[18] Cf. *Hist. Eccl. Philostorgii*, GCS 21, 71.
[19] *Homelia in Sanctam Christi Generationem*, 5, PG 31, 1468 f. Cf. PG 29, clxxiv.
[20] *Adversus Antidicomarianitas*, 1, PG 42, 700.

in partu, though St. John Chrysostom, who, as we shall see, had a peculiar view on her sanctity, defended it.[21] However, the whole question about the twofold virginity of Our Lady will soon be settled, to no small extent through the influence of the Western Fathers.

Of St. Hilary we only know his favourable attitude towards Mary's virginity *post partum*,[22] but Zeno, bishop of Verona, plainly admitted: " Maria virgo incorrupta concepit, post conceptum virgo peperit, post partum virgo permansit." [23] With St. Ambrose, the great herald of Mary, the question came to a decisive stage.

A certain Carterius, thus named in St. Jerome's *Adversus Helvidium* in praise of virginity, which was much practised in Roman ascetical circles, presented Mary as ever-Virgin. Against him Helvidius defended the matrimonial state, maintaining that Mary is not only the model of virgins on account of her virginity up to the Incarnation, but also the paragon of all married women as the perfect Mother of many children. St. Jerome launched his tract *Adversus Helvidium* to demonstrate that the virginal state far surpasses the matrimonial, forcibly arguing that Mary never had any children besides Our Lord.[24] Jovinian, who having first lived an ascetical life had later given it up, attacked this position; but his propositions were condemned as heretical by Siricius, successor to St. Damasus on the papal throne.[25] Appealing from Rome to the Emperor Theodosius, then at Milan, he got into further difficulties, for Siricius informed St. Ambrose and asked him to intervene at the imperial court; whereupon Jovinian was expelled from Milan and later on once more condemned by a council of that city.[26] On this occasion his denial of Mary's virginity *in partu* was brought up and St. Ambrose wanted to know what Rome thought about it. There St. Jerome was looked upon as not being much in favour of it.[27]

---

[21] *In Matthaeum Homilia* 5, 21, 3, *PG* 42, 700.
[22] *Comm. in Matthaeum*, 3, *PL* 9, 921 f.
[23] *Tractatus*, lib. 2, tract. 8, *PL* 11, 414 f.
[24] *Adv. Helvidium*, *PL* 23, 194-215.
[25] Letter *Optarem semper*, Mansi, 3, 663-664.
[26] Letter *Recognovimus*, ibid., 664-66.
[27] Cf. his realistic description of the birth of Our Lord in *Adv. Helvidium*, loc. cit., 212 f.

More or less forced to defend himself, he wrote his *Adversus Jovinianum* in which he again vigorously spoke up for the virginal state, but only in very vague terms touched upon the point in question of Mary's virginity *in partu*.[28] Since at the same time he vehemently wrote against matrimony, his tract was not well received, and he was even asked by one of his former fellow-students, the Roman senator Pammachius, to withdraw it. He tried to explain himself in a letter to Pammachius; but here again one cannot quite make out what precisely he held about Our Lady's virginity at the moment she brought forth her Child.[29]   However, St. Ambrose showed himself satisfied with St. Jerome's exposition. Since in the meantime Bonosus, bishop somewhere in Illyricum, was condemned, principally through St. Ambrose's influence, for not holding Mary's virginity *post partum*,[30] the whole doctrine became settled in the West, and soon also in the East. At the Council of Constantinople (553) and more expressly at that of Lateran (649) it was defined a dogma of faith.[31]

To Our Lady's perfect and perpetual virginity corresponded the highest degree of sanctity. But again, the truth concerning this great prerogative of hers became only gradually plainly manifest in the patristic age. Her sanctity was always regarded as extraordinary; nonetheless we come across a number of texts which speak of certain imperfections, short-comings, faults of the Blessed Virgin and which to some extent seem to reflect ideas and views of the faithful, since these texts are often found in sermons preached to them.

Tertullian, though defending Our Lady against more serious accusations on the part of Jews and heretics,[32] finds in her some lack of faith, even claiming that on account of this she was disavowed by Our Lord.[33] Origen does not go so far and on the whole speaks very highly of Mary, yet admits

[28] *Adv. Jovinianum*, 1, 31, *PL* 23, 265 f.
[29] *Epistola 47 seu Liber Apologeticus ad Pammachium*, 21, *PL* 22, 494-511, cf. 510.
[30] Cf. Mansi 3, 674 f.; *De Institutione Virginis*, 35, *PL*, 16, 328.
[31] Cf. Mansi 9, 377; ibid., 10, 1151.
[32] *De Spectaculis*, 30, *PL* 1, 736.
[33] *Adv. Marcionem*, 4, 19, *PL* 2, 433-35.

that she had some transitory doubts now and then.[34]   St. Athanasius also, according to the Coptic text ascribed to him and already mentioned,[35] manifests the greatest esteem for Our Lady; nevertheless certain passing expressions of his seem to allude to small imperfections of hers.   St. Epiphanius's praise is without any restriction; not the slightest weakness is to be found in Mary, though she is not to be adored as a goddess.[36]   St. Basil, answering a letter of Optimus, bishop of Antioch, on Luke ii:35, thinks that if Mary had ever been somewhat lacking in faith, her sorrows and pains on account of her divine Son's Passion would surely have restored it.[37]   St. Amphilochius of Iconium seems to have spoken in a similar way.[38]   St. Gregory Nazianzen supposes a purification of Mary at the moment of the Incarnation.[39]   St. John Chrysostom's peculiar views on Our Lady's sanctity are well known: he maintained that she found it difficult to say her *fiat*; that she was severely rebuked by Our Lord at Cana for putting herself to the forefront; that she had no proper idea about the divinity of her Son (Mt. xii:46-47); that she was lacking in faith; and if she was not disavowed by Him, it was only because of His respect for His Mother.[40]   One of St. John Chrysostom's successors, Atticus, refers to stains having surrounded her birth; and these would have contaminated her Son if God had not prevented this; but, on the other hand, he exalts Our Lady very highly, considering her the most saintly of all creatures.[41]   Again St. Cyril of Alexandria contends that Mary, pertaining to the weaker sex, had also her own weaknesses, and that the Apostle St. John had

---

[34] Cf. *Hom. 17 in Lucam, PG* 13, 1845 f.

[35] Cf. *supra*, p. 46.

[36] *Panarion, Adversus Collyridianos, PG* 42, 740-56.

[37] *Epistola* 260, *PG* 32, 965-68.

[38] *Oratio de Hypapante*, 8, *PG* 39, 56-60.

[39] *Oratio* 38 " In Theophaniam," 13, *PG* 36, 325, 633.

[40] *In Matth. Hom.* 4 and 44, *PG* 57, 44 f., 463-466; *In Joan. Homiliae* 21 and 22, *PG* 59, 129-34.

[41] J. Lebon, " Discours d'Atticus de Constantinople ' Sur la Sainte Mère de Dieu '," *Le Muséon*, 46 (1933), 190-91; M. Brière, " Une homélie inédite d'Atticus patriarch de Constantinople (406-425)," *Rev. Or. Chrét.*, 29 (1933-34), 180-82; F. S. Müller, " Die unbefleckte Empfangnis der Gottesmutter in der griechischen Ueberlieferung," *Gregorianum*, 16 (1935), 80-82.

been charged by Our Lord precisely to help her in her difficulties.[42]

In the West we come across similar opinions. St. Hilary sees in Our Lady the synagogue represented; he supposes a purification at the moment of the Incarnation and thinks that Our Lord will have found in her certain things to reprove her for at the hour of her death.[43] With St. Ambrose we again arrive at the highest idea about the Blessed Virgin; no imperfection in her, model of virgins, practising all virtues, " virgo per gratiam ab omni integra labe peccati."[44]

This question of Our Lady's sanctity now enters a decisive stage. According to St. Augustine's *De Natura et Gratia* Pelagius had declared that piety demanded that Our Lady be adjudged free from sin.[45]   Apart from St. Ambrose no one had thus far spoken so clearly and highly of her. However, that statement was a conclusion drawn from false premisses. Pelagius produced the argument that if there were so many just and holy men and women mentioned in sacred Scripture, Mary must surely surpass them all in personal sanctity; this sanctity, however, both in her case and in theirs, he ascribed to personal effort. But St. Augustine, plainly admitting Mary's perfect sanctity, pointed out that this was not due to her personal efforts, but to God's special grace; as to the case of all the other saints of the Old and New Testament, one should not extol these too much, because they would surely say: " si dixerimus quia peccatum non habemus, nos ipsos decipimus et veritas in nobis non est."[46]

With Julian of Eclanum the question of Our Lady's sanctity was brought into relation with original sin, though this point had in some measure been anticipated in St. Augustine's words against Pelagius: " Excepta itaque sancta virgine Maria, de qua propter honorem Domini nullam prorsus, cum de peccatis agitur, haberi volo quaestionem . . . "[47]

---

[42] *Comment. in S. Joannis Evang.* 12, 19, PG 74, 661-65; cf. Ph. Pusey, *Sancti Patris Nostri Cyrilli Archiepiscopi Alexandrini in D. Joannis Evangelium*, 3, 1872, 89-93.

[43] *De Trinitate*, 2, 26, PL 10, 67; *Tractatus in Ps.* 118, 12, PL 9, 523.

[44] *Expositio in Psalmum* 118, *Sermo* 22, 30, PL 15, 1599.

[45] " Sine peccato confiteri necesse est pietati," PL 44, 267.

[46] Ibid.

[47] Ibid.

In a work *Contra Florum*, known to us only from St. Augustine's *Opus Imperfectum adversus Julianum*, Julian accuses St. Augustine of Manicheism and calls him worse than Jovinian: " Ille virginitatem Mariae partus conditione dissolvit, tu ipsam Mariam diabolo nascendi conditione transcribis." [48] Julian was a strenuous defender of Pelagius. With him he held that man is good by nature, that there is no question of original sin, that consequently Mary's perfect sanctity must have originated at the very moment of her conception. In this conclusion one could even see Mary's Immaculate Conception, but here again the conclusion is drawn from false premisses. And these were attacked by St. Augustine in his reply to Julian. He did not refer to Jovinian, who denied Mary's virginity, but answered Julian's direct assault on him by retorting: " Non transcribimus diabolo Mariam conditione nascendi; sed ideo, quia ipsa conditio nascendi solvitur gratia renascendi." [49] A great deal has been written on this particular phrase of St. Augustine's, and one has to admit that it is not too clear either in itself or in its context. [50] However, in accordance with St. Augustine's doctrine it can only mean that Mary, who like all human beings should be conceived in original sin and on account of this be subjected to the devil, was at the moment of her conception released from it by God's special grace and was, therefore, never under the devil's dominion. Yet, the fact that from St. Augustine's words, cited above, it is not quite patent and obvious that this " release " from original sin means precisely preservation or protection from it, may be the reason why on this precise aspect of Our Lady's sanctity, viz. her Immaculate Conception, there remained more hesitation in the West than in the East, where it became more easily accepted. As to the Blessed Virgin's sanctity on the whole, we find that both in the West and in the East, though hesitations may still be noted, it is progressively more vigorously preached and readily acknowledged. A great factor in this development was, without doubt, the Council of Ephesus, which dealt with that other

[48] *Opus Imperfectum Contra Julianum*, 4, 122, PL 45, 1417.
[49] Ibid., 1418.
[50] Cf. Jouassard, " Marie à travers la patristique," 118, who refers to the more important literature on this point.

prerogative of Mary, the greatest one of all—her divine maternity.

On this point there were from the very beginning far fewer difficulties. Though the title " Mother of God " does not occur in the texts of the first centuries, yet, since Mary was universally known to be the Mother of Jesus Our Lord and He, in spite of some heretical views, firmly acknowledged as God, there was no serious doubt concerning her divine maternity; this was, as we may say, implicitly accepted by all, and explicitly by some e.g. St. Ignatius Martyr,[51] St. Irenaeus,[52] St. Ephraem.[53] From the fourth century the term *theotokos* quite frequently appears in the writings of the Eastern Fathers e.g. St. Alexander of Alexandria,[54] St. Athanasius,[55] St. Gregory Nazianzen,[56] St. Epiphanius.[57] Diodorus of Tarsus [58] and Theodore of Mopsuestia [59] explained it by asserting that Mary is mother of the man Jesus. This surely was not a very happy explanation and it led them into trouble—a result, incidentally, which shows that the divine maternity was commonly admitted. Again, those in favour of Mary's virginity *in partu* consequently held Our Lady to be the Mother of God; or rather, precisely because they accepted her as such, they concluded to her virginity *in partu*. St. Ambrose very much insisted on Mary's divine maternity,[60] and we heard St. Augustine already declare that he did not want to hear of any sin whatsoever in Mary " propter honorem Domini," whose Mother she was.[61]

This primary dignity of Our Lady, her greatest privilege and prerogative, was officially dealt with at the Council of Ephesus. Following upon Nestorius's rejection of the title *theotokos* and St. Cyril's subsequent spirited defence of it,[62]

---

[51] *Ephes.*, 18, PG 5, 660.
[52] *Adv. Haer.*, 3, 21, PG 7, 955.
[53] *Hymni de B. Maria*, 18, 12, T. Lamy, S. *Ephraem Syri Hymni et Sermones*, Malines, 1882-1902, vol. 2, 608.
[54] *Epistola ad Alexandrum Constantinopolitanum*, 12, PG 18, 568.
[55] *De Incarn. et Contra Arianos*, 8, PG 26, 996.
[56] *Epistola ad Cledonium*, PG 37, 177.
[57] *Ancoratus*, 75, PG 43, 157.
[58] E. Schwarz, *Acta Conciliorum Oecumenicorum*, t. 1, vol. 4, 216.
[59] *Fragmenta Dogmatica*, PG 66, 991.
[60] *De Virginibus ad Marcellinam*, 7, PL 16, 209.
[61] Cf. *supra*, p. 50.
[62] See Dr. McGreevy's paper, pp. 57 ff.

both Nestorius and Cyril applied to Rome. Rome decided that Nestorius should retract, otherwise he would be excommunicated and deposed; St. Cyril was ordered to see to this.[63] However, he himself convoked a council at Alexandria and the result of it was a document largely drawn up by St. Cyril, in which he strongly attacked Nestorius's christological views; an anathema was attached against all those who refused to consider Mary *theotokos*.[64] So the question was now officially extended to the wider one of the natures and person in Christ.

As the bishops who had to take the decisions of both Rome and Alexandria to Constantinople arrived there, they learned that the Emperor Theodosius, at the request of Nestorius, had convened an ecumenical council at Ephesus for Pentecost, 431.[65] And Nestorius claimed that the decisions against him were now suspended on account of this new council. But Rome insisted on its decisions, though at this time Nestorius was already willing to admit the title *theotokos* and had explained this to the Pope.[66] In the meantime John, bishop of Antioch, who had tried to persuade Nestorius to submit to Rome,[67] received together with the convocation to the council St. Cyril's document. He discovered traces of Apollinarianism and Monophysitism in it and denounced these with the help of Theodoret of Cyr and Andrew of Samosata.[68] So St. Cyril was now the accused, whereas Nestorius, in his reply to John, bishop of Antioch, boasted that he preached Mary as *theotokos*.[69] St. Cyril defended himself[70] and once more applied to Rome. Rome decided that Nestorius should be allowed to explain himself before the Council of Ephesus; for the time being the Roman decisions should be maintained.[71] Rome even sent three delegates;[72] but before they arrived St. Cyril had on his own accord convoked the Fathers

---

[63] PG 77, 89-93; ACO, vol. 1, 75-77.
[64] PG 77, 105-21; ACO, ibid., 33-42.
[65] ACO, ibid., 114-16; Mansi 4, 1112-1116.
[66] ACO, vol. 2, 12-14; vol. 5, 182.
[67] PG 77, 1449-1457; ACO, vol. 1, 93-96.
[68] Cf. St. Cyril's defence against Theodoret in PG 76, 385-452; ACO, vol. 1, part 6, 107-146; against Andrew, PG 76, 316-85; ACO, vol. 1, part 7, 33-65.
[69] ACO, vol. 4, 4-6.
[70] Cf. note 68.
[71] ACO, vol. 4, 27-30.
[72] About their mission cf. PL 50, 503-12; ACO, vol. 2, 22-26.

and presided, though the imperial delegate and sixty-eight bishops protested. Nestorius was summoned to appear, but did not come. In this session Nestorius was again condemned, his christological views repudiated and he himself deposed.[73] A few days later John of Antioch, arriving with his bishops, held a council which he claimed was the real ecumenical council convoked by the emperor, deposed St. Cyril with Memnon the bishop of Ephesus and excommunicated all the bishops who supported them.[74] When finally the papal legates arrived, they confirmed everything decided by St. Cyril and his bishops [75] and excommunicated John and his group. The emperor, wanting to be impartial and trying to reunite the adversaries, sanctioned both the deposition of Nestorius and that of St. Cyril and Memnon. The bishops associated with St. Cyril vehemently protested but John's followers were satisfied, since St. Cyril was condemned.[76] Of course, this condemnation came to nothing, and peace was soon restored. John recognized that he had misunderstood St. Cyril. As to dogmatic matters there was no real difference between them, as may be understood from a declaration drawn up by John and his bishops:

> The two natures (of Christ) are united (in the Incarnation). Therefore we confess but one Christ, one Son, one Lord. In virtue of this notion of indissoluble unity we confess that the Blessed Virgin is Mother of God, on account of the fact that God the Word (*Logos*) has become flesh, incarnate, and from the moment of his Incarnation has united to Himself the temple (of the flesh) He has assumed from Mary.[77]

A few years later St. Cyril approved this declaration.[78] From this time on East and West agreed about Mary's divine maternity. It still took some time, however, before this essential and fundamental doctrine had penetrated so profoundly as not only to dispel all hesitations and even errors

---

[73] About the *Acta* of this session, cf. *ACO*, vol. 1, part 5, 119-24; Mansi 4, 1260-1269.

[74] For what is known of this pseudo-council cf. *ACO*, vol. 1, part 5, 119-27.

[75] *ACO*, vol. 1, part 3, 53-63; Mansi 4, 1280-1300.

[76] Jouassard, "Marie à travers la patristique," 131.

[77] *ACO*, vol. 1, part 7, 70.

[78] *PG* 77, 173-81; *ACO*, vol. 1, part 4, 15-20.

about Mary's perpetual virginity *in partu* and *post partum* and about her perfect sanctity, but also to bring into clearer light other aspects and consequences.

How these later developments of Marian doctrine e.g. Our Lady's Immaculate Conception, Assumption, co-operation with Christ, mediation, intercession and spiritual maternity have been, from St. Justin and St. Irenaeus on, at least implicitly known in the first centuries and sometimes explicitly expressed, has been already, or is still to be dealt with in other lectures of this Summer School.

In conclusion, reviewing the whole process of " the gradual discovery of Our Lady in the patristic age," we observe that on the one hand some Fathers and ecclesiastical authors, out of intelligible and even praiseworthy antipathy towards the apocryphal writings, out of fear of and reaction against heresies, and with the sincere intention to safeguard the supreme and unique holiness of Christ, were inclined to underestimate or not to grasp fully the true sense and extension of certain prerogatives of Our Lady; whereas on the other hand the defence of these Marian privileges on erroneous principles brought other Fathers to find and give them their proper theological foundation. And we admire and gratefully acknowledge the wonderful, invisible but real working of the Holy Ghost, safely guiding and conducting the Church through so many dangerous vicissitudes to an ever clearer under-standing of the revealed truth about Our Lady as contained in holy Scripture and sacred Tradition.

Divine Maternity

BY JOHN J. MCGREEVY, D.D.

THERE are good reasons for regarding the heresy of Nestorius as the most serious doctrinal crisis in the history of Christianity. The distinction might, indeed, be claimed for the rationalism of the nineteenth century, yet the rationalism of Nestorius was, we believe, much more serious because it was much more reasonable. By denying the doctrine of the divinity of Christ Nestorianism struck at the very heart of Christianity, but it did so without doing any violence either to reason or to history. Unlike the rationalism of modern times it did not propound a theory for which the only logical basis is atheism, and it did no violence to history because it respected the authenticity and integrity of the Gospels; it denied no miracles and eliminated no texts from the Scriptures. It was rationalism that admitted the supernatural, that defended the dogma of the Trinity, that accepted, in short, all the mysteries of Christianity with the exception of the mystery of the Incarnation. And since the Incarnation was not absolutely necessary for the redemption of the world, it is conceivable that some less profound intervention of God could have taken place, resulting in a religion such as Nestorius erroneously thought Christianity to be. It was in his fundamental failure to accept the Incarnation rather than in his subsequent reasoning that Nestorius went wrong.

It was the work of the Council of Ephesus to establish the truth that the good tidings of Christianity were immeasurably better than was allowed by Nestorius—that " God so loved the world as to give His only-begotten Son " [1] and that in doing so He had raised a daughter of Eve to the sublime dignity of being the Mother of God. Thus the doctrine of the Divine Maternity of Our Lady is at the very basis of Christianity, or rather it contains the very basis of Christianity for it signifies that the Son of Mary is at once perfect God and perfect man. Little wonder, then, that in the controversy

[1] John iii:16.

which led to the convocation of the Council of Ephesus the word *theotokos*, like the word *homoousios* at the Council of Nice, should become the touchstone of orthodoxy and should be inserted in the Church's definition of the truth of the Incarnation. It thus received as honoured a place in the dogmatic formulae of the Church as it had long received in the writings of the Fathers and in the devotion of the faithful.

NESTORIUS AND THE COUNCIL OF EPHESUS

It was Nestorius's opposition to the veneration of Our Lady as *theotokos*, or Mother of God, that first drew attention to the error in his Christology. Soon after his appointment to the see of Constantinople [2] he preached a series of sermons in which he denounced the practice of honouring Our Lady as the Mother of God. *Theotokos*, he declared, was a title which was proper to the First Person of the Trinity.[3] To attribute it to Our Lady was to imply that the *Logos* derived His divine nature from a creature,[4] it was to make Mary a goddess [5] and expose Christianity to the ridicule even of pagans. The term, he pointed out, was to be found neither in the Scriptures nor in the definitions of the Council of Nice,[6] it favoured the heresies of Arius and Apollinaris;[7] and the better to safeguard the purity of the Christian faith Nestorius proposed that the following should be defined by the Church: " If any one says that Mary is the mother of God the *Logos* and not rather the mother of Him who is Emmanuel, let him be anathema." [8] Mary, he suggested, should be venerated neither as *theotokos* nor as *anthropotokos* but as *Christotokos*, that is, as " the Mother of Christ." [9] Instead of saying that " God was born of Mary "

[2] On the whole see e.g. C. Hefele, *A History of the Councils of the Church* (E. Tr.), 3, Edinburgh, 1883, 9-39; M. Jugie, *Nestorius et la controverse Nestorienne*, Paris, 1912, 19-68, 118-124.
[3] Hefele, op. cit., 16; A. Loofs, *Nestoriana*, Halle, 1905, 276.
[4] Jugie, op. cit., 119.
[5] Hefele, 12-14. Divine honours were given Our Lady at that time by the Collyridians—Epiphanius, *Panarion*, 79, PG 42, 740-756. Cf. J. Danielou, *Le Culte Marial et le paganisme*, in Du Manoir, *Maria*, 1, Paris, 1949, 172-173.
[6] Hefele, 20.
[7] Jugie, 118. " Scis hoc Apollinarem dicentem? Scis hanc vocem, *to theotokos* apud Arium plausus maximos excitare? Scis hanc quoque apud Eunomium frequentari? "
[8] Hefele, 35.
[9] Jugie, 31, 123-124.

it would be more correct to say that " God passed through Mary " [10] or, indeed, one could say that she was *theodochos*— she was one " who had received God " because God the Word had come to dwell in him who was born of her.[11] Under the pressure of controversy Nestorius relaxed to this extent in his opposition to the use of the term *theotokos*: he would allow the term provided it was rightly understood. What this right understanding was he explained in his letter to Pope Celestine I: Mary could be called *theotokos* in the sense that she is the mother of him who is the temple in which the Word of God dwells.[12] In short Mary could be called the Mother of God to the extent that Christ her son could be called God and from the writings of Nestorius it soon became abundantly clear that for him Christ was God only in the sense that he was a man united to the Word of God in an intimate and unique way.[13] But he was not the Second Person of the Trinity and his mother, therefore, could not truly and properly be called the Mother of God.

The sermons of Nestorius provoked a storm of protest in Constantinople. Several members of the clergy of the city publicly refuted the teaching of their bishop and Proclus, bishop of Cyzicus, mounted the pulpit in the presence of Nestorius and defended the popular devotion to Our Lady as *theotokos*. Feeling ran so high, indeed, that Nestorius called in the police and had several of his opponents flogged and imprisoned. The noise of the controversy soon reached far beyond the limits of the city. In the interests of peace the patriarch of Antioch, a friend of Nestorius, pleaded with him to abandon his opposition to the term *theotokos*, pointing out to him that it had been used by many of the Fathers [14] and was grounded in the teaching of St. Paul.[15] The most vigorous opposition to the new heresy came from the Church of Alexandria where the great St. Cyril defended the doctrine of the unity of Christ, vindicated the legitimacy of the title

---

[10] Hefele, 15.

[11] Hefele, 16; Loofs, *Nestoriana*, 276.

[12] E. Amann, art. " Nestorius," in *D.T.C.*, 11, 143.

[13] For Christology of Nestorius cf. Jugie, op. cit., 94-136.

[14] John of Antioch, *Ep. ad Nestorium*, PG 77, 1455-1457. John told him that this was also the mind of many other Eastern bishops.

[15] Gal. iv:4.

theotokos and expounded its true meaning in a noteworthy series of sermons and letters.[16]   Finally, Pope Celestine I convened a synod in Rome in 430 to investigate the matter and at this synod the teaching of Nestorius was condemned as heresy and the expression *theotokos* was approved.[17]   The mind of the universal Church was now revealed in these decisions of Antioch, Alexandria and Rome; and the matter might have ended there had Nestorius been less obstinate in his opinions and had the Emperor Theodosius II not intervened on his behalf. At the behest of the Emperor a general council was summoned to meet at Ephesus in June 431. Nestorius, evidently, had no intention of being martyred in defence of his convictions for he came to Ephesus with an armed body-guard provided by the Emperor.[18]   And while the bishops sat in council the troops of Theodosius paraded the streets, and Ephesus wore the appearance of a beleaguered city. The story of this council, surely one of the most dramatic in the history of the Church, must be read elsewhere; suffice it to say here that in spite of imperial intimidation the bishops under the presidency of St. Cyril assembled in the cathedral of Ephesus, dedicated to Our Lady as *theotokos*,[19] and solemnly proclaimed that Christ was the Second Person of the Trinity and that Mary was the Mother of God.[20]   The decrees of the Council were later ratified by the delegates of Pope Celestine.

[16] Hefele, 17-25; Jugie, 156-189; cf. J. Tixeront, *History of Dogmas* (E. Tr.), 3, London, 1926, 58-75.

[17] Hefele, 25.

[18] Socrates, *H.E.*, 7, 34: " As though going to battle he was accompanied by a large number of men in armour."

[19] Hefele, 45.

[20] *Denz.*, 111a. The council approved the second letter of St. Cyril to Nestorius where, *inter alia*, it is stated: " It was not that first an ordinary human being was born of the holy Virgin and then the Word descended upon that man, but in virtue of the union He is said to have been born according to the flesh from His Mother's womb . . .   Thus (the holy Fathers of the Church) have not hesitated to call the holy Virgin Mother of God." Cf. *Denz.*, 113. There is some doubt whether the anathemas of Cyril form part of the definition of Ephesus (see Hefele, 48, note 2) but, at any rate, they were adopted by the Second Council of Constantinople, 553. The teaching of Ephesus was repeated by the Council of Chalcedon (*Denz.*, 148) which also required Theodoret of Cyr to subscribe to the proposition " Anathema to Nestorius and to everyone who does not call the holy Virgin Mary Mother of God . . ." (Tixeront, 3, 88). The refusal of the bishops, who constituted at Ephesus the rival *conciliabulum* presided over by John of Antioch, to approve the teaching of Cyril does not mean that they shared the heretical views of Nestorius—they later drew up a profession of faith in which they proclaimed Our Lady as *theotokos*. See Hefele 129-131

Nestorius was the publicist rather than the author of the heresy that was condemned at Ephesus. The sermons which raised such a furore at Constantinople only served to present to the world theories which had long been current in what is known as the School of Antioch. Long before Nestorius Theodore of Mopsuestia (d. 428) had declared that it was nonsense to say that God was born of the Virgin Mary. " He who was born of the Virgin," he wrote, " is the one who was formed of her substance, not the Word who is God. He who is of one nature with the Father has no mother." [21] Mary is *theotokos* only " by relation," [22] that is to say, she is the mother of one who enjoys a unique relationship with the Second Person of the Trinity. Curiously enough, the teaching of Theodore escaped censure during his lifetime. It was only after the condemnation of Nestorius that attention was drawn to the heresy latent in the writings of Theodore and even then the question of his orthodoxy became the subject of a long and complicated controversy,[23] with the result that there was no official condemnation of his views until the Second Council of Constantinople in 553. The Council declared: [24]

> If any one says that the glorious, ever-Virgin Mary is not the Mother of God in a true sense, but only by a misuse of language,[25] or that she is the Mother of God only in a trans-ferred sense, as though a mere man were born of her and not the divine Word Incarnate . . . or if any one calls her " mother of man " or " mother of Christ " as if Christ were not God and does not admit that in the proper sense and in all truth she is Mother of God [26] . . . let such a one be anathema.

[21] Theodore, *Contra Apollinarem*, PG 66, 993.

[22] *kat' anaphoran*, *De Incarnatione*, PG 66, 992.

[23] The controversy has revived in recent times. The traditional view that Theodore was really a Nestorian has been defended in two recent studies: K. McNamara, " Theodore of Mopsuestia and the Nestorian Heresy," *Ir. Theol. Quart.*, 19 (1952), 254-278, 20 (1953), 172-191; F. Sullivan, *The Christology of Theodore of Mopsuestia*, Rome, 1956.

[24] *Denz.*, 218 (E. Tr.) from *The Church Teaches*, St. Louis, 1955, 176. This council also condemned the Letter of Ibas " which denies that God the Word was Incarnate of the Holy Mother of God . . . but asserts that a mere man was born of her." (*Denz.*, 227).

[25] *katachrēstikōs all 'ouk alēthōs*.

[26] *kuriōs kai kat' alētheian alēthōs*. The precision of this terminology was anticipated in the decree (*Denz.*, 202) in which Pope John II condemned (A.D. 534) the Acoe-metae, monks of Constantinople, who in their opposition to Monophysitism came to reject the term *theotokos*. The decree was also formulated to defend the dogma of the Divine Maternity against the teaching of Eutyches.

After the Council of Ephesus Theodore of Mopsuestia soon came to be regarded as the " Father of Nestorianism " and he was also accused of having been the first to deny to Our Lady the title *theotokos*.[27] It appears, however, that neither this paternity nor this primacy can be justly accorded to him. Theodore had learned his theology from Diodore, bishop of Tarsus (d. 392), and although the master escaped the censures visited on the pupil,[28] there is some evidence to show that there was no essential difference in their teaching.[29] Diodore expressly denies that the Word of God can be said to be the Son of Mary;[30] rather it was the temple built by the Word which was born of Mary. And like his successors Diodore too is willing enough to allow the title *theotokos* but in the sense that Mary is the mother of a man specially united to God.[31]

The history of dogma reveals more than one instance of orthodox formulae being rejected or being regarded as suspect because of the use made of them by writers who were anything but orthodox.[32] It may be some extenuation of the excesses of the theologians of Antioch that the term *theotokos* had found an ardent champion [33] in the person of Apollinaris of Laodicea (d.c. 390). In defending the doctrine of the unity of Christ Apollinaris taught that in the Incarnation the Word of God had united with Himself a human body in somewhat the same way as body and soul are united in us. He believed that in Christ the Word took the place of a human soul. In this way Apollinaris fell into a twofold christological error: he held that there was but one nature in Christ and he denied that

---

[27] Rabboula of Edessa, *Ep. ad Cyrillum*, " Iste primus exposuit non esse Dei genitricem secundum veritatem sanctam Mariam . . . ", cited by Sullivan, op. cit., 6.

[28] Cayré, *Manual of Patrology* (E. Tr.), I, Paris, 1935, 454 and P. Godet, art. " Diodore," in *D.T.C.*, 4, 1366 refer to the condemnation of Diodore at the Councils of Constantinople, A.D. 499 and Antioch, A.D. 508. These, however, were Monophysite synods convened during the Acacian schism. If they condemned Diodore they also refused to accept the decrees of Chalcedon. See Hefele, op. cit., vol. 4, 49, 87.

[29] Cf. F. Sullivan, op. cit., 181-196.

[30] Diodore, *Contra Synousiastas*, PG 33, 1560.

[31] Texts cited by Sullivan, op. cit., 189-191.

[32] Thus the reluctance of some to adopt the term *homoousios* because it had been abused by the Sabellians, Tixeront, op. cit., vol. I, 382, 403, and the reserve of e.g. Severus of Antioch in regard to the " two natures " doctrine of Chalcedon, Tixeront, vol. 3, 113.

Christ was a true or perfect man. The Christology of Antioch is in great part a reaction to this error of Apollinaris, a defence of the doctrine of the perfect manhood of Christ. And it is against this background that their opposition to the term *theotokos* must be situated. As they saw it, Apollinaris was teaching that the Son of Mary was not really a man; the nature He had was divine and this nature was formed by the union of Word and body in the womb of the Virgin Mary. In this context the term *theotokos* could signify only that Mary was the mother of one who was God but not man. Thus, for example, Apollinaris had written: " He who with his lips professes that God has come into this world, but thinks in his heart that it was a man like unto us that was born of the woman, teaches a doctrine contrary to the faith and must be counted with the infidels . . . He who was born of Mary was not a man but God." [34] Hence the insistence of the Antiochenes on the term *anthropotokos*: Mary was the mother of a man, and their vehement protest against the idea that Our Lady had begotten a divine nature. Hence also the complaint of Nestorius that the word *theotokos* favoured the heresy of Apollinaris and his willingness to allow the term provided it was rightly understood. Unfortunately neither Nestorius nor his predecessors were able to furnish this right understanding because they shared the assumption of Apollinaris that a complete nature must necessarily constitute a person.[35] Fundamentally, it was a failure to accept the mystery of the Incarnation.

The opposition of Nestorius to the term *theotokos* cannot, however, be attributed merely to concern with the theories of Apollinaris or to scruples lest the term favour the spread of heresy or be grossly misunderstood in a pagan sense. His opposition continued even after John of Antioch had pointed out that the term had considerable patristic support, and after St. Cyril of Alexandria had fully explained its true meaning.

---

[33] See C. E. Raven, *Apollinarianism*, Cambridge, 1923, 181, 211.

[34] Cited by G. Voisin, *L'Apollinarisme*, Louvain, 1901, 307. Cf. H. Manteau-Bonamy, O.P., *Maternité Divine et Incarnation*, Paris, 1949, 7: " On comprend aisément que pour Apollinaire le tître de Mère de Dieu fut dans sa christologie un argument de première valeur."

[35] Cf. Jugie, op. cit., 151.

Neither the papal approval of the term nor its adoption by the Council of Ephesus made any impression on Nestorius. His convictions on the matter remained unshaken to the end as is clear from his apologia, the *Book of Heraclides*, a work composed by him during his long years of exile in the Oasis of Egypt. There he writes: "The Virgin is by nature the mother of the man but by manifestation the Mother of God. If you say that He (the Word) is her Son by manifestation but not by nature this means that He comes from her united to him who is born of her according to the flesh." [36] It is still the doctrine of two Sons or two persons, and Mary, therefore, is properly *Christokos* but not *theotokos*.

THE WITNESS OF SCRIPTURE AND TRADITION

It is difficult to take seriously the objection of Nestorius that the term *theotokos* is found neither in Scripture nor in the decrees of the Council of Nice, seeing that the doctrine which justifies the term is clearly contained in each. Our Lady's divine motherhood is formally revealed in the New Testament, since it is taught there that Mary is the Mother of Christ [37] and that Christ is the Word made flesh.[38] "God sent His Son made of a woman," [39] writes St. Paul; and there is surely no basis in him for the supposition that the Son in question is any other than the Second Person of the Trinity. Though Our Lady is not mentioned in the Creed of the Council of Nice, the definition of Ephesus is implicit in the declaration that "the Son of God . . . consubstantial with the Father . . . for the sake of us men and for our salvation came down, was made flesh and became man." [40] The contradiction between the theories of Nestorius and the official teaching of the Church is clearly seen from the words of the Apostles' Creed, "I believe in Jesus Christ, His only Son, our Lord . . . born of the Virgin Mary." [41] Indeed, the theory of two Sons of God, one eternal and the other born in time from

---

[36] Cited by Jugie, op. cit., 122.
[37] Luke i:31-35, ii:5-7; Matt. i:18-21. Mary is called the "Mother of Jesus" eight times in the Gospels.
[38] John i:14.
[39] Gal. iv:4; cf. Rom. ix:5, Phil. ii:6-7.
[40] Denz., 54.
[41] Denz., 6.

Our Lady, was already condemned by Pope Damasus in 380.[42] Similar evidence of the belief of the Church in the doctrine of the Incarnation of the Word of God in the womb of the Virgin Mary is to be found in the decrees of the Synod of Alexandria [43] (362) and in the fourth century creeds of Epiphanius and of Constantinople.[44]

The witness of Scripture and of the official teaching of the Church is confirmed by the testimony of the Fathers. The Mariology of Antioch in the fourth and fifth centuries would surely have sounded strange to the ears of the early second century bishop of Antioch, St. Ignatius, who wrote: " Our God Jesus Christ . . . was conceived by Mary and is of the seed of David." [45] We find the same implicit testimony to the doctrine of the divine motherhood in the writings of Aristides, St. Justin Martyr, Hippolytus, Tertullian, St. Irenaeus and Origen.[46]

It is impossible to say when or where the title " Mother of God " was first expressly accorded to Our Lady, but the evidence available points to the church of Alexandria. From Alexandria we have the first record of a sermon [47] entitled " On the Mother of God," the first instance of a church dedicated to Our Lady under this title [48] and the earliest version of the hymn *Sub tuum praesidium confugimus Sancta Dei Genitrix*.[49] The title is attributed to Our Lady in the

---

[42] *Denz.*, 64. It is likely enough that this was directed against Diodore of Tarsus. Cf. Damasus, *Ad Paulinum Antiochenum*: " . . . Catholica Ecclesia anathematizat eos qui duos in salvatore filios confitentur i.e. alium ante Incarnationem et alium post assumptionem carnis ex Virgine et non eundem Dei Filium et ante et postea confitentur," Cavallera, *Thesaurus*, no. 664.

[43] *Tomus ad Antiochenos*, 7, Cavallera, no. 660.

[44] *Denz.*, 13, 86. Cf. *Fides Damasi*, *Denz.*, 16.

[45] St. Ignatius, *Ephes.*, 18, 2, Funk (1906), 85; cf. *Ephes.*, 7, 2; 20, 2; *Trallians*, 9, 1-2; *Smyr.*, 1.

[46] Aristides, *Apologia*, 15, Texts and Studies, 1, Cambridge, 1893, 110; Justin, *1 Apol.*, 63; *Dial. cum Tryphone*, 100, PG 6, 425, 709-712; Irenaeus, *Adv. Haereses*, 1, 10, 1; 3, 16, 3; 3, 21, 10, PG 7, 549, 922-924, 955; Hippolytus, *Contrt Noetum*, 17, PG 10, 825-828; Tertullian, *De Patientia*, 3, PL 1, 1252; *Apologeticus*, 21, PL 1, 399; *De Carne Christi* 18, 21, PL 2, 783, 787; Origen, *In Lucam*, Hom. 7, 8, 9, PG 13, 1817, 1821, 1822, *De Principiis*, praef. 4, PG 11, 117.

[47] By Pierius, a disciple of Origen. On this and the possible use of the term *theotokos* by Origen see G. Roschini, O.S.M., *Mariologia*, 2, Rome, 1947, 149.

[48] Roschini, op. cit., 149.

[49] In a papyrus fragment published 1938 in the *Catalogue of the Greek and Latin Papyri in the John Rylands Library*. It contains the word *theotokos* and may be as old as the 2nd century. For references see M. J. Healy, " The Divine Maternity in the Early Church " in *Marian Studies*, 6 (1955), 49-50.

writings of several bishops of Alexandria in the fourth
century and notably by St. Athanasius [50] in his work *Against
the Arians.* It was, therefore, both fitting and understandable
that in the fifth century the defence of the doctrine of the
divine maternity should be chiefly undertaken by the then
bishop of Alexandria, the great St. Cyril. But in doing so
St. Cyril was defending what was not merely a venerable
tradition of Alexandria but what was also, as the evidence
shows, a truth that belonged to the universal tradition of the
Church. Long before the rise of Nestorianism the title
theotokos is given to Our Lady by Eusebius of Caesarea, by
St. Cyril of Jerusalem, by St. Basil the Great, by St. Ephraem,
by St. Gregory of Nyssa, by Epiphanius of Cyprus and by
St. John Chrysostom. [51] Chrysostom is an interesting witness
for he was a fellow-pupil of Theodore of Mopsuestia. Indeed,
as early as 382 the anathemas of St. Cyril are anticipated by
St. Gregory of Nazianzus who seems to have the Mariology
of contemporary Antioch in mind when he writes: " If anyone
does not believe that Mary is the Mother of God, such a one
is cut off from God." [52] And the teaching of the theologians
at this period is reflected in the devotion of the faithful.
It was Julian the Apostate (d. 363) who complained that the
Christians of his time never ceased to proclaim Our Lady
as the Mother of God. [53] The accuracy of Julian's observation
is borne out some time later by St. Nilus of Sinai (d. 430)
who, with greater piety, sees in this universal veneration of

[50] Peter of Alexandria (d. 311), Roschini, 150; Alexander (d. 328), *Ep. ad Alex.*,
12, *PG* 18, 568; Didymus, *De Trinitate*, 1, 31; 2, 4; 3, 4, *PG* 39, 422, 481, 484;
Athanasius, *Contra Arianos*, *Orat.* 3, 14, 29, 33, *PG* 26, 349, 385, 393.

[51] Eusebius, *Vita Constantini*, 42, *PG* 20, 1104; Cyril of Jerusalem, *Catacheses*, 10,
19, *PG* 33, 685; Basil, *Hom.* in *Sanctam Christi Generationem*, *PG* 31, 1468; St. Ephraem,
Rouet de Journel, *Ench. Pat.*, 745; Epiphanius, *Ancoratus*, 75, *PG* 43, 157; Gregory
of Nyssa, *In Christi Resurrectionem*, *Or.* 2, *Or.* 5, *PG* 46, 648, 688; id., *In Diem Natalem
Christi*, *PG* 46, 1136; *De Virginitate*, c. 13, c. 19, *PG* 46, 377, 396; Chrysostom,
De Melchisedecho, 3, *PG* 56, 260, cf. A. Moulard, *S.* ⁴ean *Chrysostome*, Paris, 1941,
111. In addition some other Fathers who used the term but whose works are not
extant are quoted by St. Cyril of Alexandria, *De Recta Fide ad Reginas*, 10, *PG* 76, 1213.

[52] Greg. Nazianzus, *Epistola* 101, *PG* 37, 177. It is probably the doctrine of Diodore
of Tarsus to which he refers. In the same context he condemns the theory of two
Sons, one of God, the other of Mary; cf. *supra* p. 64, note 42. Cf. Gregory of Nyssa,
Epistola 3, *PG* 46, 1024. " Let none of us dare to call the Holy Virgin, the Mother
of God, ' Mother of man ' also as some recklessly do."

[53] Cyril of Alex., *Contra Julianum*, 8, *PG* 76, 901.

Mary as the Mother of God the fulfilment of her own prophecy in the Magnificat.[54]

It is interesting to note that in the Western Church in the fourth century St. Ambrose is the only writer who expressly attributes to Our Lady the title of Mother of God,[55] and this, no doubt, was due to his unrivalled knowledge of the writings of the Greek Fathers.[56]   At any rate, it was only after the Council of Ephesus that the term came into general use in the West.[57]   At the same time we can easily see that it is the formula and not the doctrine which is missing from the pre-Ephesus theology of the West when we find, for example, St. Hilary of Poitiers (d. 367) writing that " God is born from the womb of the Virgin," [58] or Zeno of Verona (d. 390) saying that the Son of God retains His divine nature when He receives a true human body from Mary His Mother.[59] St. Jerome (d. 419) refers to Our Lady as the " Mother of the Son of God ";[60] St. Augustine several times calls her " Mother of the Creator " or " Mother of the Son Omnipotent "; and when comparing the conception of Christ with that of St. John the Baptist, he writes that, while Elizabeth conceived one who was merely a man, Our Lady conceived one who was both God and man.[61]   Indeed, it was St. Augustine who was the first to take action against the heresy which would soon be immortalized by Nestorius; some years before the Council of Ephesus he induced the monk Leporius to sign a profession of faith in which he retracted his errors in regard to the Incarnation.   In this document the doctrine of the Divine

[54] Nilus, *Epistola* 180, *PG* 79, 293.

[55] Ambrose, *De Virginibus*, 2, 2, 7, *PL* 16, 209; *In Hexaem.*, 5, 20, *PL* 14, 233; cf. *In Lucam*, 2, 26; 10, 130, *PL* 15, 1561, 1837.

[56] He had studied especially the works of Athanasius, Didymus, Gregory Naz. and Cyril of Jerusalem, all of whom had used the term; cf. Cayré, 1, 522.

[57] E.g. Cassian, *De Incarnatione Christi*, 2, 2, *PL* 50, 31; Vincent of Lerins, *Commonitorium*, c. 15, *PL* 50, 658.

[58] Hilary, *In Ps.* 126, 16, *PL*, 9, 700; cf. *In Ps.* 131, 8, *PL* 9, 733; *De Trinitate*, 10, 17, *PL* 10, 356.

[59] Zeno, *Tractatus* 2, 8, 2, *PL* 11, 413.

[60] Jerome, *De Perpetua Virginitate B.V.M.*, 2, *PL* 23, 185; cf. *Comm. in Isaiam*, 3, 7, 15, *PL* 24, 110.

[61] *Sermo* 186, 1; 188, 4; 189, 2; 289, 2; 290, 4; *PL* 38, 999, 1003, 1005, 1308, 1314. *De Trinitate* 15, 46, *PL* 42, 1093.

Maternity is clearly asserted in the statement that " God became man and was born of Mary ever Virgin." [62]

St. Cyril of Alexandria had history, therefore, on his side when he pointed out to Nestorius that the term *theotokos* was no novelty, that it had strong patristic support, and that it was rejected by none who belonged to the orthodox stream of tradition. [63] Exactly the same warning was given to Nestorius even by those who were disposed to support him in his opposition to the patriarch of Alexandria. His friend, John of Antioch, was quick to inform him that " none of the teachers of the Church has rejected the term *theotokos*. Many indeed of the greatest among them have used it and those who did not use it have not censured those who did." [64] Theodoret of Cyr likewise declared that " the most ancient heralds of the Catholic faith have proclaimed, on the strength of apostolic Tradition, that the Mother of the Lord is to be praised and venerated as the Mother of God." [65] But Nestorius was deaf to this appeal to Tradition and affected to see in the term *theotokos* a catchword that belonged to the systems of Arius and Apollinaris. For his own position he could, of course, claim some support too in tradition, [66] but it was the narrow tradition of a school, a thread of rationalistic thought that ran in a section of the church of Antioch [67] and that stemmed ultimately from the theories of a much earlier bishop of Antioch, Paul of Samosata. The Nestorians might repudiate

[62] Leporius, *Libellus Emendationis*, PL 31, 1224. Leporius was a native of Southern Gaul and was accused of holding both Pelagian and Nestorian opinions. The theologian of Pelagianism, Julian of Eclanum, also appears to have had Nestorian leanings in Christology—see Augustine, *Opus Imperfectum Contra Julianum*, 4, 84, PL 45, 1386.

[63] Cyril, *De Recta Fide ad Reginas*, 11, PG 76, 1217; *Epistola* 14, PG 77, 97; *Apolog. pro 12 Cap.*, Anath. 1, PG 76, 324-325.

[64] *Epist. ad Nest.*, PG 77, 1455. The Nestorian, Alexander of Hierapolis, also admitted that the term *theotokos* had long been used by the faithful—Roschini, op. cit., vol. 2, 152.

[65] Theodoret, *Haereticarum Fabularum Compendium*, 4, 12, PG 83, 436.

[66] It is not very clear how well acquainted Nestorius was with the writings of the Fathers. Socrates, *H.E.*, 7, 32, PG 67, 809 accuses him of considerable ignorance in the matter. Cf. Jugie, op. cit., 21.

[67] Eustathius of Antioch (d.c. 330) appears to be the link between the teaching of Paul of Samosata and that of Diodore, Theodore and Nestorius. Though he first accepts the term *theotokos* he later rejects both the divine maternity and the communication of idioms; cf. F. Sullivan, op. cit., 165-169; R. V. Sellers, *Eustathius of Antioch*, Cambridge, 1928, 109-114.

the teaching of Paul,[68] but the filiation of ideas can be traced unmistakably from the fragments of his writings that survive. In one of these we read: " The Word is from heaven. Jesus Christ the man is from here below . . . Mary is not the Mother of the Word . . . Mary, rather, has received the Word and is not older than the Word. She is the mother of a man like us, only he was better than us in every way."[69] Granted the wide differences in their teaching in other respects, one can only conclude that in regard to the doctrine of the Divine Maternity Nestorius had inherited the mantle of the heresiarch of Samosata.

Little more need be said on the history of the doctrine of the Divine Maternity except to note its intimate connection with the dogma of the true manhood of Christ. For the reality of Our Lady's maternity implies the reality of the flesh taken by the Son of God and is the basis of our assurance that Christ is truly our brother, truly a member of our race. The denial of this dogma has had a long and curious history. Born of the conviction that matter was evil and shrinking from the idea of any intimate contact between God and this world, it made its appearance very early in the history of Christianity in the systems of Docetism and Gnosticism. In its extreme form it maintained that Christ had only an apparent body;[70] in a modified form it admitted the reality of Christ's body but attributed to it a heavenly origin and a quasi-spiritual nature.[71] In both instances it denied the doctrine of Mary's maternity; at the most it would allow that Christ passed through Mary but He was not of her substance nor was He her Son. This theory was inherited from the Gnostics by Marcion of Pontus and was propagated by the Manicheans. It crept into the Christology of some of the followers of Arius [72] and Apollinaris,[73] and it turned up in Spain with

---

[68] Cf. Jugie, op. cit., 214-217. " Angelus diaboli est Samosatenus Paulus " was how Theodore of Mopsuestia described him. Jugie, 3, note 2.

[69] *Apud* Leontius of Byzantium, *Contra Nestorium et Eutychen*, PG 86, 1389.

[70] Thus Saturninus and the Eastern Gnostics. Irenaeus, *Adv. Haer.*, 1, 24, 2, PG 7, 674; Hippolytus, *Philosophumena*, 7, 28, PG 16, 3322.

[71] So Valentinus and the Western Gnostics. Cf. F. Cayré, *Manual of Patrology*, vol. 1, 104 ; G. Barcille, art. " Docétisme," *D.T.C.*, 4, 1492.

[72] Athanasius, *Ep. ad Epicteutm*, 2, PG 26, 1052.

[73] C. E. Raven, op. cit., 212. The accusation of Docetism made against Apollinaris

Priscillianism.[74] Hence the truth of Our Lady's maternity and the reality of the human body of Christ are emphasized and defended in the letters of St. Ignatius of Antioch, in the works of St. Irenaeus and Tertullian, in several of the writings of St. Athanasius and in St. Augustine's refutation of Faustus the Manichean.[75] The theory re-appeared, however, in the fifth century in the Christology of Eutyches and long continued in favour with certain sections of Monophysite opinion.[76] In the seventh century it was propounded by the Paulicians and by some of the Monothelites.[77] It is the persistence of this theory, therefore, that explains the fact that the teaching of the Church on the divine maternity should be solemnly re-affirmed by Pope John II in 534, by the Lateran Council in 649, and by the Third Council of Constantinople in 681.[78]

Finally, to come to more modern times, the dogma of the Divine Maternity is again proclaimed against the Socinians [79] by Pope Paul IV in 1555, by Pope Benedict XIV in 1743 in the Profession of Faith required of the Maronites [80] and in our own time by Pope Pius XI in 1931 in his encyclical Lux Veritatis.[81] This encyclical was issued to commemorate the fifteenth centenary of the Council of Ephesus and it announced the institution of a new liturgical feast of Our Lady, the feast of her Divine Maternity, to be celebrated each year on 11 October. In this encyclical the Pope recalls the events that led up the definition of this dogma at the Council of Ephesus, and in regard to recent attempts to rehabilitate Nestorius [82] he points out that the traditional verdict stands,

---

himself appears to have been unjustified; cf. J. Tixeront, op. cit., vol. 2, 101, 103; G. L. Prestige, St. Basil the Great and Apollinaris, London, 1956, 63-64; C. E. Raven, op. cit., 217 f.

[74] Denz., 235, 242.

[75] Ignatius, Trall., 9, 1; Magnes., 11; Smyrn. 1; Irenaeus, Adv. Haer., 3, 21-22, 2, PG 7, 945-956; Tertullian, Adv. Marcionem, 4, 10; 4, 21; 5, 9, PL 2, 379, 411, 493; De Carne Christi, 1-4; 6-7; 17; 20-23, PL 2, 754-760, 763-768, 782, 786-790; Athanasius, Ep. ad Epictetum, 4, 5; Ep. ad Adelphium, 4-6; Ep. ad Maximum, 2-3, PG 26, 1056-1057, 1076, 1080, 1088-1089. Augustine, Contra Faustum, 11; 23, 5-10; 29, 2-4, PL 42, 245-254, 469-472, 488-490.

[76] Tixeront, op. cit., vol. 3, 78-80, 108, 111.

[77] Tixeront, vol. 3, 438-439, cf. Hefele, op. cit., vol. 5, 104.

[78] Denz., 202, 256, 290.

[79] Denz., 993.

[80] Denz., 1462, 1463.

[81] AAS, 23 (1931), 493-517.

[82] Cf. M. Jugie, op. cit., 7-17.

viz. that Nestorius was really guilty of the heresy condemned
at Ephesus.   And having explained the true meaning of the
doctrine of the Divine Maternity he refers to some of its
consequences.   He points out that because Mary is the Mother
of the Redeemer she is also the Mother of the redeemed, and
because she is the Mother of God her dignity is the highest
after that of God Himself. [83]   In this connexion the encyclical
quotes with approval the declaration of St. Thomas Aquinas:
" Because of the fact that she is the Mother of God, the Blessed
Virgin has a certain infinite dignity from the infinite good
which God is." [84]   This it is which justifies the Catholic
veneration of Our Lady so severely criticized by Protestants
and so unjustly described by them as mariolatry.   The
encyclical points out, however, that a change for the better
could be discerned latterly in Protestant opinion on this
matter, [85] and this, it was hoped, would hasten the day of
their return to their mother, the Church.

THE DIVINE MATERNITY AND REDEMPTION

As we have already remarked, God could have redeemed
the world in the manner imagined by Nestorius, that is,
without the Incarnation.   Or, if He did will the Incarnation,
He could have entered the world in the manner contemplated
by Marcion, that is, He could have come suddenly upon earth,
with a body not of this earth, a full-grown man ready to enter
immediately upon His ministry.   To a certain way of thinking
that would have been more divine because more miraculous,
more in the nature of a theophany.   In that way, too, the
glory of the Ascension, the splendour that attended the Lord's
leaving the world, would also have announced His entry into it.
Different, however, were the designs of God.   The Kingdom
of Heaven was to come " not with observation," [86] nor was
the Son of God to descend from heaven borne up in the hands
of angels. [87]   Miraculous, indeed, would be His coming into

---

[83] " Summa post Deum dignitas," *AAS*, loc. cit., 513.
[84] *Summa Theol.*, 1, 25, 6.
[85] Cf. P. Palmer, S.J., " Mary in Protestant Theology and Worship," in *Theological
Studies*, 15 (1954), 529-540, with special reference to Karl Barth and Max Thurian.
[86] Luke xvii:10.
[87] Matt. iv:6.

the world but it would be a hidden miracle like that of His coming in the Eucharist, a miracle that would pertain to the content rather than to the basis of men's faith.

"God sent His Son," writes St. Paul, "made of a woman."[88] By taking flesh in the womb of the Virgin Mary the Son of God became not merely man but a member of the human race, a descendant of Adam, of the seed of Abraham and of the royal line of David, His father.[89] It was, therefore, a completely human Incarnation and in virtue thereof the Word of God integrated Himself with the humblest realities of our human existence. He had come to save a sinful race and so He came "in the likeness of sinful flesh," "in the form of a servant," like to His brethren in all things, sin excepted.[90] This was necessary in order that the Saviour of men, "taken from amongst men,"[91] might be a perfect high-priest and mediator, truly human as well as being truly divine. It was also necessary in order that He might become the Second Adam, the new Head of mankind who would restore to men the supernatural life which their first head had failed to transmit to them.[92] From the Virgin Mary the Word Incarnate inherited Adam's nature without inheriting Adam's sin, and so the blood of sinners ran in the veins of the Redeemer of the race, to be shed by Him for the remission of their sins. The motherhood of Mary is essentially related, therefore, to the redemption of the world. Divine justice decreed that the pattern of the redemption should retrace the pattern of the Fall. This disaster had its origin in the disobedience of Eve and its repair would begin with Mary's consent to the Incarnation. Thus would the devil's victory be changed into defeat by the co-operation of the Woman with her Seed.[93] Mary, then, is the Second Eve, the second "mother of all the living,"[94] associated with her Son, the Second Adam, in the reversal of the Fall.

Such is the mystery of Mary's election to the highest office

[88] Gal. iv:4.
[89] Heb. ii:16; Rom. i:3; Luke i:32.
[90] Rom. viii:3; Phil. ii:7; Heb. ii:17; iv:15.
[91] Heb. ii:17, v:1.
[92] I Cor. xv:21-22, 45; Rom. v:12-21.
[93] Gen. iii:15.
[94] Gen. iii:20.

and dignity ever conferred on a creature. Whether or not
that dignity would still have been hers, had Eve not yielded
to temptation and had Adam retained his innocence, is
a matter of theological controversy. At any rate, it can
be said that the doctrine of the Divine Maternity is not
entirely limited by the horizon of the Fall. As it recalls
the tragedy of sin and the reality of Satan, so also it testifies
to the essential goodness of creation and the falsity of all forms
of dualistic pessimism. For the Incarnation of the Son of
God in the womb of the Virgin Mary constituted an emphatic
Amen to the refrain of the first chapter of Genesis: " And
God saw all the things He had made and they were very
good." [95] Through Mary He by whom and in whom the
world was made [96] became part of the world He had made;
from her He who is the " image of the invisible God " took
to Himself that which He had made to His " own image and
likeness; "[97] in her, He who was " the first-born of every
creature " became " the first-born among many brethren " [98]
and the Head of a new creation, His Mystical Body, the
Church.[99] Thus, in the mystery of the Divine Maternity
there is revealed at once the meeting-point of heaven and
earth, the harmony of grace and nature, the unity between
the New Testament and the Old. It is a mystery which holds
the key to the theology of history.

It is an article of the Christian faith, defined by the Second
Council of Constantinople, that the Blessed Virgin Mary is
the Mother of God in the true and proper sense.[100] This
means that she is related to the Second Person of the Trinity
in exactly the same way as any mother is related to her Son,
that is to say, she has given Him the human body which is truly
His, and is united to Him by the same physical and spiritual
ties as unite any mother to her son. Indeed, it is true to say
that, both physically and spiritually, the maternal relationship
that exists between Mary and her Son is more intimate and

---

[95] Gen. i:31.
[96] John i:3, 10; Col. i:16; Heb. i:2.
[97] Col. i:15; Gen. i:26.
[98] Col. i:15; Rom. viii:29.
[99] Col. i:18; cf. Eph. i:23, v: 23; 2 Cor. v:17; Gal. vi:15.
[100] Denz., 218. ". . . proprie et vere Dei genitricem."

more perfect than any other in history. Because she is the Virgin-mother of Christ it follows that she is the single principle of His sacred humanity—His flesh is completely hers. She is also the solitary example of a mother who has been chosen by her son to be his mother, and in virtue of that choice she has been endowed by Him with the extraordinary graces that prepared her for so exalted an office. She is a Mother indeed who has received all from her Son, and the remarkable privileges accorded her are the measure of His unique love for her. She is a Mother too who knew her Son before He became her Son.[101] Great as the honour of being the Mother of God was for Mary it was not conferred on her without her consent. It came to her by way of an invitation in the divine courtesy of the Annunciation. As St. Augustine says, Mary " conceived the Word in her mind before she conceived Him in her womb." [102] Her conception of Christ was an act, therefore, of the spiritual and of the physical order, an act which engaged her whole being both body and soul, a holy and supernatural act of the virtues of faith, obedience and the love of God. And as she knew who her Son would be, so also must she have known what His mission would be. From the words of the angel Gabriel it was clear that He who would be born of her would establish the long-awaited messianic kingdom; and His name, Jesus, signified that He would save His people from their sins.[103] With that mission of salvation she was invited to associate herself by becoming the Mother of the Redeemer, by providing Him with the flesh in which He would redeem the world. In effect, she was being asked by her Son to be not merely His Mother but His partner also, to be to Him what Eve was to Adam, " a help like unto himself." [104] We may, therefore, regard

[101] Luke i:31-35. Certainly Our Lady knew that her Son would be the Messias and it is most probable that she also knew that He would be God. Fr. Peter, O.F.M. Cap., art. " When did Our Lady know she was the Mother of God? " in *Ir. Eccl. Rec.*, 67 (1946), 145 states that this is " the common doctrine of theologians "; cf. G. Smith, *Mary's Part in our Redemption*, London, 1954, 61-62; W. G. Most, *Mary in our Life*, Cork, 1955, 257-258. For the controversy on this question between Fr. Peter and Fr. E. Sutcliffe, S.J., see *Ir. Eccl. Rec.*, 66 (1945), 421-434, 67 (1946), 145-153, 68 (1946), 123-128, 69 (1947), 807-814, 113-124.
[102] Augustine, *Sermo* 215, 4, *PL* 38, 1074.
[103] Luke i: 31-33.
[104] Gen. ii:18.

the Incarnation as the term of a contract between the Second Person of the Trinity and the Virgin Mary, a contract that was sealed by her acceptance of the proposal made to her by the angel Gabriel, by her acquiescence in the choice made of her by the Word of God. Hence Mary's *fiat* constituted a union of will with, and an act of love of the divine Person who would be her Son; and of this spiritual union her divine motherhood and the temporal generation of the Word of God are the fruit and consequence. To that extent we can follow the line of thought so richly developed by Scheeben [105] and distinguish a twofold aspect or modality in the relationship that obtains between Our Lady and her divine Son—a bridal and a maternal aspect. She is both Spouse and Mother of the Word, she is the bridal Mother of God; and her motherhood, therefore, implies a union with her Son more complete and more complex than is possible between an ordinary mother and her child. This was possible in the case of Our Lady because her maternal relationship with her divine Son was preceded by their mutual knowledge, mutual love and mutual choice.

By being born of a woman the Son of God became a member of the human race, by His birth from a Virgin He avoided the sin of the race. Our Lady's conception of Christ was therefore partly natural and partly supernatural: natural insofar as it was the production in the ordinary way of the initial cell from which Christ's body would develop, supernatural insofar as this was accomplished without the co-operation of a human father. It was thus a miraculous [106] conception, a messianic sign fulfilling the prophecy of Isaias: "Behold a virgin shall conceive and bear a son." [107] Hence, the formation of the body of the Second Adam, like that of the first Adam, was due to a special intervention of God, an intervention that was revealed to Mary in the words of the angel, "The

---

[105] M. J. Scheeben, *Mariology* (E. Tr.), 1, St. Louis, 1954, 154-183. Cf. C. Dillenschneider, *Le Principe Premier d'une théologie mariale organique*, Paris, 1955, 45-49.

[106] Some theologians also teach that the instantaneous formation of the body of Christ was miraculous, e.g. A. M. Lépicier, *Tractatus de Beatissima Virgine Maria*, Paris, 1912, 88.

[107] Isaias vii:14.

Holy Ghost shall come upon thee and the power of the
Most High shall overshadow thee." [108]   This divine action
was common to the three Persons of the Trinity, but is
appropriated to the Holy Spirit because it was a work of love
and of sanctification.   The Holy Spirit, however, can in no
sense be called the Father of Christ because the divine action
in question was not an act of generation, a communication
of the divine nature by one Person to another.   It was rather
an act *ad extra*, a purely spiritual influence which made the
virginal conception possible.   From this it follows that the
body of Christ was completely formed from the substance of
His Mother; and His temporal generation is therefore an image
of His eternal generation, for in both instances it proceeds
from a single principle.   And since both the conception and
the birth of Christ were virginal it follows (according to the
traditional interpretation of the *virginitas in partu*) that His
earthly origin from His Mother resembles His heavenly origin
from His Father in that it involved for His Mother no physical
change, no loss of bodily integrity. [109]

One can see a further, though imperfect, analogy between
Mary's motherhood and the divine Fatherhood in the fact that
her conception of her divine Son was preceded by, and was the
outcome of her act of faith in the word of God brought to her
by the Angel.   Thus she knew her Son and accepted Him as her
Son before she actually conceived Him, and for that reason He
can be said to be the fruit of her faith as well as being the fruit
of her womb.   In that limited sense His earthly origin from His
Mother receives an added likeness to His eternal origin from
the Intellect of His Father.   But the closest relationship
between the Mother of God and the First Person of the Trinity
comes from the fact that the divine and human generations
terminate in the same Person.   It is the one Person who is
related as Son to God the Father and to the Virgin Mary; and
as He is the only-begotten of the One, so is He the only-
begotten of the other.   And since the procession of the Son
from the Father is an eternal action, one can say that at the

[108] Luke i:35.

[109] See, however, Father Ryan's examination of the meaning of *virginitas in partu*
in his paper on Our Lady's Perpetual Virginity.

mysterious moment of the Incarnation the two generations coincided, that Mary begot her Son being begotten by the Father. With the Father she could then declare " Thou art my Son, this day have I begotten thee." [110]

THE MEANING OF DIVINE MATERNITY

Mary's motherhood can be called divine for three reasons. First of all, being virginal it was miraculous and was a work, therefore, of divine omnipotence. Secondly, it was divine in its exemplar: it was, as we have seen, an image of the divine paternity. But obviously, the principal and indeed the one essential reason for saying that Mary's motherhood is divine is that she is the Mother of a divine Person. Jesus Christ was as truly God as He was truly her Son and she, consequently, is truly God's Mother. For this all that was necessary was that she confer on her divine Son whatever other mothers confer on their children. And in giving Him His body, in nourishing Him of her substance, in caring for Him as her Child, Mary has given as much to the Second Person of the Trinity as any mother has ever given her child.

Nor does it make any difference to the reality of Our Lady's motherhood that the Person, whose Mother she is, existed and was a person before He became her Son. It is sufficient that He did not exist as man before He became her Son. Strictly speaking, no mother confers either personality or existence on her child. In the act of generation the parents provide the body which their child will possess. This body is made for union with a spiritual principle, the soul, and for that reason the parents can be said to be the dispositive cause of the union of body and soul and of the existence, therefore, of the person who will be related to them as their child. But it is God who is the efficient cause of the existence of the person, for the union of body and soul is an act, not of the parents, but of God who creates the soul and infuses it into the body prepared for it by its parents. In this union it is the soul, the higher and active principle, which informs the body and confers existence on it. A person, therefore, owes his existence as

[110] Ps. ii:7.

such to the creative act of God, but the manner of his existence he owes to his parents. For, in giving him a body they make him an embodied spirit, a rational animal. Hence, they are said to confer on him the nature he possesses, and in doing so they make him a being like unto themselves. Generation, then, is an act whereby one person transmits to another the nature he himself possesses, and for that reason it is the nature rather than the person which is the product of the act of generation. The person, on the other hand, is rather the subject of the act of generation; he is, as it were, clothed with the nature given him by his parents, and thus receives from them the power to live and to act as a human being. Ultimately, his nature is like an instrument given him by his parents, a *principium quo operandi*. And as all the acts of that nature are ultimately referred to him as their subject, so also is the initial act of taking possession of that nature, just as the initial act of the writer is to take hold of his pen. Thus, while it is the nature which is the direct product or immediate term of the act of generation, it is nonetheless the person who is conceived by his parents and who is the subject or ultimate term of this act. We conclude, therefore, that the prior existence of her divine Son in no way diminishes the reality of Our Lady's maternity or makes it less complete than that of other mothers in the generation of their children. She, too, has given her Son a complete human nature and in doing so she made it possible for a divine Person to become a perfect man.

"Just as any woman," writes St. Thomas Aquinas, "is a mother from the fact that her child's body is derived from her, so the Blessed Virgin Mary ought to be called the Mother of God if the body of God is derived from her." [111] This principle, so lucid and so simple, implies that the divinity of her Son is the one thing necessary and sufficient to constitute Mary the Mother of God, and that, consequently, Mary's maternal activity, the virginal conception apart, was as perfectly natural as that of any other mother. And it is, indeed, the more common teaching of theologians that in order to be God's Mother Mary herself did not require any

[111] *Compendium Theologiae*, c. 222.

higher powers, nor did she need to accomplish any more than other mothers do in the generation of their children.[112]

It must be mentioned, however, that the sufficiency of this principle as an explanation of Mary's divine motherhood has been questioned recently by a number of theologians.[113] They argue that Mary's maternal activity was not limited merely to the production of the human nature of Christ, but must also have extended to the union of this nature with the divine Person of the Word, that Our Lady was an instrumental cause of the Incarnation. But since such activity would be clearly beyond the natural powers of Mary, it follows that she must have received some supernatural power which raised her maternal activity to a new plane and made her capable of being the Mother of a divine Person. This supernatural reality, infused into Mary's soul either at her conception or at the moment of the Annunciation, is described as being a formal participation in the divine paternity of the First Person of the Trinity. As such, it gave Our Lady's activity a direct orientation towards the generation of the same divine Person who is the term of the Father's act of generation. As a result of this Mary's act of conception could produce in the human nature of Christ some supernatural perfection or disposition which made it impossible for this nature to belong to any but a divine Person. Furthermore, this supernatural reality in the soul of Mary is the permanent basis of her maternal relationship with her divine Son, and according to some authors it is for Our Lady a formal principle of sanctification, producing in her all the formal effects of sanctifying grace.[114] Thus Our Lady's motherhood is super-

[112] Cf. L. Billot, *De Verbo Incarnato*, Rome, 1942, 409-411; L. Lercher, S.J., *Institutiones Theologiae Dogmaticae*, 3, Barcelona, 1951, 287.

[113] G. Bitremieux, "Utrum B. Virgo Dici Potest Causa Efficiens Instrumentalis Unionis Hypostaticae," *Eph. Th. Lov.* 21 (1945), 167-180; J. Bover, "La Gracia de la divina maternidad," in *Estudios Marianos*, 5 (1946), 147-164; G. Rozo, *Sancta Maria Mater Dei*, Milan, 1943, 21-39; G. M. Roschini, *Mariologia*, 2, Rome, 1947, 196; J. M. Alonso, "Hacia una Mariologia Trinitaria," in *Est. Mar.*, 10 (1950), 141-191, 12 (1952), 237-267; J. M. Delgado Varela, "Maternidad formalmente sanctificante," *Est. Mar.*, 8 (1949), 133-184; C. de Pamplona, "Naturaleza de la maternidad divina . . .," *Est. Mar.*, 8 (1949), 65-92; J. Chiodini, "The Nature of the Divine Maternity," *Marian Studies*, 6 (1955), 21-40.

[114] Cf. G. Van Ackeren, S.J., "Does the Divine Maternity Formally Sanctify Mary's Soul?" in *Marian Studies*, 6 (1955), 63-101.

natural not merely in its term but in its entirety. Such in broad outline and without attempting to do justice to the considerable differences in expression and argument as found in different authors is a theory of the divine maternity which has latterly attracted some attention.

De Maria nunquam satis. As every theologian knows there is no tract in theology which contains so many opinions to which the note " pious and probable " is attached as does the treatise on Mariology. This, of course, is as much evidence of the still unfinished nature of this treatise as it is also, at times, the expression of a well-known tendency to magnify Our Lady's privileges, to attribute to her as the Mother of God all supernatural perfections consonant with the power of God and the capacity of a creature.[115] In justice to the present theory, however, it must be said that, while appeal is made to the argument that " this adds to Our Lady's dignity," in the main it is proposed rather as a solution to what these theologians consider a real problem. Nor is it exactly a new theory: in one form or another it is to be found in the works of Suarez and Vasquez, Saavedra and the Salmanticenses; and it is this fact, no doubt, which accounts for the strong Spanish cast in the modern presentation of the theory. Logically, if not historically, it has some radical affinity with the Suarezian theory of the Hypostatic Union for, according to Suarez, the human nature of Christ was in fact terminated by some supernatural disposition which determined it for union with a divine Person.[116] On the other hand, insofar as these theologians teach that Our Lady somehow shared in the divine paternity of the First Person, their theory is closely connected with, and labours under the same difficulties as a somewhat novel explanation of the nature of sanctifying grace, which has likewise attracted some attention recently.[117]

This theory, as we have said, has been proposed as a solution to a problem, to what Suarez described as " a grave diffi-

---

[115] Cf. E. Dublanchy, art. " Marie," in *D.T.C.*, 9, 2359-2362.

[116] Suarez, *De Incarnatione*, disp. 8, 3, 8. Cf. A. Michel, art. " Incarnation," *D.T.C.*, 7, 1525; E. Dublanchy, art. cit., 2362.

[117] See e.g. A. Tanquerey, *Synopsis Theologiae Dogmaticae*, 2, ed. 27, Paris, 1953, 71-74.

culty," [118] namely that it is difficult to see how Mary is truly the Mother of God if her activity was limited to the generation of the human nature of Christ. It is not sufficient, they say, that the human nature produced by Mary should be united at that instant to the divine Person of the Word, for the production and the union are two distinct actions and the latter is logically or " by nature " subsequent to the former.[119] Consequently, if Mary's maternal activity is logically or " by nature " complete before the unitive action takes place, then she is only indirectly or accidentally the Mother of God— much as a woman might be said to the mother of a bishop because her son subsequently became a bishop. Hence they conclude that Mary must also have influenced the unitive action and in this way came into direct contact, so to speak, with her divine Son, and is therefore truly and properly His Mother.

On the face of it, this statement of the matter looks dangerously like saying that Mary, in virtue of her generation of the human nature of Christ, is a mother indeed, but yet nobody's mother, which would be contradictory. There is, nonetheless, a certain inner logic in this theory once it is granted that the problem it purports to resolve really exists. And the problem, we believe, does exist only if, in the act of generation, the parents not merely provide the body which their child will possess but determine also the identity of the person who will possess this body. But we have already argued that this is not so. The most that can be said is that the nature which is the term of the act of generation is disposed for union with a person and must, therefore, of course, belong to some person. If it is assumed by a divine Person there is no need to postulate the presence in it of some supernatural reality making that assumption possible. For this one thing alone is necessary and sufficient, namely, that divine personality be capable of conferring on this nature whatever actuation would be conferred on it by human personality.[120]   That a divine Person could supply this

[118] Suarez, *De Mysteriis Vitae Christi*, disp. 1, 1, 14.
[119] Salmanticenses, *De Incarnatione*, disp. 11, n. 17, Lyons, 1686 (9, 706); J. Chiodini, " The Nature of the Divine Maternity," *Marian Studies*, 6 (1955), 24-28.
[120] As a human nature it would have a capacity, a *potentia obedientialis* for such union or actuation.

actuation follows from the truth that God possesses in an eminent way the perfections He has bestowed upon creatures. Nothing more, therefore, is required of Mary's act of generation than that it be a perfectly natural act productive of a perfect human nature. But it is a truth of faith that Christ was a perfect man, and that, we suggest, is the only criterion by which to judge the perfection of Mary's maternity. She is perfectly God's Mother if she has given God a perfect human nature.

In conclusion, it seems that the problem we have been discussing arises not so much from the mystery of the Incarnation as from a particular theory of the Incarnation. Ultimately, and I suppose inevitably, it goes back to that evergreen conundrum, the distinction between essence and existence. Scotus and Suarez denied that there is here a real distinction and they held, consequently, that the human nature of Christ had its own proper existence. But a being so complete as one having its own connatural existence can, and indeed must be considered as logically or " by nature " in existence before it is united to another being which has its completely separate existence—the existence of the two is logically prior to the union of the two. If this view-point is adopted, and if Our Lady's maternity is considered as confined to the generation of the human nature of Christ, then there is a sense in which it can be said that her maternal act is complete before the Incarnation takes place. Indeed the gap between Mary's act of generation and the divine unitive action is even wider in the theory of the Incarnation as proposed by Suarez. In his view the human nature of Christ not merely possesses its own human existence but is further completed or terminated by a supernatural and created perfection which constitutes the link uniting the humanity to the Second Person of the Trinity. It is thus an extrinsic link which separates as well as joins the parties to the union, for it is a reality distinct from both. To that extent it also separates the productive act of Our Lady and the unitive act of God. How then is Our Lady the Mother of God? One obvious way to meet the difficulty would be to extend Our Lady's maternal activity to the realization of this supernatural perfection in the humanity of Christ. This could be envisaged in two ways: God as the principal agent could have used Our Lady as a physical instrumental cause [121] in the production of this supernatural reality which is the basis of the Hypostatic Union, or her maternal act could be related to this effect as a dispositive cause.[122] In either event, Our Lady's maternal activity would need to be raised to a new plane by the reception of some supernatural power commensurate with the production of such a supernatural effect.

Although he regarded this solution as being both " pious and probable," Suarez himself did not adopt it because he felt that such activity would be of a different order from Mary's maternal activity.[123] Instead, he suggested that the problem could be solved by saying that the body and soul of Christ were each united to the Word before being united to one another and that, consequently, the unitive action was logically prior to the formation of the human nature.[124] It may have been the echo of Abelard in this ready solution which deterred Saavedra, Suarez's eminent contemporary, from embracing it. At any rate, he came forward with a theory to meet the difficulty before which Suarez retreated.   He argued that Our Lady's influence on the Hypostatic Union could be related to her act of generation if the supernatural perfection she received made her share in the divine paternity.[125] This perfection itself, although supernatural and a formal principle of sanctification, was explained by Saavedra as being a corporeal or material reality.[126]   This view of the matter is rejected, however, by the modern exponents of the theory who maintain that the perfection in question is a spiritual reality inhering in the soul rather than in the body of Our Lady.   But even

---

[121] Thus e.g. Novati, de Vega, de Rhodes.   See E. Dublanchy, art. cit., 2362. P.I. de Guerra Lazpiur, O.F.M., *Integralis Conceptus Maternitatis Divinae iuxta C. Del Moral*, Rome, 1953, 70-71 denies Ragazzini's assertion that this was the common Scotist teaching.

[122] Cf. e.g. G. M. Roschini, op. cit., 2, 196.

[123] Cf. J. A. de Aldama, S.J., " Mariologia," in *Sacrae Theologiae Summa*, 3, Madrid, 1953, 380.

[124] Suarez, *De Mysteris Vitae Christi*, disp. 1, 1, 14-16, edit. Vives, Paris, 1877, t. 19, 6-7.

[125] P. de Guerra Lazpiur, op. cit., 37-43, 139-143. Cf. H. Lennerz, S.J., *De Beata Virgine*, Rome, 1957, 19-20.

[126] De Guerra Lazpiur, op. cit., 40.

in this modified form the theory is open to what most theologians would regard as an insurmountable difficulty, namely,
that it is impossible to see how a creature could really
participate in something that is proper to the First Person
of the Trinity. Nobody who propounds this theory would
suggest that Our Lady has any share in the divine generation
of the Word, but could any satisfactory explanation of this
be given if it is stated that she formally participates in the
principle of this generation? Besides, such formal participation
implies some special union between Our Lady and the First
Person of the Trinity, and for that reason this theory appears
to by-pass the accepted teaching, recently re-affirmed in the
encyclical *Mystici Corporis*, that all acts *ad extra* are common
to the three divine Persons.[127]

In view of these difficulties, many theologians would be
disposed to apply to this theory the judgment expressed by
De la Taille in a different context, namely, that it is an impossible solution offered to resolve a non-existent problem.
Most theologians, no matter what their philosophical allegi-
ance, are satisfied that no problem exists—that the simultaneity
of the productive action and the unitive action is sufficient
to constitute Our Lady the Mother of God.[128] In addition,
if one accepts the Thomistic theory that the human nature
of Christ did not possess its own human existence but was
immediately actuated by the divine existence of the Second
Person of the Trinity, then it cannot be said that Our Lady's
act of conception was even logically prior to the Incarnation
—the human nature she produced had no other existence but
that of the divine Person whose nature it is. Our Lady is
therefore immediately the Mother of God or, to put it in
another way, in the Incarnation it was God who became man,
not a man who became God.

[127] *Mystici Corporis*, AAS, 35 (1943), 231. In addition, some theologians deny even
the possibility of Our Lady's being an instrumental cause of the Hypostatic Union,
cf. V. Contenson, O.P., *Theologia Mentis et Cordis*, 9, 2, 2, ed. Vives, Paris, 1875,
vol. 3, 36-38.
[128] C. Pesch, S.J., *Compendium Theologiae Dogmaticae*, 3, Friburg, 1924, 92:
" Logica autem illa prioritas nihil attinet ad quaestionem, num Maria sit mater Dei,
quia maternitas constituitur physica causalitate." Cf. H. Lennerz, op. cit., 21;
J. de Aldama, op. cit., 382.

Immaculate Conception

By MGR. H. FRANCIS DAVIS, D.D.

DIFFICULTIES OF NON-CATHOLICS

W E Catholics in these islands cannot be entirely indifferent
to the fact that much of our Marian theology, notably
the doctrines of the Immaculate Conception and the Assumption, together of course with that of Our Lady's Mediation,
have met with some degree of bewilderment and incom-
prehension among our Protestant neighbours. Their realization
of what these doctrines mean to Catholics has brought home
to many of them with a shock the extent to which Protestants
have in a few centuries lost sympathy with the tradition of
their mother Church. To large numbers of them the whole
Marian aspect of Christianity is unfamiliar or even forgotten.
They come across it perforce, not only when they meet
Catholics, but also when they have conversations with the
separated Christians of the East. For it is not the property
of schism in general to forget Mary, but only of the Protestant
heresy. To Protestants the new definitions appear as " new "
doctrines. They profess to wonder where and when it will
stop. Even Pusey, the very Anglo-catholic one-time companion of Newman in the Oxford Movement, wanted the
Catholic Church to declare openly the ultimate limit of future
possible Marian definitions.

Their shock has been the greater perhaps because they have
felt that in many respects there had been a growth of mutual
understanding. German and French Catholics, in particular,
have taken many occasions to make clear to Protestants that
Catholics put their trust in Christ as utterly as any Lutheran
or Calvinist. A Fr. von Balthasar or a Fr. Bouyer have even
praised the more orthodox theologians of the Lutheran and
Calvinist traditions for their zealous and almost prophetic
defence of God's glory, and their proclamation of salvation
by the grace of Christ alone. And yet, inconsistently, as it

seems to some of these Protestants, Catholics return from their eirenic discussions with Protestants to ever more magnificent manifestoes and zealous discussions of Mariology.

To make confusion more confounded, while some Protestants in this spirit protest against what they regard as the Catholic intrusion of unwritten tradition and pious opinion into the faith, and appeal for a return to the simple truths of Scripture, and other Protestants say they would not mind tradition so much if only Catholics would base it upon historical evidence, Catholics for their part are increasingly finding the basis of their mariological progress in the very Scriptures which the Protestants declare to be so uncompromisingly against it. However, I do not want this lecture to be an attack *in absentia* on Protestants not here to defend themselves. Many Protestants—and not only Anglo-catholics —have been led in recent years to recognize that they have themselves in the past neglected the paying of due honour to Our Lady. One could quote from many of their statements, but perhaps it will be enough to recall what one German Lutheran said to me in Birmingham. " We Lutherans have certainly not been of the generations that call her blessed." And we all know that not many years back a Lutheran wrote a book on Mary, the Mother of God.[1]

DUE TO DIFFERENT UNDERSTANDING OF FAITH

There is a difference of approach which it would be helpful for us to notice, in order the better to understand our Catholic position. There does exist a reason why Catholics manage to be so confident that the basis of Mariology is in the Scriptures, and Protestants remain so confident it is not there ! On both sides there are scholars of first rank, and we have outlived the days when scholarship was one-sided and subjective. It is certainly not lack of Scripture scholarship that makes Protestants blind to what we see there.

The basic difference between us, it has long seemed to me, lies, more than either side generally realizes, in the different notions of faith that have prevailed on either side of this

[1] H. Asmussen, *Maria, die Mutter Gottes*, Stuttgart, 1950.

barrier.   Though few Protestants have entirely lost the
traditional idea of faith, their whole approach to the Scriptures
has been influenced by the Protestant emphasis on faith as
exclusively recognition of sinfulness, and trust in Christ.
This emphasis has, in turn, facilitated a general weakening of
their hold on the idea of revelation.   Bultmann, still with
a stress on utter faith in Christ, is capable of a calm rejection
of Christ's divinity and bodily Resurrection, which he would
regard as symbolical " myths " rather than facts.   This, to a
Catholic mind, must surely be the *reductio ad absurdum* of the
Protestant position.

The Protestant tends to understand the Scriptures in the
light of his doctrine of faith.   This doctrine was recently thus
expressed by a group of Heidelberg professors: " In faith a
sinner places himself in the hands of Jesus Christ as his Lord,
in whom God calls him, promises him forgiveness, and binds
him to His service." In harmony with this definition, where
the Scriptures speak of Our Lord turning away from his
Mother when she stood outside seeking him and devoting
Himself alone to His public mission, the Protestant is impressed.   To him this is interpreted as a turning away of Our
Lord from His Mother, and a concentrating of our attention
on Himself.   On the other hand, where Our Lady is referred
to as Mother of the Saviour, as full of grace, as blessed among
women, as winning from her Son His first miracle, as standing
at the foot of the Cross and having St. John commended to
her, as the one from whom the Messias was made, as the
Woman clothed with the sun,—when Our Lady is referred
to in these ways, the Protestant exegete looks for one thing
alone—what he regards as the central message of faith in
Christ who by His blood justifies sinners.   Protestants will
fail to find any privileges of Mary in the deposit of faith until
they notice that God has included Mary herself as an important
part in that deposit.

ONE-TIME OPPOSITION FROM SOME THEOLOGIANS

The two Marian doctrines in question have during their
history met with opposition also on the part of Catholic
theologians.   A curious but significant fact will however also

be noticed as a result of historical investigation. Responsible opposition has always come from the professional, never from the untrained theologian. This is not due to a special incompetence of the trained, as contrasted with the untrained theologian, but because the trained theologian was for a time impeded from a steady, clear contemplation of the positive reasons by a greater realization of the apparent difficulty of reconciling one or other of these personal privileges of Mary with some doctrine of the faith either already defined or already boasting a strong independent witness. Another difficulty sometimes seen more clearly by the trained theologian was his fear that the " doctrine " was too much dependent on unreliable apocryphal accounts. The theologians could not rest satisfied till they had removed these seeming stumbling-blocks; whereas the simple faithful merely saw the apparent obviousness to the popular mind of the connection between the " doctrine " and the revealed facts.

Our Lady, as the village girl of Nazareth, must have a special joy in the thought that God in his Providence made clear through the simple faith of little ones the glory and dignity of her person and vocation, even in the face of theological scruples of the professional. Eadmer in the twelfth century, the first to put up a theological defence of the Immaculate Conception against theological attack, thus defends the claims of unsophisticated faith: " Pure simplicity and simple purity of love towards God and His most sweet Mother is not afraid to pass judgement on the conception of the Mother of God herself." [2] An anonymous German writer of the same period wrote: " Without fear, and without diffidence, with the piety of the Christian religion, come and worship the footstool of His feet, namely Mary, the Mother of the Saviour." [3]

This phenomenon of the great part played by the non-theologian in Marian doctrinal development is also due greatly without doubt to the fact that a deep understanding of the ways of God as recorded in Scripture and a deep appreciation of the greatness of the girl He chose as Mother are sometimes

---

[2] Eadmer, De Conceptione, 2 (ed. Thurston, 7); cf. P. Henri Barré, " Immaculée Conception et Assomption au XII siècle," in Virgo Immaculata, Acta Congressus Mariologici mariani Romae Anno MCMLIV Celebrati, 5, Rome, 1955, 156 (my translation).
[3] Quoted by H. Barré, op. cit., 157, from manuscript (my translation).

likely to come to the pious Christian praying and meditating in the spirit of faith independently of the theologian busy syllogizing in his study. Newman, himself by long choice a Marian theologian, fully realized this, and was at pains to point out that in actual fact the faith and love of Christians will sometimes reach a deeper understanding of Christian truth without formal theologizing. " The inquirer into heavenly truths," he wrote, " dwells in the cell and the oratory, pouring forth his heart in prayer, collecting his thought in meditation, dwelling on the idea of Jesus, or of Mary, or of grace, or of eternity, and pondering the words of holy men who have gone before him till before his mental sight arises the hidden wisdom of the perfect, which God predestined before the world unto our glory, and which He reveals to them by His Spirit." [4] Is it not something like this that Our Lord had in mind when he said that, if we remained faithful to his word, " so you will come to know the truth, and the truth will set you free "? [5] St. Thomas understood the gifts of the intellect as dependent upon faith and charity. It is with the help of these gifts that our reason enlightened by faith penetrates more deeply into the truths of faith. St. Augustine spoke of God's part in leading us to a full understanding: " God then by Himself, since He is the Light, enlightens devout minds to understand the divine truths that are spoken to them or shown them." [6] St. Ambrose liked to describe faith as a grace giving true light to the mind.

The Scriptures left us a message concerning Our Lady, which was inexhaustible in its richness, yet extremely concise in its expression. " There is so little about Mary in the Scriptures," once complained a group of Methodists to whom I was talking. " In one sense, yes," I replied, " but what little there is contains more than is said about any other creature of God. In a few words of Scripture, she was Mother. Her Son was God. She was Mother co-operating with her God and Son. What other office could Scripture have recorded which would have added to her greatness? "

[4] *Discourses to Mixed Congregations*, London, 1893, 343.
[5] Jo. viii:32.
[6] *Enarr. in Ps.* 118, Sermo 18, 4, PL 37, 1553.

EARLIEST STATED GROUNDS OF ACCEPTANCE

The method of this lecture will be to show from certain selected instances the manner in which Catholics were led to the firm conviction that God dwelt in His Mother with His grace, not merely at some moment of her conscious life, but from the first moment of her existence.

May I first take you to a sermon preached by St. Andrew of Crete on the feastday of Our Lady's birthday in the eighth century? The fact that he was celebrating Our Lady's birthday is significant. The Church does not normally keep the birthdays even of her saints, for even saints are born in a state of sin. Exceptionally, the Church kept the birthday of Our Lord, and that of St. John the Baptist, who, according to the Scriptures, was sanctified in his mother's womb. St. Andrew of Crete, incidentally, was one of those who struggled against the Iconoclasts in defence of Catholic honour paid to images. Our Lady's birthday was already well established before the time of which we speak. Suppose we listen in for a moment to his sermon. What will he take as his subject? It will not be Mary's freedom of sin at birth, still less at conception. An obvious reason for this is that Eastern writers up to the eighth century and beyond rarely referred to original sin as such. We can only deduce their faith in it by implication. No, we shall have to guess his meaning from his proclamation that, when Our Lady was born, it was the beginning of our salvation. He quotes from the liturgy: " Be of good cheer, it is the feast of the birth and restoration of the race. For a virgin is now born, suckled and formed, and a Mother is prepared for God, the King of all ages." [7] Here and throughout the sermon, he makes it clear that Mary is a new beginning. " Today," he says, " Adam offers to God from among us and on our behalf the first part of the sacrifice, and he gives Mary as the firstling." [8] Mary, then, is the first part of the sacrifice which will restore our race. We need not draw any technical conclusions as to her part in the redemption, but she is certainly here understood as the new beginning. " The only

[7] S. Andreae Archiep. Cret., Oratio 1, 1, PG 97, 805a.
[8] Op. cit., 812a.

part," he continues, " that is not kneaded in with the whole lump is through Mary made into bread, for the sake of the remaking of the race." [9]   Our race, he further tells us, is about to return to its first beauty, that beauty which had been disfigured by the fall, and had lost the purity of its first creation.   The race had in the first instance been made from virgin earth.   Here is virgin earth again.   " So also here and now he chooses as new earth, for the bringing about of the Incarnation, this pure and immaculate one, the Virgin chosen from the whole of nature." [10]   He also calls her the new seed, and the new heaven in which the Word came to dwell.

No sermon has come down to us from St. Andrew precisely on Our Lady's conception, but he did have a part in the newly introduced feast of St. Anne's conceiving of Mary, adopted about a century earlier on the analogy of St. Elizabeth's conceiving of St. John the Baptist, and influenced by a legend that the conceiving of Mary was also miraculous.   But, though he left no sermon, he did leave a liturgy for the feast. In this liturgy he divided his attention between his praise of Anne's conceiving and his prayer of adoration to her holy child.   But there was in these prayers no specific mention of Mary's initial purity.

The first sermon that has come down to us on the new feast of the Conception is one of John of Euboea in the ninth century:

> We celebrate first of all glorious feastdays the day on which the Blessed Joachim and Anna received the glorious tidings of the generation of the fully immaculate Mother of God.   Then comes that of the most august Birthday of Mary . . . Another feastday most worthy of honour and service is that on which Gabriel treading the earth with immaterial feet pronounced the Hail to the Virgin.[11]

Continuing with his sermon, John protests that this feast, though not everywhere recognized, is not without sanction or useless.   For the first time he put forward a consideration, often to be used since his time, based on the Psalms and

[9] Op. cit., loc. cit.   [10] Op. cit., 815a.
[11] Joannes Euboeensis, *Sermo in Conc. Deiparae*, 10, PL 96, 1475a.

Wisdom literature, as a foundation for Our Lady's privileges. Mary was the dwelling-place of God, chosen out from eternity from among mankind for that purpose. The idea that Mary was predestined as the dwelling-place or *habitaculum* survives gloriously for us in the age-old prayer after the *Salve Regina*, where we ask for the intercession of her who had been prepared as a worthy dwelling-place of the Son of God.

On this day, to go back to John of Euboea's sermon,

> the foundations were laid; neither with stones, nor by the hands of men was the temple of God built. But Christ, the Son of God, the corner-stone, Himself by the good pleasure of the Father, and with the co-operation of the all-holy and life-giving Spirit, built it and Himself dwelt within it, that He might fulfil the law and the prophets and so save us." [12]

He concluded with regard to Mary's heavenly gifts:

> Truly blessed and many times blessed Joachim and Anne, but a thousand times more blessed offspring and daughter of David that came forth from your loins and womb. For you are earth and she is heaven. You are of the earth, through her they become heavenly. Truly are you blessed, for the King of Glory, whom Moses could not see, coveted the beauty of your daughter. [13]

DIFFERENCES BETWEEN EAST AND WEST

These passages illustrate the truth of a remark made by M. Guitton that the Eastern writers saw Mary as the beginning of a new race, while the Western ones saw her as an enclave protected from the contamination of the world's sin. St. John of Damascus was another witness to the Eastern view from the same period. He spoke of Mary as the holy firmament in which the Son of God would appear, holy from the first moment in her mother's womb. She was the holy seed of St. Joachim, the holy child in St. Anne's bosom. In conceiving Mary, they conceived a holy mountain of God, more holy than Mount Sinai. Mary was the spiritual Eden, holier and more divine than the original one. In the latter the earthly Adam

[12] Op. cit., 23, *PG* 96, 1499a & b.
[13] Op. cit., 12, *PG* 96, 1478.

dwelt; but in Mary dwelt the Lord who came down from heaven. Like St. Andrew of Crete, he called Mary the virgin earth from which the new Adam was made, the immaculate flesh and blood from which His body was taken.[14] In all this there was no hint that Mary was not already holy, already sanctified, already the fit dwelling-place of God, already the abyss of grace from the first moment of her being. Nothing indeed was lacking from the witness of St. John of Damascus except for him to say explicitly that she had no original sin. And that he would not say, since he never said with full explicitness that other sons and daughters of men had original sin. But he did say that Mary was incorruptible, while others were subject to corruption.

It has been objected that some of these Fathers appear virtually to contradict the Immaculate Conception by saying that Christ alone was sinless. The difficulty is however only apparent, for their meaning was that Christ alone was by nature unable to sin. Another difficulty comes from their saying that Mary was purified in the Temple, but the following words of St. Sophronius show that one should not conclude too much from such a statement. " The Holy Ghost will come upon thee, O Immaculate One, to make thee purer and give thee the power which renders fruitful." [15] Notice that he calls Mary the Immaculate One in the same breath as he speaks of her further purification.

These eighth and ninth century Eastern Fathers saw that Our Lady's privileges were involved in her uniqueness. They accepted her as one who had always been proclaimed as holier than Eve and purer than the virgin earth from which the first Adam was taken. They were moved not by conscious theological reasoning, but by a devout recognition that one they loved and honoured was indeed what God had made her.

EARLY ANTICIPATIONS OF THE DOCTRINE

If time allowed, it would be inspiring to go back from the eighth to the earlier centuries and see in more detail the stages of realization of Our Lady's uniqueness, as reflected

---

[14] See especially Hom. 2 in Dormitionem B. V. Mariae, PG 96, 722d.

[15] Or. in S. Deip. Annun. 43, PG 87(3), 3273d. Cf. V. A. Mitchell, S.M., The Mariology of Saint John Damascene, Maryhurst, Mo., 1930, 119.

in the extant early literature. Just as St. John of Damascus did not go so far as to say in so many words that Mary was never stained by original sin, so the earlier Fathers did not say explicitly as much as St. Andrew of Crete, John of Euboea, St. Germanus and St. John of Damascus. One reason undoubtedly must have been that these earlier Fathers had no occasion to preach on Our Lady's birthday, still less on her conception. We all know, even today, what a stimulus to devotion is a new feast or a new definition. We straightway are confronted with a challenge. Such a challenge is the 1958 Lourdes centenary, and it has been accepted. What the early Fathers did proclaim was that God had predestined Mary from eternity, and that she was greater than Eve or any other of God's creatures. St. Sophronius in the seventh century proclaimed that she had " grace beyond all grace." " No one was given a fullness of grace such as was given to thee." [16] St. Augustine, as is well known, was unwilling that any question of sin should be raised in connection with Mary, out of respect for her Son. St. Ephraem, as Pope Pius XII reminds us, declared that " Only Thou, in fact, and Thy Mother are wholly beautiful. For neither in Thee nor in Thy Mother is any stain." [17] Even back in the third and second centuries we still find, as other lecturers have reminded us, a Mary proclaimed who was uniquely pure and holy beyond the purity and holiness of Eve at the time of creation.

It is true that the problem of Christ's universal redemption led some not only of more modern, but even of the early Fathers, to feel bound to attribute some sin, however slight, to Mary, in order that there might be something in her to redeem. But even these theologians and Fathers did not deny her uniqueness by original vocation. St. John Chrysostom, for instance, thought she might have been guilty of vanity. Newman has pointed out how in all such cases they were moved, not by a tradition that Mary was ordinary, but rather by a false theological understanding of the way Mary fell under redemption, joined to a wrong exegesis of two passages in the gospels.[18] But, when all is said and done, error regarding

[16] Op. cit., 3248a.   [17] Carmina Nisibena, 27 (ed. Bickell, 122).
[18] Cf. Newman, Difficulties o Anglicans, 2, London, 1896, 143 ff.

Our Lady's subsequent sanctity is compatible with a soundness at least by implication regarding her personal uniqueness.

However, it cannot be denied that the eventual development of Marian doctrine began with the enthusiasm and confidence which followed throughout Christendom on the definition of Ephesus.

THE WEST

At this stage we must fill in our picture of the living faith and devotion which led the way surely to the established explicit faith in the Immaculate Conception by saying something as to the manner in which this devotion and doctrine found its way to the West, where it was to reach a clearer theological result than it ever had done in the East.   St. Augustine's influence was to dominate the whole period during which this happened.   His forthright statement of Mary's sinlessness, though it is uncertain how far he applied it to the case of original sin, was a clear signpost in the right direction.   His witness to original sin also helped to clarify theological statement, when one came eventually clearly to express Mary's exemption from it.   Nevertheless his manner of explaining the handing down of original sin through the concupiscence which accompanies generation was to have an unfortunate retarding effect, on account of special difficulties to which it was thought to give rise.

During the years following St. Augustine, the love of the pure Virgin grew in the West as well as in the East.   For wherever the Catholic faith is found, the following words of Newman are verified:

> Our heart yearns towards that pure Virgin, that gentle Mother, and our congratulations follow her, as she rises from Nazareth and Ephesus, through the choirs of angels, to her throne on high, so weak, yet so strong; so delicate, yet so glorious; so modest and yet so mighty. [19]

I will pass over the years between St. Augustine and the time when the conception of Our Lady begins to find liturgical mention in the West.   Apart from its appearance from the

[19] Newman, op. cit., 85.

East in Naples in the ninth century, it is in these islands that it is first found. The earliest in date is an Irish martyrology, where it appears on 3 May. How it got there, or what was thought of it at the time, whether it sprang, as is likely, from popular devotion or from a desire for theological completeness, whether it was based on the legendary story of St. Anne's miraculous conceiving of Mary or on pure theological conviction, no one knows. An older Irish martyrology, that of Oengus, had on the same date, "The great feast of Mary," without further clues.

A memory of the conception appeared about a century later in England, but has left more details about its meaning. Also, at least as far as we know from records, they made more of it, for they introduced it into their Mass calendars, and made it a feast.

You would naturally like to think that we English got it from you. But you must be satisfied with having recognized the conception liturgically at a notably earlier date. For, if we had taken it from you, we would hardly have kept it five months from the Irish date on 8 December, only one day removed from the date of the feast in the Eastern Church. Very little is known about how it arrived or why. The present lecturer has argued in recent years [20] that it must have come direct from the Eastern Church, together with several other feasts only found in England and the East for several centuries before they appeared generally in the West.

Doubtless the English, apart from Providence, would have been as reticent as the Irish appear to have been about the meaning they attached to the feast had it not been for the historically fortunate accident that the Normans suppressed the feast when they invaded England. This fact, followed by its gradual re-introduction, meant that those who re-introduced it had to defend their action.

From that time through a couple of centuries there was a series of writers in England defending Our Lady's privilege, and culminating in the final triumphant removal of the last difficulties in the theology of the Celtic Duns Scotus. It is now known that gradually a group of less known devotees

[20] Cf. H. Francis Davis, *The Dublin Review*, 118th year (1954), 375 ff.

of Our Lady sprang up also in France and Germany. After Scotus it was slowly to win over the whole Church, and indeed in a mounting wave of unprecedented fervour and enthusiasm.

WESTERN DIFFICULTIES

The earlier defenders of the doctrine were pious, simple folk for the most part, with little claim to fame except for the part they are now known to have played in defence of this doctrine. They had perforce to become theological because the objections of the great continental theologians found their defenders in these islands and had to be answered.

These objections were mainly the following: (1) How could carnal lust, which many thought was unavoidably bound up with the use of marriage, fail to cause sin in the offspring of Joachim and Anne? Even St. Bernard, the great Marian doctor, said: " How can anything be holy without the presence of the Sanctifying Spirit, and how can the Holy Spirit have any part in sin, and how can there not be sin where there is carnal lust? " Others modified this view by saying that, even if there were no formal sin in marriage, there was material sin, which still causes contamination in the offspring's flesh. (2) How could Mary be said to be redeemed if she never had sin? This difficulty was greater now that everyone agreed that Mary committed no actual sin.

If we expurgate from these difficulties St. Augustine's theory of the transmission of original sin and its connection in theologians' minds with the parents' carnal lust—a connection eventually seen anyhow to be beside the point—we could say that their objections in modern terms came from the difficulty of exempting Mary from original sin and from the need of redemption. St. Anselm it was who really prepared the way to a reconciliation of these doctrines with the Immaculate Conception, by his explanation of original sin as being merely due to membership of the race of which Adam was head, without any relationship to whether it was passed on by carnal lust or was due to a taint in the flesh. For him the sin was simply the sin of the race, a sin belonging to all members of the race. It was not seen immediately, but eventually would appear clearly, that this meant the possibility of an application of Christ's merits to Mary's preservation from sin. The idea of " preservation " saved them from the theological need of postulating any contamination from which Mary was to be redeemed. The stock from which Mary came was not as such physically contaminated, it was just spiritually in exile.

St. Anselm also enunciated the principle that the greatest conceivable purity outside the Godhead must be attributed to Mary.

Yet, in spite of these Anselmian pointers to a doctrine of initial sanctity in Mary, it is not certain whether he ever attained its clear enunciation. It is also not clear whether or not he favoured the celebration of the feast.

PIONEER THEOLOGICAL DEFENCE

The first full-length treatise dealing with the matter was written by Anselm's secretary, Eadmer. He both boldly protested the doctrine, and replied to objections. His strongest protestation was on the basis of Our Lady's predestination. We must not imagine that God, after the manner of men, must wait until He finds one worthy for His vocation. From all eternity God chose Mary to be His dwelling-place —and here like St. Andrew of Crete he thought of the passage in Wisdom where Wisdom is said to build for herself a house —He chose her to be the temple of the Holy Spirit in a very special way. How could He have allowed her to be stained by sin? " The foundations " of His palace " would be weak if the conception of Mary were in any way corrupted by stain of sin." [21] " Until God shows me something more worthy of my Lady's excellence, I will say what I say: I will not change what I have written." [22] " For nothing, Lady, is equal to thee, nothing comparable. All that is is either above thee or below thee. Above thee is God alone." [23] He saw references to this purity of Mary in many Old Testament texts.

Further, it was of this conception of Mary that the prophet

[21] Eadmer, *Tractatus de Conceptione S. M.*, 13, ed. Thurston (cf. *infra*, p. 103), 15, PL 159, 401.
[22] Op. cit., ed. Thurston, 24; PL 159, 404.
[23] Op. cit., 17; PL 159, 401.

Isaias spoke in his famous text concerning the branch of Jesse. Truly this branch is the Virgin Mary: and the flower which came from it is her blessed Son on whom and in whom rested essentially all the fullness of the Godhead.[24]

He applied the principle of co-redemption. Did not Mary come that by the fruit of her womb the world might be saved from sin? Could she be conceived bearing the burden of the sin with which the earth was filled by the envy of the devil, whom she was sent to crush?[25]

He sought an argument from the meaning of the Incarnation. Was not her flesh the flesh which would provide a fitting body for the Word? God could keep her pure and unstained. He certainly willed it. *Si ergo voluit, fecit.*[26]

Against the objections stemming from the Augustinian idea that sin begets sin, Eadmer replied: " If there was any sin, it would be in the parent, not necessarily in the offspring."[27] " Where the Spirit is, there is freedom from sin."[28] " But the Spirit could not be absent from the beginnings of Mary."[29]

Other writers followed Eadmer's example. Eadmer had implied an application of Genesis iii:15 about the enmity between the serpent and the woman and the final victory of the woman. Osbert of Clare explicitly applies it. " Nor can there be found any other woman than this in the whole series of human generations, concerning whom God in the beginning of His offspring world would make so glorious a prophecy."[30] St. Aelred applied the word " blessed among women ": " While all women are under the curse, thou alone among them art counted worthy of this blessing."[31]

Eadmer, Osbert, and Nicholas of St. Alban's use another argument. If God gave the special privilege of a sanctified birth to Jeremias and St. John the Baptist, as traditionally people believed, how much more must He have given it to His Mother.

[24] Op. cit., 7, *PL* 159, 398.
[25] Ibid., 15-16, *PL* 159, 400, 401.
[26] Ibid., 11, *PL* 159, 399.
[27] Ibid., 10, *PL* 159, 398.
[28] Ibid., 9, *PL* 159, 398.
[29] Ibid., loc. cit.
[30] Osbert de Clara, *Sermo de Conc. S. Mariae*, cf. ed. Thurston, *Eadmeri Tractatus*, 67.
[31] S. Aelred, *Sermo 17 in Ass. B. Mariae*, *PL* 115, 305.

We might conclude concerning this period of witness by some words from the recently published opus of Nicholas of St. Alban's:

> Thou art all beautiful, because in thee is nothing disgraceful, for thou were built by Wisdom. Thou art all beautiful, because everything that is beautiful is in thee, since thou art full of grace, and there is no stain in thee, neither original handed down to thee, nor stain brought on by the will, because thou art founded by Him, than whom there is no other foundation. Thou art all beautiful by nature, thou art all beautiful by grace.[32]

It has often been objected against these earliest theologians that they did not persuade Christendom through their failing to include Our Lady under the redemption, that it was left to Scotus to explain how all this was possible through Our Lady being redeemed by anticipatory preservation. Perhaps they did not express themselves sufficiently theologically. They were simple and devout children of Mary, convinced of the glorious truth about her, but little versed in theological subtleties. Yet I am not convinced that they withdrew her from the redemption. They do say that her sinless conception was the first fruits of the redemption. They insist that her purity was on account of the dignity of her Son. None is purified but by Mary's Son, said Eadmer. Nicholas said that Mary was a foundation built, not by the old nature of Adam, but the new nature of Christ. Would they not assume that the application of Christ's new nature to men became possible through its sanctification on the Cross? Finally Nicholas stated that the reason for this conception is that which transcends reason, the sacrament of our redemption.

FINAL DEVELOPMENT

There is no time to carry the story further. It is henceforward a story of triumph upon triumph. Popes and faithful vie with one another in honouring this privilege, and gradually the difficulties of the theologians are universally seen to be

---

[32] Nicholas of St. Alban's, *De Celebranda Concepcione Beate Marie contra Beatum Bernardum*, *Revue Bénédictine*, 64 (1954), 1-2, 112.

unreal scruples. Perhaps it might, however, be pleasing, in
these troubled days, to note that in this year of the Lord 1958
there was published in the Catholic University of Lublin,
Poland, an account of the Immaculate Conception in mediaeval
Polish liturgy.[33] The enthusiasm there reflected is equivalent
to the enthusiasm found in any part of the world. In the very
Gloria of the Mass were introduced the words: " Quoniam tu
solus Sanctus Mariam fabricasti. Tu solus Dominus Mariam
praeservasti. Tu solus altissimus Mariam sublimasti, Jesu
Christe. Cum Sancto Spiritu in gloria Dei Patris. Amen." [34]

There is also a most attractive sequence of which the following verses give an idea:

> Virga florem conceptura, stella solem paritura, hodie concipitur.
> Flos de virga processurus, sol de stella nasciturus, Christus
> intelligitur.
> . . .
> O quam felix, quam praeclara, mundo grata, Deo cara, fuit
> hec concepcio,
> Qua, salute destitutis, redit vere spes salutis, luctus cedit
> gaudio.[35]

There was even a special *Invitatorium*: " Adoremus Dei
Patris Natum ex pura Virgine, qui conceptum sue Matris
preservavit a crimine." [36]

THE MANNER OF DEVELOPMENT

The development of the doctrine concerning this privilege
of Mary is an example of what Newman described in his
Sermon on Development:

> . . . the mind which is habituated to the thought of God, of
> Christ, of the Holy Spirit, naturally turns . . . with a devout
> curiosity to the contemplation of the Object of its adoration,
> and begins to form statements concerning Him before it knows
> whither, or how far, it will be carried.[37]

[33] Ks. Julian Wojtkowski, *Wiara w Niepokalane Poczecie Najswietszej Marii Panny,
studium historyczno-dogmatyczne*, Lublin, 1958.
[34] Op. cit., 133.
[35] Op. cit., 142.
[36] Op. cit., 167.
[37] Newman, *Oxford University Sermons*, London, 1892, 329.

The Immaculate Conception came to be realized through the contemplation of God, His Christ and His Spirit. It is not the feast of what Mary did, but of what God did for her and our race. It is sublimely a feast of grace. The mind habituated to the thought of God's providence and enlightened by what the Book of Wisdom tells us of God's ancient pre-destination of all things in His wisdom, came to realize God's providence regarding His Mother. This must have been why these passages found a place in the liturgy of God's Mother. In this way was shown forth the Catholic mind of the Church.

> I do not claim (wrote Newman) for the generality of Cath-olics any greater powers of reflection upon the objects of their faith than Protestants commonly have; but, putting the run of Catholics aside, there is a sufficient number of religious men among whom, instead of expending their devotional energies (as many serious Protestants do) on abstract doctrines, such as justification by faith only or the sufficiency of Holy Scripture, employ themselves in the contemplation of Scripture facts, and bring before their minds in a tangible form the doctrine involved in them, and give a substance and colour to the sacred history as to influence their brethren; and their brethren, though superficial themselves, are drawn by the Catholic instinct to accept conclusions which they could not indeed themselves have elicited, but which, when elicited, they feel to be true.

The writers I have mentioned, typical of many in every age of the Church, lived and died in the faith and contem-plation of Jesus Christ, what He was, what He did, and how God gave Him to us through His Mother Mary, what God did for our race in Mary; and they glorified God the more, the more they saw His wonders. This vision came to them not in the way of syllogistic reasoning, nor by any formal conscious process, but by that informal reasoning on the basis of revealed facts, which is best described as the interplay of mind on mind, until the Holy Spirit brings to all a deeper understanding. It is then at this final stage that the theologian comes to explain, to reduce to argument, to answer ob-jections, to describe the manner in which the understanding of our faith has been preserved and even deepened among us.

But I hope to explain more fully in relation to the doctrine of the Assumption the part played by simple faith, the gifts of the Holy Ghost, the Catholic principles of dogma, theology, and grace, and the spontaneous simple reasoning of the sincere Christian believer in the development of doctrines. For these great Christian doctrines were recognized as relating to living persons and realities which were part of a great world which God has revealed to us, in which we all live and die. This world is much greater than could be contained in the bare confession that we are sinners, and that we are saved by faith in Christ's name. It is a world which already finds reflected in redeemed human beings something of the victory over evil brought about by Christ's death and Resurrection.

SELECT BIBLIOGRAPHY

(1) The doctrine was of course defined in the Bull *Ineffabilis, Denz.*, 1641; in English, *The Immaculate Conception of the Most Blessed Virgin Mary*, Dublin (M. H. Gill), 1953. The Encyclical *Fulgens Corona*, 1953, also dealt with the Immaculate Conception, *AAS*, 45 (1953), 577-92; in English, London, CTS, 1953.

(2) The history of the doctrine is well covered in the columns of the Bibliotheca Immaculatae Conceptionis, 5 vols., Rome, 1950-1954.
Note especially vol. 3: Jugie, M., A.A., *L'Immaculée Conception dans l'Ècriture Sainte et dans le tradition orientale*, and vol. 5: Balić, C., O.F.M., *Ioannes Duns Scotus Doctor Immaculatae Conceptionis*.

(3) Equally important from a theological point of view are the Acts of the first Mariological Congress in Rome:—
Virgo Immaculata (Acta 1 Congressus Internationalis Mariologici, Romae Anno Sancto MCML Celebrati), 12 volumes, of which vol. 4 (on the growth of the doctrine), vol. 5, fasc. 1 (on the early theology), and vol. 5, fasc. 2 (on Eastern theology) are of the greatest interest in this subject.

(4) On the mediaeval controversies and theological development, the following are recommended:—
The writer of this chapter has written the following articles:—
   (a) " The Origins of Devotion to Our Lady's Immaculate Conception," *Dublin Review*, 118th year (1954), no. 466, 375-392.
   (b) Our Lady's Conception: A Mediaeval Manuscript," *Clergy Review*, 30 (1948), 85 ff.
   (c) " The Defence of the Immaculate Conception a National Heritage," *Clergy Review*, 31 (1941), 311 ff.
   (d) "Theologia Immaculatae Conceptionis apud Primos Defensores, scil. in Anglia, Saec. XII," *Virgo Immaculata*, vol. 5, fasc. 1, 1-12.
   The whole volume in which the last-quoted article appears is concerned with the mediaeval controversies and growth of doctrine.
Eadmer's treatise, together with what remains of Osbert of Clare on the Immaculate Conception are pul·lished in Thurston, H., and Slater, T., *Eadmeri Mon. Cant. Tractatus de Conceptione Sanctae Mariae*, Herder, 1904. Eadmer's treatise is also found in *PL* 159.
Nicholas of St. Alban's treatise was published recently in the *Revue Bénédictine*, 69 (1954), C. H. Talbot, " Nicholas of St. Alban's and Saint Bernard."

(5) For the development of the doctrine in general, see:
J. Duhr, S.J., " L'évolution du dogme de l'Immaculée Conception," *Nouv. Rev. Théol.*, 73 (1951), 1013 ff.
Cl. Dillenschneider, C.SS.R., *Le Sens de la foi et le progrés dogmatique du mystére marial*, Rome, 1954.
J. H. Newman, *The New Eve*, Oxford, The Newman Bookshop, 1952. This gathers together what Newman wrote in answer to Pusey on the subject.

(6) For this and other Marian doctrines, cf. J. B. Carol, O.F.M., *Mariology*, Milwaukee, 1956-57 (2 vols. published).
Cf. also *The Dogma of the Immaculate Conception, History and Significance*, Edward D. O'Connor, C.S.C. (Ed.), Notre Dame, 1958.

Perpetual Virginity

By DERMOT RYAN, M.A., L.S.S.

INTRODUCTION

Miraculous births in the Old Testament period were usually indicative of a special divine mission for the child born in such circumstances (Abraham, Samson, John the Baptist). It was therefore fitting that the entry of Christ into the human race should so far transcend the entry of other beings, as the function for which He had come—and His own dignity— far surpassed any particular act of salvation of Old Testament times. The sterility of the Old Testament mothers was but a faint reflection of the fruitful virginity of Mary.

A new beginning becomes possible with the New Adam. The first Adam was created by the direct intervention of God. As head of the human race, he thwarted the designs of God and begot a blighted race which at times reflected so little of the image of their Creator that He was tempted to destroy them. God intervened once again to create the New Adam, who by His obedience begot a blessed race, who so perfectly reflected their Creator's image that they are become worthy to be called and to be the sons of God (1 John iii:1).

The virginal conception is also indicative of the purely gratuitous nature of Christ's redemption. In a sense, it is the first act which is immediately concerned with Christ in His redemptive mission. It is completed without the aid of man; it can only happen because God has freely chosen to intervene. Man is unable to free himself from his state of sin. The act of redemption is not accomplished by his willing—"not by the will of the flesh, nor of the will of man,"—and only those to whom God gives the strength, have power to become the sons of God (John i:12-13). By His unique conception and birth, Christ taught this mystery of His new creation.[1]

Our Lady's virginity is therefore a great privilege and an integral part of the mystery of the Incarnation. The perfection of this state in Mary is frequently emphasized by the addition of the word " perpetual "; it was a privilege which Mary was to enjoy forever.

When considering this privilege of Our Lady, theologians distinguish neatly between *virginitas mentis*, *virginitas sensus*, and *virginitas corporis*. *Virginitas mentis* is the determination (*propositum*, *votum*)[2] of Our Lady to refrain from any thought, word, or act contrary to perfect chastity. *Virginitas sensus* describes Our Lady's freedom from disordered movements of the flesh, and is included in her freedom from concupiscence. *Virginitas corporis* refers to the virginal state of Our Lady's body, which, according to Merkelbach,[3] excludes " all damage to or violation of the genital organs, and all experience of venereal pleasure."[4]

The bodily virginity of Our Lady is further discussed under the three heads: *virginitas ante partum*, *in partu*, and *post partum*. The *virginitas ante partum* implies the virginal conception of Jesus and the absence of marital relations between Our Lady and St. Joseph up to the time of the birth of Christ. *Virginitas post partum* excludes marital relations, and therefore the generation of other children, after the birth of Christ. *Virginitas in partu* includes non-rupture of the hymen at the moment of birth, which takes place without opening of the membranes or damage to Our Lady's body, and without pain. This description of *virginitas in partu* involves a miraculous birth, in the course of which Christ passed from His Mother's womb, as He later passed from the closed sepulchre.[5]

Such then are the distinctions to be found in a modern

[1] Cf. M. Schmaus, *Katholische Dogmatik*, 5: *Mariologie*, Munich, 1955, 137 ff.

[2] Discussion of the nature of Our Lady's *propositum* (whether a vow or not, when elicited etc.) is outside the scope of this article. These matters, which are highly controversial at the present time, are touched on in Fr. Kearns's article, " Our Lady in the New Testament." See p. 35, n. 12.

[3] It is not necessary to multiply references to the standard theology textbooks, as the treatment of this subject does not vary greatly. B.H. Merkelbach's *Mariologia*, Paris, 1939, may be taken as representative of the usual exposition.

[4] Op. cit., 216.

[5] Op. cit., 216-217.

theological text-book. It would surprise us to find these distinctions ready-made in the earliest witnesses to Revelation, and, of course, they are not there. A fairly long process of development took place before these several aspects of Our Lady's virginity emerged from the clash of truth and error, and some of the important phases in the clarification of this doctrine may now be considered.

I

THE DEVELOPMENT OF THE TEACHING ON *VIRGINITAS IN PARTU*

The earliest records we have, viz. the Gospels of St. Matthew and St. Luke, leave us in no doubt about the virginal conception of Christ. They are, in a sense, independent witnesses in that they narrate the same event from different standpoints. St. Matthew (c. 1) describes the re-action of St. Joseph on his discovery of this stupendous miracle, while St. Luke (c. 1) depicts Our Lady's consent to the entry of God into her virginal womb. St. Mark does not deal with the Infancy of Christ, which may not have been part of the earliest catechesis, but by describing Christ as the Son of Mary (Mark vi:2) he *may* be hinting at the virginal conception of the Saviour.[6] Strangely enough, St. John, the virgin disciple, has nothing to say on Our Lady's virginity, unless one accepts the variant reading in i:13—" who *is* born not of blood, nor of the will of the flesh, nor of the will of man, but of God " instead of " who are born . . . " There would then be a clear reference to the virginal conception rather than to our re-birth to the life of grace. Some theologians deduce the doctrine of Our Lady's perpetual virginity, i.e. *virginitas post partum* from the act of Christ on the Cross in entrusting Mary to the care of St. John. When we are already aware of Our Lady's perpetual virginity, this gesture of Christ becomes an important detail in the complete picture, but of itself it could hardly warrant the conclusion that Our Lady remained a virgin after the birth of Christ.

[6] This mode of reference may have been used because St. Joseph was already dead.

The evangelists, or rather two of them, give more than abundant proof of the virginal conception of Christ, but phrases which reflect the general ignorance on this point at an earlier period are faithfully recorded by them, and provided the starting point for heretics, when later they launched attacks on this privilege of Mary. Christ is described as " the son of Joseph " (Luke iv:22; John vi:42) and " the son of the carpenter " (Matt. xiii:55), phrases which merely reflect the popular belief of the time. Our Blessed Lady, for obvious and practical reasons, uses a similar mode of address when she says to Christ: " Thy father and I have sought thee sorrowing " (Luke ii:48).

It need not surprise us that the virginal conception was not immediately publicized. It was first of all necessary that the divinity of Christ and His mission should be clearly established, lest premature revelation of His miraculous origin should endanger His own and His Mother's lives before His mission was accomplished. He might well be stoned as a blasphemer, while His Mother might suffer the same penalty for adultery.

If one interprets Our Lady's words " How can this be for I know not man? " as the expression of her determination always to remain a virgin, then the words teach implicitly the *virginitas in partu* and the *virginitas post partum*. A number of scholars, however, consider that Our Lady's words do not involve such a *propositum*, and still less a *votum*,[7] and consequently provide no evidence for the *virginitas in partu* and *post partum*. In view of the uncertainty which surrounds this text, one may sum up the evidence of the Gospels by saying that they provide clear and explicit testimony for *virginitas ante partum*, but no *explicit* support can be got from them for the *virginitas in partu* and *post partum*.[8]

The fundamental truth of the virginal conception of Christ, so clear in the Gospels, eventually finds its way into the baptismal creeds. When this happened is not certain; it may have been about the end of the first century.[9] The words

---

[7] For a discussion of this problem cf. " Our Lady's Vow of Virginity " by Rev. Neal M. Flanagan, O.S.M., in *Marian Studies*, 7 (1956), 103-21.

[8] The text in Isaias vii:14 is fully discussed in Fr. Duncker's second paper, see pp. 13 ff. Cf. also p. 126 for a comment on this text.

[9] Cf. St. Ignatius of Antioch, *Trallians*, 9, 1; *Ephesians*, 19, 1; *Symrnaeans*, 1, 1.

"ex Maria virgine" are found in the Creed for the Roman rite of Baptism described by Hippolytus in his *Apostolic Tradition*, written about A.D. 200, but it was composed long before this date.[10]   The early creeds, like the Gospels, therefore concerned themselves especially with the virginal conception of Christ, and did not include any article concerning *virginitas in partu* or *virginitas post partum*; neither do the creeds of the present day include explicit reference to these aspects of Our Lady's virginity.

Even while the creeds were being formulated, errors about the virginity of Our Lady began to appear. More often than not, direct attacks were not made on this doctrine, but its denial followed from christological errors of one kind or another. Cerinthus, at the end of the first century, asserted that Jesus was the Son of Joseph and Mary, and that at the time of His Baptism He became possessed by the Holy Spirit, who, however, abandoned Him before His Passion. This doctrine necessarily involved the denial of Our Lady's virginity, and although many hold that St. John wrote his Gospel to combat the errors of Cerinthus, one looks in vain for a defence of the virgin birth in the fourth Gospel. This omission on the part of St. John may be a confirmation of the view that he was not immediately concerned with the errors of Cerinthus.[11]

Shortly after the death of St. John St. Ignatius of Antioch (died c. 107) testifies that Jesus was "truly born of a virgin," [12] and writes in his letter to the Ephesians: ". . . the prince of this world was in ignorance of the virginity of Mary and her childbearing, and also of the death of the Lord . . . three mysteries loudly proclaimed to the world, though accomplished in the stillness of God." [13] Because St. Ignatius puts the childbearing of Our Lady (*ho tokētos autēs*) in the same category as the mysteries of her virginity and Christ's death, some commentators see a reference to a mysterious parturition, in other words to *virginitas in partu* in these words.

---

[10] For the origin and growth of the Apostles' Creed cf. J. Quasten, *Patrology*, 1, Westminster, Md., 1951, 23 ff.
[11] Cf. R. Schnackenburg, *Die Johannesbriefe*, Freiburg, 1953.
[12] *Smyrnaeans*, 1, 1.
[13] *Ephesians*, 19, 1.

The interpretation of the whole passage is, however, exceedingly difficult. In what sense is the prince of this world in
ignorance of these three mysteries? Why are they called
" the three mysteries of shouting," which is the literal translation of the words " three mysteries loudly proclaimed to the
world "? Or are the " three mysteries of shouting " distinct
from the virginity and childbearing of Our Lady and the death
of Our Lord? These and other questions concerning the
textual criticism of the passage make it a very unreliable
witness for *virginitas in partu* as generally conceived by
theologians. [14]

A text often quoted in support of the doctrine of Our
Lady's virginity, and especially of *virginitas in partu*, is the 19th
Ode of Solomon, written about the middle of the second
century:

> The womb of the Virgin caught (it),
> And received conception,
> And brought forth;
> And the Virgin became a Mother with many mercies;
> And she travailed and brought forth a Son,
> Without incurring pain.
> Because it happened not emptily,
> And she had not sought a midwife
> For He brought Her to bear,
> She brought forth
> As if she were a man,
> Of her own will. [15]

This text clearly teaches the virginal conception of Christ,
and also His painless birth, something which is quite different
from what the theologians describe as *virginitas in partu*. It
is also worth recording that the writer had no doubt that Our
Lady was active in the birth of Christ: " she travailed and
brought forth," as indeed had already been implied by St.
Ignatius, when he spoke of Our Lady's childbearing. While

---

[14] Cf. Joseph C. Plumpe, " Some Little-known Early Witnesses to Mary's *Virginitas
in partu*," *Theological Studies*, 9 (1948), 567ff. Plumpe, however, tends to identify
painless birth with the doctrine of *virginitas in partu*.

[15] The translation is taken from J. H. Bernard, *The Odes of Solomon*. The difficulties
of this passage are obvious even in translation. The edition of J. R. Harris and
A. Mingana should be consulted.

then this *Ode* of Solomon may be quoted in favour of Our
Lady's virginity and the painless birth of Christ, it is not
evidence for the *virginitas in partu* in the sense that this phrase
has in the textbooks.[16]

St. Justin Martyr contributes a new element to Mariology
when he contrasts Mary with Eve, and emphasizes their
virginity, when each made her fateful contribution to the plan
of salvation:

> Christ became man by the Virgin in order that the disobedi-
> ence which proceeded from the serpent might receive its
> destruction in the same manner in which it derived its origin.
> For Eve, who was a virgin and undefiled, having conceived the
> word of the serpent, brought forth disobedience and death.
> But the Virgin Mary received faith and joy when the Angel
> Gabriel announced the good tidings to her . . .[17]

The Fathers and ecclesiastical writers up to the middle of
the second century add little to the evidence of the Gospels,
and continue to stress the virginal conception of Christ, while
not hesitating at the same time to speak of the reality of His
birth and Our Lady's active part in it (Ignatius; *Odes*).
During the latter half of the second century, other aspects of
Our Lady's virginity find mention in the literature.   The
Protoevangelium of James (end of second century), the well-
known apocryphal Gospel of the Infancy, surrounds the birth
of Christ, as indeed His whole childhood, with the most
extravagant miracles.   Unfortunately, the passage is too long
to quote here, but the description of the birth is such as to
make the author suspect of the heresy of Docetism, according
to which Christ did not have a real body, but only an apparent
one.   The writer of this document shows peculiar interest in
the virginity of Our Lady, before, in and after the birth of

---

[16] The *Ascensio Isaiae* is sometimes quoted as a witness to *virginitas in partu*.   Its
evidence, however, is not direct, and its witness of doubtful value.   Quasten describes
this " Christian adaptation of Jewish writings " as a " rhapsodical description of the
seven heavens, and of the incarnation, passion, resurrection, and ascension of Christ,"
(*Patrology*, vol. 1, 110).   The relevant text is: " It came to pass that when they (Joseph
and Mary) were alone, Mary straight way looked with her eyes, and saw a small
babe, and she was astonished.   And after she was astonished, her womb was found
as formerly before she had conceived."   R. H. Charles, *The Ascension of Isaiah*, 59.

[17] *Dialogue*, 100.   Cf. J. Quasten, *Patrology*, vol. 1, 211.

Christ, and describes in almost offensive detail the intervention of a midwife to testify to the physical integrity of
Our Lady after the birth.   This midwife is hardly a historical
person, as the evidence for her existence is contradicted by
the testimony of the 19th *Ode* of Solomon, already quoted,
and by the Fathers who deny the presence of a midwife at
the birth of Christ, as e.g. St. Jerome.   Clement of Alexandria
(156-215), when speaking of Our Lady's virginity *in partu*
and *post partum*, shows that he is aware of the story of the midwife in the *Protoevangelium* of James: " For after she had brought
forth, some say that she was attended by a midwife and was
found to be a virgin." [18]

The apocryphal gospel of James was probably written in
Alexandria,[19] and from the same period we have a witness
from the other side of the Mediterranean in the person of
St. Irenaeus, from whom we may quote the well-known
passage: " Filius Dei filius hominis; purus pure puram aperiens
vulvam: the son of God is also son of man; He who is pure
purely opens the pure womb." [20]   These words are rather
illogically quoted by some as an indication of the *virginitas in
partu* of the textbooks.   The word " aperiens " is denied its
ordinary meaning and " pure " is interpreted to mean " vir-
ginally." [21]   Elsewhere, St. Irenaeus testifies to the painlessness
of the birth of Christ,[22] and speaks of the birth of Christ from
Mary " who was yet a virgin." [23]

The clear evidence of the *Protoevangelium* of James for the
virginity before, in and after the birth is in contrast to the
position adopted by Tertullian (155-c. 223), who, when faced
with Docetist errors, denied that the birth of Christ was
miraculous, and limited the virginity to the absence of marital
relations with St. Joseph before the birth of Christ.   He

[18] *Stromata*, 7, 93, 7, *PG* 9, 530.
[19] Cf. J. Quasten, *Patrology*, vol. 1, 121.
[20] *Adv. Haereses* 1, 4, c. 33, n. II, *PG* 7, 1080.
[21] As the Greek original of this passage is missing, it is not possible to ascertain
with certainty the word or words used by St. Irenaeus for " purus pure puram."
[22] *Proof of the Apostolic Preaching*, 54.
[23] " Jouassard has also noted that it is very difficult to know what St. Irenaeus
thought, or even if he gave any thought, relative to the virginity *in partu* and *post
partum*." Quoted from *Marian Studies*, vol. 7, p. 78, n. 19. The work of Jouassard,
which I have not seen, is " La Théologie mariale de Saint Irenée," in *Congrès Marials
Nationaux, VIIe Congrès, Lyon,* 1954.

therefore denied the virginity in and after the birth. He says:
" She was a virgin, so far as her husband was concerned; she
was not a virgin, so far as her childbearing was concerned." [24]
" If she was a virgin when she conceived, in her childbearing
she was a wife." [25]   Tertullian also held that Our Lady had
other children by St. Joseph,[26] and it is surprising to learn
that this doctrine does not seem to have provoked the violent
reaction one would expect if he were teaching open heresy on
these points. In fact, he underlines the position of the *virginitas
ante partum* as a dogma of faith in contrast to the *virginitas in
partu* and *post partum*.[27]

While Origen speaks of Our Lady as the first-fruits of
virginity among women as Christ was among men,[28] his
teaching on the virginity of Mary is not perfect in every
respect. He defends her reputation against the blasphemous
assertion of Celsus that Jesus was her illegitimate son,[29] and
he rejects the view that Our Lady had other children besides
Jesus, without however, branding it as heretical:

> . . . for this body, chosen to serve the Word of God who
> had said: " The Holy Spirit shall come upon thee, and the power
> of the Most High shall overshadow thee," should not have
> intercourse with man after the Holy Spirit came upon Mary
> and after the power of the Most High had overshadowed her.
> In my opinion it was logical that the first flower of the life of
> purity should be Jesus among men and Mary among women;
> for it would have been unbecoming to attribute to anyone
> other than Mary the title of " The First of Virgins." [30]

With regard to the virginity in the birth of Christ, Origen
differs from his predecessor in the school of Alexandria, when
he says that the womb of Our Lady, as distinct from other

[24] *Liber de carne Christi*, c. 23, PL 2, 790.
[25] Ibid.
[26] *Adv. Marc.* 3, 11, PL 2, 335bc; 4, 19, ibid., 404b-406a.
[27] *De Praescr. Haeret.*, 13, PL 2, 26b; 44, ibid., 60a.
[28] *Comm. in Matth.*, 10, 17, PG 13, 877a.
[29] *Contra Celsum*, 1, 32ff., PG 11, 719ff.
[30] *Comm. in Matth.*, 10, 17, PG 13, 876-877. The translation is found in *Marian
Studies*, vol. 7, 80-81, and is taken from Emil Neubert, S.M., *Mary in Doctrine*, Milwaukee, 1954, 185-6.

mothers, remained closed until the birth of Christ,[31] but not afterwards. While therefore Origen grasped the relationship between Our Lady's holiness and her virginity, and from her intimate association with the Holy Ghost in the work of the Incarnation concluded to her *virginitas post partum*, he did not see that there was any contradiction between an act of birth which was natural and this perfect state of virginity.

The doctrine of Our Lady's *perpetual* virginity was incorporated into the eastern version of the Nicene Creed by including the words *aei parthenos*—" ever virgin " (*Denz.*, 13). This addition was due to St. Epiphanius (315-402),[32] who was engaged in rebutting the errors of the Antidicomarianites (opponents of Mary). They taught the by now common error that Our Lady had of St. Joseph other children besides Jesus, and added to it an unusual interpretation of St. John xix:27. " He took her unto his own " would mean that he took her unto him as wife. Epiphanius bases his arguments on the tradition of the perpetual virginity which had been handed down, and on Scripture. In dealing with the problem of the " the brethren of the Lord " (Mark iii:31 etc.), he takes the view which occurs frequently in the Fathers, that St. Joseph had already six children by a previous marriage, when he was wedded to Our Lady.[33] This opinion probably derives from the apocryphal gospel of Peter and the book of James referred to by Origen,[34] but is not the explanation which ultimately found favour with St. Jerome and the scholars of the present day.

St. Ephraem (305-c.372)[35] in his Hymns in honour of Our Lady, insists that the seals of virginity remained unbroken during and after the birth of Christ. His evidence is exceed-

---

[31] " Omnium mulierum non partus infantis, sed viri coitus vulvam reserat. Matris vero Domini eo tempore vulva reserata est, quo et partus editus." *In Lucam Hom.* 14, *PG* 13, 1836c.

[32] He did not hesitate to say that Christ opened his Mother's womb, *Haer.*, 78, 19, *PG* 42, 730.

[33] *Haer.*, *PG* 42, 707-711. So also Hilary of Poitiers, *Comm. in Matth.*, c. 1, *PL* 9, 922.

[34] *Comm. in Matth.*, 10, 17, *PG*, 13, 876-877.

[35] For St. Ephraem cf. Paul Krüger, " Die somatische Virginität der Gottesmutter im Schrifttume Ephraems des Syrers," in *Alma Socia Christi*, vol. 5, fasc. 1, 46-86; E. Beck: " Die Mariologie der echten Schriften Ephräms " in *Oriens Christianus*, 40 (1956), 22-39.

ingly difficult to assess, as the authenticity of many of his
writings is called in question.   Due allowance must also be
made for the customary extravagances of Syriac poetry, and
for the peculiar position which St. Ephraem takes in regard
to the privilege of Our Lady's virginity.   He is only concerned
with the physical virginity of Our Lady, and finds the perfection of this privilege in complete and absolute physical
integrity.   He develops his argument from a comparison with
the Resurrection, and describes the birth in the following
terms: " When the glorious Spouse wished to go forth, He
left the virginal organs asleep, so that they should not feel
His going forth." [36]   In these words, he seems to exclude all
activity on the part of Our Lady in the birth of her Son.

St. Jerome was mainly concerned with the defence of the
virginitas post partum against the errors of Helvidius and
Jovinian.   Both held that Our Lady had children by St. Joseph
after the birth of Christ, and were motivated by the desire to
put virginity and the married state on the same plane, and
establish Our Lady as the perfect model of both states.   In
this they were reacting against the emphasis laid on the virtue
of virginity by the ascetic tradition of which we have already
heard representatives in the persons of Origen and Athanasius.
St. Jerome, like Epiphanius, argued from Tradition:

> Might I not array against you the whole series of ancient
> writers? Ignatius, Polycarp, Irenaeus, Justin Martyr, and many
> other apostolic and eloquent men, who against Ebion, Theodotus
> of Byzantium and Valentinus, held these same views, and wrote
> volumes replete with wisdom. If you had ever read what they
> wrote, you would be a wiser man . . . [37]

He solved the difficulty from Scripture derived from the
" brethren of the Lord " by saying they were children of a
sister of Our Lady: " fratres propinquitate, non naturae." [38]
He gives a long list of instances in the Old Testament where
" brethren " is used for relatives.

These arguments of St. Jerome are concerned with *virginitas
post partum*.   Once in the course of his *opusculum* against

---

[36] S. *Ephraemi Syri Hymni et Sermones*, ed. T. I. Lamy, vol. 2, 573-4; 575-6.
[37] *Adv. Helvidium*, PL 23, 201.   [38] Ibid., 199.

Helvidius, he refers to the birth of Our Lord in terms which could only describe a natural process:

> Add, if you wish, the other afflictions of nature: the swelling womb for nine months, the upsets, the birth, the blood, the swaddling clothes. He is described to you as an infant enveloped in the customary wrapping of membranes. The hard wood of the crib, the wailing of the infant, the circumcision on the eighth day may be included, and even the time of purification, that He may seem unclean. We are not ashamed, we are not reduced to silence. The greater the humiliations He suffered on my account, the more do I owe Him. And when you have exhausted all arguments in reply, you will have produced nothing more shameful than the Cross, which we gladly profess, on which we pin our faith, and in which we see our enemies defeated.[39]

This is admittedly a rhetorical passage, but it is interesting that St. Jerome permits himself the use of phrases which later writers find disturbing.[40] Elsewhere St. Jerome uses the customary formula, " januis clausis," but it seems to apply only to the virginal conception, which occurred " januis clausis," just like Our Lord's *entry* into the supper room after the Resurrection: " Let them tell me how Jesus *entered* with the door closed, and I will answer how Mary is virgin and mother." [41] Even here, however, he seems to avoid the question of *virginitas in partu* in the technical sense of non-rupture of the membranes and the hymen, for he continues " Virgo post partum, mater antequam nupta."

In his *Adversus Jovinianum* he refers the " hortus conclusus " of the Canticle of Canticles (iv:12) to Our Lady, but once again he does not treat of the *virginitas in partu*: " That which is closed and sealed bears the likeness of the Mother of the Lord,

---

[39] " Junge si libet et alias naturae contumelias: novem mensibus uterum insolescentem, fastidia, partum, sanguinem, pannos. Ipse tibi describitur infans, tegmine membranorum solito convolutus. Ingerantur dura praesepia, vagitus parvuli, octavae diei circumcisio, tempus purgationis, ut probetur immundus.   Non erubescimus, non silemus. Quanto sunt humiliora quae pro me passus est, tanto plus illi debeo. Et cum omnia replicaveris, cruce nihil contumeliosius proferes; quam profitemur, et credimus, et in qua de hostibus triumphamus." *PL* 23, 202.

[40] E.g. St. Ildephonsus.   Cf. *PL* 23, 202, note h.

[41] *Epist.* 48, *PL* 22, 510.

(who was) both Mother and Virgin." [42] In fact, his treatment
of this question in the *Adv. Jov.* is such that one author says
that at the end of it, one is uncertain if he agrees with St.
Ambrose,[43] who stoutly maintained the *virginitas in partu* in
the technical sense. This attitude of St. Jerome was probably
due to his dislike of the apocrypha:

> No midwife was there; no fussing of handywomen. She
> herself wrapped Him in swaddling clothes. She was mother
> and midwife. "She laid Him in a manger because there was
> no room for them in the inn." This sentence confounds the
> ravings of the apocrypha. [44]

After St. Jerome's lively and telling defence of Our Lady's
virginitas post partum, it only remained for St. Ambrose to
state clearly his view of *virginitas in partu*. This he did on
many occasions, and especially in his *De Institutione Virginis*,
from which are taken the words:

> Who is this gate but Mary, closed because (she is) a virgin?
> Therefore Mary is the gate through which Christ entered this
> world, when He was delivered by a virginal birth without
> opening the portals of virginity. The shield of modesty
> remained intact, and the seals of integrity inviolate, when He
> went forth from the Virgin. [45]

He lays particular stress on the fact that the womb was not
opened,[46] and may well have been motivated by his desire to
preserve the traditional physical sign of virginity in Our Lady
even after the birth of Our Lord. This would put him in an

---

[42] "Quod clausum est, atque signatum, similitudinem habet matris Domini,
matris et virginis," *PL* 23, 254.

[43] G. Jouassard, "Marie à travers la patristique," in *Maria*, ed. H. du Manoir,
vol. 1, 110.

[44] "Nulla ibi obstetrix; nulla muliercularum sedulitas intercessit. Ipsa pannis
involvit infantem, ipsa et mater et obstetrix fuit. Et collocavit eum in praesepio,
quia non erat ei locus in diversorio. Quae sententia et apocryphorum deliramenta
convincit." *Adv. Helvidium, PL* 23, 192a.

[45] "Quae est haec porta nisi Maria; ideo clausa, quia virgo? Porta igitur Maria,
per quam Christus intravit in hunc mundum, quando virginali fusus est partu, et
genitalia virginitatis claustra non solvit. Mansit intemeratum septum pudoris, et
inviolata integritatis duravere signacula cum exiret ex virgine." *De Institutione Virginis*,
8, 54, *PL* 16, 320. The words are a commentary on Ezechiel xl:2 ff.

[46] But cf. *Expos. Ev. sec. Lucam*, 2, 57, *PL* 15, 1655, where he says: "Hic ergo solus
aperuit sibi vulvam . . . hic est qui aperuit matris suae vulvam ut immaculatus exiret."

even stronger position when dealing with the errors of Jovinian and Bonosus.

St. Augustine, as we might expect, depends largely on St. Ambrose for his Mariology, and we frequently find in his writings the triple formula, used also by Zeno of Verona (d. 380): " Virgo concepit; miramini; virgo peperit, plus miramini; post partum virgo permansit." [47] Elsewhere he says after comparing the passage of Christ from His Mother's womb to His entry into the supper room after the Resurrection: " infans de . . . utero virginali, illaesa matris virginitate procederet." [48]

From this time on the teaching concerning Our Lady's *virginitas in partu* includes a miraculous birth, and there is little variation in the manner of presenting this teaching, even at the present day.[49]

This brief study of the development of the teaching on *virginitas in partu* shows that the earliest records do not teach anything on this subject, and do not seem to have thought of the question at all. The earliest documents to teach the *virginitas in partu* are the apocrypha, which do so in such an extravagant fashion that they seem to contradict the earlier records concerning the birth of Christ. Many of the Fathers, however, developed their teaching on the *virginitas in partu* along the lines suggested by the apocrypha, and postulated a miraculous birth in order to safeguard the virginity of Our Lady. Although St. Jerome would have none of " the ravings of the apocrypha," the teaching found in St. Ambrose and St. Augustine became almost universal. The Fathers seem to have accepted without discussion the current concept of bodily virginity.

---

[47] *Sermo* 196, *PL* 38, 1019.   [48] *Sermo* 191, *PL* 38, 1010.

[49] Limitations of time and space preclude a review of the controversies in which Ratramnus and Paschasius Radbertus were engaged, as well as the opinion of Durandus concerning the birth of Christ. For an introduction to these topics, cf. *D.T.C.*, 9, 2383-5. Georg Söll, S.D.B., " Die Mariologie der Kappadozier " in *Alma Socia Christi*, vol. 5, fasc. 1, pp. 137ff., should be consulted for the evidence from the Cappadocian Fathers.

II

The third canon of the Lateran Council of 649 reads:

> Si quis secundum sanctos Patres non confitetur proprie et secundum veritatem Dei genitricem sanctam semperque virginem et immaculatam Mariam, utpote ipsum Deum Verbum specialiter et veraciter, qui a Deo Patre ante omnia saecula natus est, in ultimis saeculorum absque semine concepisse ex Spiritu Sancto, et incorruptibiliter eum genuisse, indissolubili permanente et post partum eiusdem virginitate, condemnatus sit. (*Denz.*, 256).[50]

This council was not in fact a general council, although Hefele says that it has almost the same authority as a general council.[51]   Its canons were repeated in a letter of Pope Agatho to the Third Council of Constantinople [52] as a clear statement of orthodox doctrine.   It should be noted that the council was concerned principally with the Monothelite heresy, and on the occasion of the rebuttal of the errors of this particular heresy it took the opportunity to state the traditional doctrine concerning the Trinity and the Incarnation, including the traditional statement of the doctrine of Our Lady's perpetual virginity.   As far as one can see, there is no clear intention of defining the doctrine of Our Lady's perpetual virginity in precisely those terms.

The words " absque semine concepisse ex Spiritu Sancto " clearly teach the virginal conception which had been a dogma of faith from the beginning. The *virginitas post partum* is also

---

[50] " If anyone refuses to confess, in agreement with the holy Fathers, that the holy and immaculate Mary, ever Virgin, is properly and truly Mother of God, inasmuch as, at the end of ages, by the power of the Holy Spirit and without the agency of human seed, she truly and in a special manner conceived God the Word Himself, who was born of God the Father before all the ages, and gave birth to Him without experiencing corruption, her virginity remaining ever inviolable and abiding intact after His birth—let him be condemned."

[51] Hefele, *Histoires des Conciles*, vol. 3, I, 435.

[52] Cf. *Denz.*, 254, n. 1.

clearly defined, but as to the phrase "incorruptibiliter genuisse" one reading it for the first time would understand by it
that the virgin who brought forth had not had intercourse, for
that was the normal meaning of *corruptio virginis*. The phrase
therefore would only add to the virginal conception a normal
act of parturition.[53] The history of the doctrine, however,
which has been briefly considered, and the use of the words
"secundum sanctos Patres," may indicate that the phrase
"incorruptibiliter genuisse" reflects the teaching of the Fathers
when they spoke of *virginitas in partu*. They used phrases like
"utero clauso et obsignato, signaculo virginitatis intacto et
inviolato," etc. to indicate non-rupture of the hymen. The
Council uses a phrase which is more indefinite, and while it
wishes to state the absence of any physical corruption of Our
Lady's virginity in the birth, it does not say precisely what are
the physical elements of this "incorruptibilitas."

The other document of the Magisterium which should be
considered here is the Constitution of Paul IV dealing with
the errors of the Unitarians concerning the Trinity and the
Incarnation. He condemns those who would deny that Mary
was truly the Mother of God, or say "nec perstitisse semper
in virginitatis integritate, ante partum scilicet, in partu, et
perpetuo post partum." (*Denz.*, 993). Once again the doctrine
is stated in general terms, and again there is no difficulty
about *virginitas ante* and *post partum*, but we are not enlightened
concerning the precise meaning of "integritas virginitatis in
partu." For this reason a recent dogmatic textbook [54] states
that the preservation of "integritas corporalis" is a necessary
element of the dogma of Our Lady's virginity *in partu*, but
the author refrains from any further determination of this
"integritas corporalis."

In this Constitution of Paul IV the word "integritas" is

---

[53] Prof. Dr. Christine Mohrmann of Nijmegen University has kindly forwarded
the following note on the phrases "incorruptibiliter genuisse" and "indissolubili
permanente . . . virginitate": "The adverb 'incorruptibiliter' and the adjective
'indissolubili' have here a sense they often have in late texts: the original meaning
of the suffix '-bilis' has been weakened very much, so that 'incorruptibiliter'
has got the meaning 'incorrupte,' that is to say 'as a virgin,' and nothing more.
In the same way, 'indissolubili' is the equivalent of 'indissoluta,' meaning intact.
As far as I can see there is nothing in these words to suggest a birth *ex utero clauso*."

[54] I. A. Aldama, *Mariologia*, in *Sacrae Theologiae Summa*, 3, Madrid, 1953, 392.

linked univocally, or indifferently, to the virginity *ante partum*, *in partu*, and *post partum*. A brief analysis discovers a difficulty in this phrasing. Virginity before birth implies the absence of intercourse, and the non-rupture of the hymen for this very reason—if indeed the rupture of the hymen would necessarily follow on intercourse—for only such a rupture of the hymen would be destructive of *virginitas ante partum*. If one then says that " integritas virginitatis in partu " involves the non-rupture of the hymen by the act of parturition, one is giving a second meaning to " integritas," which makes it rather difficult to predicate it equally of *virginitas ante partum* and *in partu*.

Alternatively, one may say that the loss of " integritas virginitatis " consists in the rupture of the hymen from any cause whatsoever, and that is something which would seem to require proof—a proof which is not found in the theology textbooks.

A third possibility presents itself, viz. that " integritas virginitatis " is lost only through intercourse. This gives a perfectly straightforward meaning to the statement that Our Lady always remained " in integritate virginitatis," but would mean that the *virginitas in partu* would not necessarily involve the preservation of an intact hymen.

A fourth explanation may be given. One might say that the notion of virginity is to be applied to Our Lady in an unique sense, for while in the case of other women virginity is lost by intercourse, it would be lost by Our Lady through the rupture of the hymen in the course of a natural birth, and that therefore the words " integritas virginitatis " necessarily exclude the rupture of the hymen. This reasoning attaches great importance to the hymen as an essential part of Our Lady's bodily virginity, and demands some kind of defence and explanation.

This fourth explanation might also be stated thus: the act of parturition in the case of Our Lord was unique in that it did not involve the rupture of the membranes or the hymen, and this unique event considered in relation to Our Lady is known as her *virginitas in partu*. It is, therefore, an unique use of the word virginity. When put in this way, the reasoning depends on the establishing of a historical fact, viz. that the birth of Our Lord was miraculous and did not involve the rupture of the membranes or the hymen.[55]

Most theologians follow either form of the fourth explanation and therefore tacitly assume, without proving, that Our Lady's virginity was unique in requiring the non-rupture of the hymen in childbirth, or that Our Lord's birth was miraculous in that it did not involve rupture of the membranes and hymen.

Some theologians begin by defining virginity like this: "Castitas perfecta in subiecto non voluntarie corrupto."[56] This definition includes no reference to the hymen, (which is regarded—even by theologians—as one of the signs of virginity), and as a definition of virginity it applies perfectly to the *virginitas ante* and *post partum*. But those same theologians speak of the *virginitas in partu* as consisting in the non-rupture of the hymen and the non-opening of the membranes enclosing Our Lord's body.[57] In other words, they introduce a new concept of virginity which is not covered by their original definition. Even St. Thomas himself says that the hymen pertains to virginity only *per accidens* and that its rupture by any other means than " delectatio venerea " is no more destructive of virginity than the loss of a hand or foot.[58] He does however hold that the birth of Our Lord did not involve " adapertio vulvae." [59] He gives as one of the *rationes convenientiae*: " Conveniens fuit ut de incorrupto virginis utero nasceretur," in which he presupposes that rupture of the hymen and membranes in the birth would involve " corruptio virginitatis," and

---

[55] In a note on the words (see note 47, above), Prof. Dr. Mohrmann says: " ' In virginitatis integritate ' is an example of a simple *genetivum inhaerentiae* (type: *in proelio certaminis*), which means that the two words have practically the same meaning, ' integritas ' being synonomous with ' virginitas.' This *genetivum inhaerentiae*, a mere rhetorical pleonasm, is very usual in ecclesiastical official style and in Roman liturgy. In these words I do not see a trace of a birth *ex utero clauso*. If theologians base their views (i.e. that Christ was born *ex utero clauso*) on these *documenta ecclesiastica*, *philological* evidence is against them." (Italics mine).

[56] E.g. P. Aloisius M. Maestu Ojanguren, O.F.M., " De voto virginitatis Mariae," *Alma Socia Christi*, 11 (1953), 115 f.

[57] Cf. ibid. This author says that bodily virginity is " integritas carnis quae nullo actu libidinoso fuit violata," yet goes on to say that corporal virginity *in partu* excludes the rupture of the hymen etc. To be logical he should therefore prove that parturition is an *actus libidinosus* or re-define corporal virginity.

[58] 2-2, 152, 1 ad 3.   [59] 3, 28, 2.

in this he is not consistent with his teaching on virginity already referred to.

Other theologians use a descriptive method; Merkelbach, for example, simply begins by saying that Our Lady's corporal virginity includes " integritas carnis, absque ulla laesione aut violatione organorum genitalium ac sumpto experimento delectationis venereae." [60] He then says that this is found *ante partum* because Christ was not generated by a man. It was found *in partu* " because Our Lady brought forth her Son without violation, rupture, perforation or laceration of the seal of virginity, and therefore from a closed and sealed womb, and, *a fortiori*, without pain." The " integritas" continues *post partum* because Our Lady abstained from marital intercourse and never had any other children nor, he adds, did she " ever lose this ' integritas carnis ' even accidentally." He also states that Our Lady conceived and gave birth in such a way that her body was as undamaged (" illaesum ") as if she had never conceived or borne a child. In accordance with these statements which are based on Patristic texts, he expounds the *documenta ecclesiastica* already quoted. At no stage does he consider the notion of bodily virginity in general, nor does he ask if and why the bodily virginity of Our Lady should be different from bodily virginity in other persons. His proof of this view involves the establishing of a historical fact, viz. that the birth of Our Lord did not involve the rupture of the hymen. This fact is not defined in the ecclesiastical documents, and theologians must establish it from historical sources, the Scriptures and the Fathers, or from Tradition. [61]   Some elements of their proof will be examined at a later stage.

[60] *Mariologia*, 216.

[61] A historical event which is not attested in the earliest surviving sources may still be preserved in Tradition, e.g. the Assumption. It can hardly be said that the miraculous *birth* of Christ is handed on by the Tradition which is a source of Revelation. There are many traditions in the Catholic Church which are not part of Tradition. See below pp. 128 ff.

III

A NEW APPROACH

The matter may now be approached from another point of view. The following question and answer appeared in the *Catholic Herald* on Friday, 30 December, 1955:

> Is it true that we must believe that Our Lady gave birth to Our Lord without violation of her physical virginity, and that the birth of Our Lord was miraculous and painless?
>
> It is true that we must hold as of Faith that Our Lady bore her Son without any violation of her virginal integrity, but the dogma, according to modern theologians, merely asserts the fact of the continuance of Our Lady's physical virginity without determining or detailing more closely *how* this is to be physiologically explained.
>
> The Fathers of the Church, with very few exceptions, and the Scholastic theologians, in general, thought of physical virginity as intimately connected with non-injury to the hymen. Accordingly they taught that Our Lady gave birth to Our Lord in a miraculous way, without opening the womb or injury to the hymen, and consequently without pains.
>
> However, according to modern natural scientific knowledge, the purely physical side of virginity consists in the non-fulfilment of the sex act, and is not necessarily connected with any particular state of the hymen. Injury to the hymen in birth would not then destroy even physical virginity, while on the other hand it would seem necessarily to belong to complete natural motherhood.
>
> It would follow from this that the miraculous process of Our Lord's birth cannot be immediately inferred from the continued physical virginity of His Mother, but must be derived from other facts of Revelation. The Gospels, however, bear witness to Our Lady's active rôle at the birth of her Son (" she brought forth "), which does not seem to point to a miraculous process.
>
> The almost unanimous testimony of the Fathers of the Church to the miraculous character of the birth of Our Lord raises the question, according to one modern theologian, " whether in so doing they attest a truth of Revelation, or whether they wrongly interpret a determined truth of Revelation, Mary's virginity, from an inadequate natural scientific point of view.

It seems hardly possible to demonstrate that the dignity of the Son of God or the dignity of the Mother of God demands the supernatural character of the birth."

The modern theologian referred to in the letter is probably A. Mitterer, who re-examines St. Thomas's teaching concerning the Holy Family in the light of modern biology.[62] He shows how St. Thomas drew certain conclusions from the application of the biological knowledge of his own age of the data of Revelation, and how some of these conclusions would now need revision.

He examines St. Thomas's treatment of Our Lady's *virginitas in partu* at some length. He accuses [63] the Angelic Doctor of being illogical when he says in one place that the rupture of the hymen otherwise than by " delectatio venerea " is no more prejudicial to virginity than the loss of a hand or a foot,[64] and then elsewhere says that this " integritas corporalis " belongs to the perfection of virginity.[65]

Mitterer then shows that from a modern biological standpoint the unruptured hymen can be considered only a sign of virginity, and a very uncertain sign at that. Some women are born without it; in others, it remains intact even after intercourse has taken place. It is therefore related to virginity as the *res significans* to *res significata*; the *res significans* may be present, even when the *res significata* is absent, and vice-versa. He says that one must therefore distinguish between injury to the organs of a virgin and the corruption of virginity.[66] The latter is found only when voluntary sexual intercourse has taken place.

In the course of his discussion on motherhood, Mitterer says that bodily changes and the pains which accompany motherhood are more closely bound up with full physical motherhood than is the preservation of the hymen with the perfection of virginity.[67]

St. Thomas thought that perfect virginity and full maternity

---

[62] The full title of his book is: *Dogma und Biologie der heiligen Familie nach dem Weltbild des hl. Thomas von Aquin und dem der Gegenwart*, Vienna, 1952.
[63] Op. cit., 108.　　[64] 2-2, 152, 1 ad 3.　　[65] *Quodl.*, 6, 18c.
[66] Mitterer asks whether the virginity of Our Lord was any less perfect as a result of circumcision, op. cit., 111.
[67] Op. cit., 112.

in the birth were not compossible, apparently because of the
importance which he attached to the hymen, so he sacrificed
an element which seems to belong to perfect motherhood.
Mitterer says he ought to have insisted with the same force
on the rupture of the hymen by the act of birth as a sign of
maternity, as he had insisted on its preservation as a sign of
virginity. [68]

St. Thomas goes even further and denies that Our Lady was
active in the birth of Christ. He says: " Corpus Christi quod
ad discipulos januis clausis intravit, potuit eadem potestate de
utero clauso exire." [69] In other words, he substitutes a
miraculous act of Christ for the act of giving birth which
should belong to Our Lady as Mother. In this, however, he
is not followed by most theologians who hold Our Lady was
active in the birth of Her Son.

To be brief, Mitterer says that since corporal virginity
consists in the absence of voluntary sexual intercourse, it is
possible to hold that Our Lady gave birth to Jesus in the normal
way without any violation of her virginity. He explains the
use of the formula *virginitas in partu* [70] in conjunction with
the *virginitas ante* and *post partum* as being merely the unfolding
of the doctrine of the perpetual virginity of Our Lady. This
particular statement of the doctrine became necessary as
various heresies arose, and emphasis was placed on the
virginitas in partu because " partus " is normally the most
decisive sign of lost virginity.

What is to be said about this view which maintains that
the actual birth of Christ was a natural process, in other words
that it may have involved the opening of the membranes and
the rupture of the hymen?

In the first place, it must be considered in relation to the
evidence of Scripture. The texts in St. Matthew and St. Luke
simply state that Our Lady brought forth her Son, at least
implying that she was active in the birth, just as active as
when she wrapped Him up in swaddling clothes. Some
interpret these words as hinting at a miraculous birth, but

[68] Op. cit., 113.
[69] *Compendium theologiae*, 1, 225. In this he follows S. Ambrose. See above p. 116.
[70] Op. cit., 123.

such an interpretation is not at all necessary. Many women give birth to their children with little effort and are quite well able to attend to the child immediately after birth.

The text of St. Luke says nothing on the subject of a painless birth, but once again it should be remembered that painless births are not necessarily miraculous. [71] In this connection, a *non sequitur* sometimes found in the textbooks may be noted. [72] They teach that since the pains of childbirth are a penalty for original sin, Our Lady who was free from original sin did not experience these pains. The fact may be true, but the reasoning is not necessarily valid. Suffering is also a consequence of original sin, and yet Our Lady suffered. Death entered into the world with sin, and although all theologians teach and believe that Our Lady was preserved from original sin, many of them say Our Lady died. Our Lady's Immaculate Conception does not therefore necessarily guarantee the painlessness of Our Lord's birth.

The text from Isaias (vii:14) may not be invoked in proof of a miraculous parturition, as the same three verbs are predicated of Anna in the same way in the first book of Samuel (i:20) and thus imply a normal, active birth. The unusual character of the event foretold in Isaias is guaranteed by the virginal conception alone. If the text tells us anything about *virginitas in partu*, it is simply that the act of parturition was performed by a virgin, but not that this act was miraculous in the manner of its accomplishment.

The words in St. Luke ii:23, " Every male opening the womb shall be called holy to the Lord," are usually stated not to refer to the manner of the birth, as the phrase " opening the womb " really only means first-born. [73] In resorting to

---

[71] On the 8 Jan., 1956 His Holiness Pope Pius XII gave an *Allocutio* entitled: " L'Accouchement sans douleur " (cf. *AAS*, 48 (1956), 82 ff.). The sections headed " Appréciation théologique " (p. 89) and " La Nouvelle Methode et l'Écriture Sainte " (p. 90) are of interest here. The translation of this allocution in the *Clergy Review*, 1956, 365 is headed: " Painless Natural Childbirth." An article by Fr. J. H. Crehan, S.J. (*Clergy Review*, 1956, 719-726), " The Painless Birth of Christ," seeks to establish Our Lady's *virginitas in partu* by proving that the birth was painless. Even if he has proved that the birth was painless, he has not proved that it was miraculous, nor does his proof establish the *virginitas in partu* as understood by theologians.

[72] E.g. Hugh Pope, O.P., in The Cambridge Summer School Lectures for 1933, *Our Blessed Lady*, London, 1934, 141.

[73] E.g. Merkelbach, *Mariologia*, 246.

this explanation, the theologians give one the impression of doing what they sometimes accuse Scripture scholars of doing, viz. stating that the words of Scripture do not really mean what they say !

Theologians sometimes say that St. Luke refrained from quoting the law of Leviticus, c. 12, concerning the " sin " or legal impurity contracted by childbirth because it did not apply in the case of Our Lady. They do not, however, explain why Our Lady offered two doves, one of which, according to the law (Leviticus xii:8), was a sin-offering, i.e. made on account of the legal impurity contracted in childbirth.

On the basis of St. Luke's account, one might ask how Our Lady knew her time was come? Mitterer would answer that the natural process of birth had begun.

When preaching on Our Lady, priests often quote the words of the unknown bystander in the Gospel: " Blessed is the womb that bore thee, and the breasts that gave thee suck " (Luke xi:27). They have therefore no hesitation in accepting the fact that Our Lady nourished her Child at her breasts. [74]

Again on the basis of Scripture, one might ask how St. Joseph knew Our Lady was with child, and again Mitterer would reply that it was by the ordinary manifestations of pregnancy. He therefore feels that it is quite illogical to hold that the birth was miraculous. The development of the Child in His Mother's womb went on naturally for nine months. His Mother was active during the birth, but here one interposes a miracle in order to save the *sigillum virginitatis* and to prevent Our Lady contracting an impurity from the so-called *sordes nativitatis*. Immediately after the birth the natural process begins again with the natural feeding of the Child Jesus. Mitterer asks is it logical to invoke a miracle to save one of the signs of virginity when other and more important signs of virginity are already lost? He also asks is it a Christian view of childbirth to say that the mother becomes thereby in some way impure? The Scriptures, then, can hardly be quoted against Mitterer's view.

[74] The theologians who state that Our Lady's body after the birth was the same as if she had never borne a child (e.g. Merkelbach) may be overlooking the fact that lactation involves bodily changes that are not normally found in a virgin.

What about the *documenta ecclesiastica*? We have seen already that while they assert *virginitas in partu* they are not clear on the physiological meaning of Our Lady's virginal integrity *in partu*. Neither is there any document which *defines* that the act of parturition was in itself miraculous, except in so far as it was being effected by a virgin. Mitterer's teaching is therefore not opposed to any defined doctrine. Nor is it condemned by the ordinary and universal Magisterium of the Church. It would be foolhardy to state that all the bishops of the Church in communion with the Roman Pontiff teach that the act of parturition was in itself miraculous. Many bishops do not teach anything on the subject, and at least two theologians say " that the *virginitas in partu* (and *a fortiori* the miraculous birth) does not pertain to the common and public preaching of the Church to the people." [75]

An investigation of the belief of the ordinary faithful in this matter might well surprise the theologians. Many presume that the actual birth was a natural process. When presented with the arguments usually adduced by theologians in favour of a miraculous birth, they do not understand the importance attached by the theologians to the unruptured hymen; still less do they appreciate the viewpoint that there was something sordid and unworthy about the act of childbirth. Indeed, the devotion to Our Lady of many women in childbirth seems to be based on the assumption that she gave birth to her Son in the usual way, just as she had borne Him in her womb for nine months.

The unanimous teaching of theologians is a certain criterion of divine Tradition when there is question of *res fidei et morum*,[76] and since the majority of theologians have taught a miraculous parturition, one may reasonably ask if they taught it as a matter of faith. Few would claim this degree of certainty for their teaching, and a recent dogmatic textbook says that the *more probable* view is that " Christ came into this

[75] J. P. Junglas, *Die Lehre der Kirche*, Bonn, 1936, 143, which is quoted with favour by Fr. Gerard Owens, C.SS.R., in *Marian Studies*, vol. 7, 44, in the course of his article on " Our Lady's Virginity in the Birth of Jesus."

[76] Cf. J. Salaverri, *De Ecclesia Christi*, Madrid, 1952, in *Sacrae Theologiae Summa*, vol. 1, p. 785.

world in a miraculous way, as a ray of sunlight passes through glass without breaking it." [77]

The approach of theologians to the nature of the parturition is largely determined by the traditional importance attached to the hymen or *signaculum virginitatis*. They accept the position that an unruptured hymen is essential to bodily virginity, and since the hymen does not usually survive parturition undamaged, [78] they conclude to a miraculous birth in order to safeguard it. They establish their position by reference to the Scriptures and the Fathers, but since the Scriptures favour rather than reject a natural birth, [79] their proof is of the same value as the witness of the Fathers which they invoke. Here there is need for solid work before one could say that the Tradition of the Church excludes the possibility of a natural birth. It is a long and laborious task and the following points may help towards clear thinking on the subject.

It may not be out of place to recall at this juncture that the manuals of theology do not always provide a proof *ex consensu Patrum*. Usually they argue from the authority of the Fathers by quoting a few short passages, or sometimes even by giving a list of names. The proof that a doctrine is *de fide ex consensu Patrum* is much more difficult; it may be reduced to the following pattern:

(1) The writers cited qualify for the title " Father of the Church."

(2) The Fathers certainly teach this doctrine.

(3) This is a doctrine of faith and morals.

---

[77] P. Xaverio de Abarzuza, O.F.M. Cap., *Manuale Theologiae Dogmaticae*, 3, Madrid, 1956, 236.

[78] Cf. however: " Physicians have described cases in which women who have given birth to a child have afterwards shown no physical evidence of marital contact or of childbirth." In other words the hymen has been known to survive natural childbirth. For the quotation cf. Joseph C. Fenton, " Our Lady's Virginity *in partu*," *American Ecclesiastical Review*, 130 (1954), 46-53. The words quoted are found on p. 52. Fr. Fenton holds they are irrelevant to a discussion of Our Lady's virginity *in partu*. This article was written in answer to a contribution from Clifford E. J. Henry, M.D., " A Doctor Considers the Birth of Jesus," published in the *Homiletic and Pastoral Review*, 54 (1953), 219-223. Fr. Fenton's article reproduces the exposition found in the textbooks. Other items in this controversy are to be found in *Homiletic and Pastoral Review*, 54 (1954), 446-447 and 636-638.

[79] See above, pp. 125 ff.

(4) It is taught by the Fathers as witnesses to the faith, or as *doctores authentici*, and not simply as private persons.

(5) The Fathers are morally unanimous in teaching this doctrine to be of faith.

If these points are established with certainty, one can say that the doctrine in question is *de fide ex consensu Patrum*, and belongs to the deposit of faith.

Each one of these points involves a critical examination of the texts which must be considered in their literary, historical, and religious contexts. Due account must be taken of the scope and aim of the works in which they occur, and the teaching must be considered in relation to the philosophical, scientific, historical, and religious *praesupposita* of the Fathers. It must also be remembered that the authority of the Fathers in profane matters, concerning philosophy, the natural sciences etc., is of no greater weight than the reasons they advance in support of their views. [80]

Mitterer asks [81] whether the Fathers accepted as a *praesuppositum* that the non-rupture of the hymen pertained to the perfection of virginity, and therefore interpreted the perpetual virginity of Our Lady as involving non-rupture of the hymen at the moment of birth. They would, therefore, explain a dogma in the light of a premise accepted unquestioningly from a natural science, or popular tradition. The dogma of Our Lady's Perpetual Virginity obviously belongs to Revelation, but what about the explanation of it which includes a miraculous birth?

Before one could think of giving assent to Mitterer's view one must subject the evidence of the Fathers to a critical examination. One cannot lightly cast away 1500 years of tradition, and until cogent arguments against its acceptance are produced, it would be unreasonable to reject it. The length of the tradition, while not decisive, gives a certain strength to its position, and the onus is on those who reject

---

[80] This account of the requirements for a proof *ex consensu Patrum* as a certain criterion of revelation is taken from J. Salaverri, S.J., op. cit., p. 782 f.

[81] Op. cit., 128.

it to show that it is unacceptable. It should, however, be remembered that this tradition in so far as it concerns the miraculous parturition does not seem to constitute a matter of faith. [82] In the course of a critical examination of the tradition, it is important to take into account the errors against which the teaching of the Church was being defended. The early Fathers stated the reality of Christ's birth when opposing the Docetists and developed the miraculous aspects of Christ's entry into the world when proving His divinity.

The distinction between virginal conception and virginal birth must be carefully maintained in assessing the texts from the Fathers. Similarly, texts which speak of a painless birth do not necessarily prove the virgin birth in the sense of non-rupture of the hymen. [83] A thorough study of the influence of the Apocryphal Gospel of James on the Fathers' teaching concerning the *virginitas in partu* must be made. Its influence was certainly considerable, but it should be borne in mind that St. Jerome had uncomplimentary things to say about it, and it was condemned as heretical by the *Decretum Gelasianum de libris recipiendis et non recipiendis* of the sixth century. [84] It has been a fruitful source of inspiration for painters and poets, but a theologian must exercise great care before he uses it as a witness to Revelation. [85]

It should also be remembered that in developing the doctrine of Our Lady's virginity, sometimes to the detriment of her maternity (e.g. St. Ambrose), the Fathers were emphasizing what was new in the Christian Revelation. Maternity was commonplace and ordinary, whereas perpetual virginity as an ascetical practice was most infrequent, and of course, had never been found simultaneously with maternity in the

---

[82] See above p. 128. The mere length and universality of a tradition are not enough to constitute an article of faith; the doctrine must be taught as of faith. The teaching that Our Lady died was supported by long-standing tradition, but Pope Pius XII carefully refrained from including it in the definition of the Assumption, and it remains a matter for discussion among theologians. Similarly, other views which enjoy the authority of the Fathers and earlier theologians are now presented by theologians with less assurance, e.g. the universality of the flood; the formation of Eve from Adam's rib.

[83] See above, pp. 125 f.

[84] *PL* 19, 790 ff.; cf. 59, 157 ff.

[85] The question of how far apocryphal works reflect the popular beliefs of the faithful is a difficult one, but it surely has relevance here.

same person. In defending the virginity of Our Lady, therefore, the Fathers sometimes give the impression that they regarded childbirth as something impure and unworthy of the entry of God into the human race.[86]

Mitterer, then, would regard the birth of Christ as miraculous in that an act which is proper to a non-virgin, and is usually a sign of lost virginity, is being performed by a virgin. The birth would involve a normal, uncomplicated parturition. It may well have been painless and resulted in exceedingly slight damage to the organs of Our Blessed Lady, without thereby being miraculous. In any event, Mitterer feels that these latter elements—absence of pain and absence of lesions —are not essential to the doctrine of Our Lady's *virginitas in partu*. Theologians must ask themselves if Mitterer's case does justice to the words *in partu*, in the traditional presentation of the dogma: *virgo ante partum*, *in partu*, *et post partum*. Some may feel that his view renders them superfluous. Discussion will also centre on the relationship of even the slightest lesions resulting from childbirth to perfect virginity. Such changes may not touch the essence of bodily virginity, but may take from its perfection.

While the arguments advanced by Mitterer are not necessarily and immediately convincing, they are of sufficient strength to demand a re-examination of the Fathers and a more careful statement of the meaning of virginity and maternity in this section of the dogmatic textbooks. Some elements of the customary proof of *virginitas in partu* do not bear close examination, and a re-assessment of terms and authorities would make it possible to attach a more accurate theological note to the various parts of the doctrine.[87]

It is no harm perhaps to add that if this re-consideration of the doctrine of Our Lady's virginity should be favourable to a normal birth, it would not seem to derogate from the honour

---

[86] Cf. especially St. Ambrose. The Fathers may have been influenced to some extent by Old Testament ideas concerning legal impurities.

[87] Dr. Ludwig Ott in *Fundamentals of Catholic Dogma* (E. Tr.), Cork, 1955, 203, outlines Mitterer's view without recording any disapproval. Rahner, in *Zeitschrift für Katholische Theologie*, 75 (1953), 500 f., and Semmelroth, *Scholastik*, 28 (1953), 310 agree that Mitterer's arguments are strong and demand the attention of positive theologians. Cf. also *The Clergy Review*, 41 (1956), 545 for a review of Ott's work.

due to Our Lord or to Our Lady. In the case of the former, it would simply emphasize the reality of the Incarnation and add strength to the words of St. Paul: " It behoved him in all things to be made like unto his brethren " (Hebrews ii:17), while it would do honour to the perfection of what Pope Pius XI called the " gravissimum maternitatis munus " of Our Lady.[88] The pastoral value of this view is obvious at a time when the dignity of motherhood is often lightly spurned by women in the married state.

If, however, the investigation should confirm the traditional presentation of Our Lady's virginity *in partu*, this privilege of Our Lady will have acquired a new clarity and a new certainty. The investigation should therefore be carried out in a spirit of calm and with a consciousness that whatever the result, neither Our Lord's nor Our Lady's dignity will in any way be diminished.[89]

CONCLUSION

Our Lady's bodily virginity has been considered at some length. The purpose of this detailed study was not to stress certain aspects of this privilege, but rather to examine a view which, by attaching less importance to these aspects, showed Our Lady's virginity and maternity in a clearer light. When all is said and done, it would be disappointing if long discussion of the physical virginity should distract us from the more important theme of the virtue of virginity in Our Lady, which alone gives meaning and point to her physical virginity. When Christ spoke of virginity, He emphasized that it was a gift of God, that only those to whom it had been given could practise it. To Mary it was given in her function as Mother of God, and of no other could it be said with the same perfection, that she practised this virtue for the sake of the Kingdom of heaven (cf. Matthew xix:12). No other creature fulfilled the Pauline ideal of virginity as Mary did: " The

[88] *AAS*, 23 (1931), 516.
[89] Cf. *The Clergy Review*, 41 (1956), 701-704.

virgin thinks on the things of the Lord that she may be holy both in body and soul " (1 Cor. vii:34).

Called to a unique vocation, Mary responded with complete generosity, and gave herself entirely to God. Henceforth, she belongs to God and to God alone. Her virginal life finds its fulfilment in the accomplishing of her divinely given task. It occupies her completely; she has no other interest in life. This dedication touches her innermost being so that, in a sense, she has no capacity for any other function. The perfection of her virginity is the measure of the fruitfulness of her maternity, for in consenting to become the Virgin Mother of Christ, she became also the Mother of His Mystical Body, and left herself free to attend to the wants of His many brethren.

In her virginal life Mary is the perfect model of those who live lives of complete self-surrender to God. It is to her that our Holy Father says we must direct our prayers that our priestly lives may reflect the same dedication to our divinely given tasks,[90] for virginity is not to be honoured for its own sake, but only when it is dedicated to the service of God: " Neque enim et ipsa quia virginitas est, sed quia Deo dicata est, honoratur." (St. Augustine, De Sancta Virginitate, c. 8).

[90] The Encyclical Sacra Virginitas, CTS translation, par.58 ff.

Mary's Rôle in Redemption

BY MICHAEL O'GRADY, S.J.

INTRODUCTION

CATHOLIC teaching on Our Lady is summarized in that brief dogma of our faith which says that she is the Mother of God. Throughout the centuries this mystery has been pondered, its riches gradually unfolded and a new insight gained into the many and varied splendours of grace which it involves. In the process hidden aspects have been brought to light and in time have come to be enshrined in new definitions, but always as serving the same essential purpose, namely, to emphasize and illumine the fundamental truth from which they stem.

Thus Mary was the Mother of God, invested with the fullness of grace; she was in consequence immune from original sin, which is what the doctrine of the Immaculate Conception implies. Her pure body was preserved from corruption and transferred to glory in heaven, which is the doctrine of the Assumption. Mary was the Mother of the Redeemer, and as such she is seen to have a place apart in the mystery of the redemption. This in its widest significance is what we mean by the doctrine of the Mediatrix of Grace which it is our purpose to examine and explain in the course of the two papers today. Of deliberate purpose I have chosen to describe the whole field to be covered in terms of mediation. The subjects " Our Lady's Rôle in Redemption " and " Our Lady's Mediation of Graces " are so interwoven and interdependent that their coherence will, I think, be more appropriately and clearly appreciated by seeing them both as aspects of the mediation of Our Lady. This will, I hope, become more evident in the course of what I have to say.

GENERAL PRINCIPLE GOVERNING EXAMINATION OF QUESTION

Meantime I would preface a few words on the attitude and method which should govern an investigation in a question of this kind. We enter on a field that is to a certain extent uncharted. We are on different ground from that which is covered by the *definitions* of the Church, as in the dogmas of the Immaculate Conception and the Assumption. Our attitude has, accordingly, to be modified. While in its general tenor the doctrine of Our Lady, Mediatrix of Grace, is held by the faithful throughout the Church, there are certain features and aspects of it—as one can readily appreciate from the vast and growing bibliography on the question—which remain under discussion and will continue to do so until such time as the issues are clarified by the Church's decision.

What is to be our attitude in the face of such discussions? Mary as Mother of God enjoys the greatest dignity that any creature does or could enjoy. Conscious of this, the Catholic instinct is to give to Mary every grace and privilege compatible with her unique position, and that in the highest measure. The instinct is proper; it remains, nevertheless, that it must be subject to the divine will and order of things. The sole cause and arbiter of Our Lady's privileges is God. It is not what *we* may think, but what *He* thinks and freely decrees, that determines the disposition of grace; and that divine decree we can know through Revelation and through Revelation only. Hence it is that in considering such a privilege of Our Lady as is embodied in the doctrine of her mediation, we should be concerned primarily with what Revelation has to tell us. Presently the Church may solve our doubts on this or that aspect of the matter. Meantime we take what we find; we discipline interpretation and deduction to essential harmony with the other truths of our faith, and thus strive towards a conclusion which will serve at once to promote the interest of sound piety and doctrine.

This is all the more important at the present time when Catholics must be prepared to give the reasons for the faith that is theirs, and especially in regard to a new development of doctrine such as is involved in the mediation of Our Lady. In addition there is the fact that no child of the Church has the right to urge with the force of a dogma any doctrine or aspect of a doctrine until it is defined. Neither the good of the Church nor the honour of Our Lady is promoted by a zeal which is not firmly rooted in the truth of Revelation. As St. Bonaventure has said: " Beata Virgo non indiget nostro mendacio quae tanta plena est veritate." [1]

EXPLANATION OF THE TERM " MEDIATOR "

The connotation of mediator is familiar. The term explains itself. A mediator is one who holds a middle position between two other persons or groups of persons, and whose function is to promote the union of those persons or groups. Generally this process of unification will imply the aspect of reconciliation. The mediator must have a title or qualification which accredits him to his rôle as intermediary. The exercise of that function to achieve the union of the other parties is what we understand by *mediation*.

An illustration will serve to clarify our meaning. Consider the case of Mr. Dag Hammarskjold who was appointed by UNO to mediate in the Israel-Arab dispute. By his position as mediator he had to represent both sides while identifying himself with neither. His duty was to strive for the reconciliation of both parties. His title and qualification derived from the legitimate authority vested in him by UNO. In his efforts to promote understanding and effect the reconciliation of the Jews and Arabs he exercised his function as mediator.

Transferring the application of the terms from the natural to the supernatural sphere, we find that " mediator " has its highest and most perfect fulfilment in the person of Jesus Christ. He was God and man, and in virtue of this transcendent union of natures He was uniquely qualified for the rôle of mediator. As man He was able to stand as representative of Adam and all his sinful progeny; as God He was able to make satisfaction that was condign and adequate, nay that

---

[1] *In 3 Sent.*, d. 3, p. 1, a. 1, q. 2, 3.

was superabundant and infinite, for being God each action of His was of infinite moral value, according to the axiom *actiones sunt suppositi.*

Some scripture texts, notably 1 Tim. ii:5 and Acts iv:12, which embody this very doctrine of Christ's unique mediation, are invoked by Protestant critics to urge a difficulty against the Catholic teaching of all secondary agents of mediation in general, and of Our Lady in particular: " There is only one God and only one Mediator between God and man, Jesus Christ who is a man like them and gave Himself a ransom for them all." Thus they assert Christ is the sole Mediator; neither is there salvation in any other name but His (Acts iv:12). The difficulty is superficial and need not detain us long. The fact is that in extending the term mediator to those other than Christ we are making use of analogy, by which one and the same word is expressive of concepts that are partly the same and partly different. Christ is the one supreme, necessary and adequate Mediator between God and men; He alone offered the sacrifice which in accordance with the mandate of His Father was the price of our redemption, and which made condign, sufficient, superabundant satisfaction for the injury wrought by the sin of Adam; but this unique mediation does not exclude secondary and subordinate mediators, nor is there anything in the thought of St. Paul to imply such exclusion. The apostles co-operated with Christ; the saints and the faithful co-operate with Christ, and so in a sense are mediators with Him, though obviously in a minor and dependent rôle. The fact that God is our Father does not exclude the existence of earthly fathers; the fact that Christ is the one High-priest does not prevent His sharing His priesthood with the apostles and their successors throughout the centuries; no more does the unique and necessary mediation of Christ rule out a mediation which is subordinate and dependent. All this has been set forth by Pope Leo XIII in a passage of the encyclical *Fidentem Piumque*, in the course of which he invokes the teaching of St. Thomas:

> Undoubtedly the name and attributes of the absolute mediator belong to no other than Christ; for being one person, and yet

both God and man, He restored the human race to the favour of the heavenly Father: " One Mediator of God and men; the man Jesus Christ who gave Himself a redemption for all."

And yet as the Angelic Doctor teaches, there is no reason why certain others should not be called in a certain way mediators between God and man, that is to say, in so far as they co-operate by predisposing and ministering in the union of man with God. Such are the angels and saints, the prophets and priests of both Testaments; but especially has the Blessed Virgin a claim to the glory of this title. For no single individual can ever be imagined who has ever contributed or ever will contribute so much toward reconciling man with God. To mankind heading for eternal ruin she offered a Saviour when she received the announcement of the mystery of peace brought to this earth by the message of an angel and, in giving her consent, gave it in the name of the whole human race. She it is from whom Jesus is born. She is therefore truly His Mother and for this reason a worthy and acceptable mediatrix to the Mediator.[2]

THE NATURE OF OUR LADY'S MEDIATION

We shall have occasion later to refer again to this passage. For the present it is sufficient that it serves to confirm the truth that Christ's unique mediation does not exclude secondary mediators and that among these latter Mary holds primacy of place. The question is: In what does this mediation of Our Lady consist? How are we to understand it? Obviously it must be interpreted in relation to the mediation of Christ. What is relative and dependent can be understood only with reference to what is absolute and necessary. As a first step, therefore, in the solution of our problem it is essential that we have clearly defined what we mean by the mediation of Christ.

Christ fulfils His rôle as Mediator by the redemption of the human race. The whole plan of redemption centred on Christ, whereby the evil of original sin was undone and the reign of grace restored, was the result of the free decree of the Blessed Trinity. Out of several possible choices the divine Wisdom

---

[2] *D.M.*, 444.—References to papal documents, except where otherwise stated, are given to the volume *Documentos Marianos*, B.A.C., Madrid, 1954, thus: *D.M.*

ordained that redemption should be wrought by way of condign satisfaction and merit. As the insult offered to God was in a certain sense infinite, so the reparation, to be adequate, had to be made by a person who was divine. Thus the Word was made flesh, lived His life among us and died the victim for sin on the Cross. It is true, as we have said, that every action of the God-man Christ was of infinite moral value. Nevertheless it remains that, as Scripture and Tradition testify beyond doubt, it was by His final sacrifice of the Cross that Christ achieved the redemption of mankind. By that oblation the price of sin was paid, grace was again available to man and with it the possibility of assimilation to the image and likeness of God and incorporation into the Body of Christ. This is what we mean by *objective redemption*. It is the act by which sin was repaired and grace purchased. It marked one phase in the redemptive plan. Another was to follow. Christ having died and ascended glorious into heaven was henceforth to ensure by His intercession that the merits which He had acquired should bear fruit in the souls of men, and that the graces made available should be applied to each and every member of the human race. This is what we understand by *subjective redemption*. There is, we may remark, some difference of opinion as to the usage of these terms, subjective redemption and objective redemption. The matter is not of importance as the realities expressed by the terms are beyond dispute.

THE MEDIATION OF OUR LADY

Now in the second phase of redemption Christ has admitted others who act as co-operators with Him. It is part of Catholic dogma that in virtue of the merits of Christ the just *in statu viae* (wayfarers) can merit condignly for themselves and in equity for others. Likewise it is part of Catholic belief that the angels and saints, and in particular Our Blessed Lady, by their intercession co-operate with Christ in bringing grace to the members of the Church militant. In our later paper we shall consider the scope and the nature of her co-operation in this phase of redemption. Our present concern is entirely to determine Our Lady's part in the first phase, i.e. objective redemption.

THE *STATUS QUAESTIONIS*

The state of the problem can be briefly stated in the following query: What did Our Lady by her activity during her lifetime contribute to the redemptive sacrifice of Christ?

What now are the facts of Our Lady's life which we must keep in view? They are familiar to all of us. By her free acceptance of the angel's message she became the Mother of God. She brought Him into the world at Bethlehem. She nurtured and cared for Him as an infant. She figured with Him in many of the mysteries of His life. She presented Him in the Temple. She suffered the sorrow of losing Him when He was twelve years old, when at the cost of such pain to His Mother the Child vindicated the claims of His Father's business. She was present at Cana, where the power of her influence was testified to by the miracle which changed the water into wine. Finally, she was present at Calvary when, as the Gospel says, " There stood by the Cross of Jesus, Mary His Mother " (Jo. xix:25). Such in brief is the record of Mary's life up to the act of redemption. What now is the relation between them?

The answer demands that we distinguish clearly between the different forms of co-operation. Thus there is physical co-operation and moral co-operation: the one in the order of physical activity, the other in the order of intentional and volitional activity which can be either by way of entreaty, command, or persuasion.

Again co-operation, whether physical or moral, can be either immediate or mediate; immediate if the effect depends on it immediately, mediate if it depends on it remotely. To illustrate our meaning, we might consider the example of a mother who helps her infant to make its first efforts to walk. The walking is achieved by the efforts of the child and the help of the mother. She thus co-operates physically and immediately in the movement of the child. Or again she may urge or command the child to turn his attention to his books; in this case she co-operates morally and immediately in the study of the child. On the other hand she may persuade the

father to be the helper in one or other of the ways we have
described; in which case it is the father who immediately
co-operates with the child, the mother only mediately and
through the father.

There are still further aspects of co-operation: it can be
meritorious either with a title of justice (*de condigno*) or a
title of equity (*de congruo*). The labourer has a strict title in
justice to his wage; the child who gives a special proof of his
piety has a claim in equity to some testimony of appreciation
from his parents. Again, co-operation may have an aspect of
satisfaction and reparation: the man who enables another to
restore stolen property or repair an injury that he had done
to his neighbour in any way can be said to have co-operated
in the reparation.

To revert now to our question of the co-operation of Our
Lady and the part she played in the redemption of the human
race which was effected by Christ on Calvary. As we have
seen she co-operated physically and morally in the mystery of
the Incarnation. But we must keep in mind that the Incarnation, while it initiated the process which terminated in
redemption was not in itself formally redemptive. Thus Our
Lady's co-operation in as far as it arises from the Incarnation
could not be immediate but mediate in regard to the final
redemption of Calvary. The same holds true of her activity
throughout her lifetime up to the scene on Calvary. Her
co-operation with her Son whether physical or moral at
Bethlehem, at Nazareth, in the Temple, at Cana, did not
immediately effect the redemption which was effected by
Christ's sacrifice on the Cross.

What now of her activity on Calvary? Can we say that the
redemption wrought on Calvary immediately depended on her
co-operation with Christ? If for the moment we consider
merely the hypothetical order of things, there are various
possibilities that can be envisaged:

Firstly: Our Lady may be conceived in the capacity of co-
offerer and co-priest with Christ the great High-priest, in
which case her co-operation in redemption would be physical
and immediate. Such a possibility, however, we submit has
no foundation in fact. To have offered the sacrifice of the

Cross would imply that Our Lady was endowed with the character of priest. Tradition, however, has not considered this possibility except to reject it.[3] Mary's priesthood is of a kind with that enjoyed by all who are baptized in Christ.

Again: We might conceive the possibility of Our Lady persuading Christ to offer the sacrifice that was required for our redemption. In this hypothesis redemption would be in part the immediate effect of Mary's moral co-operation with Christ. Just as at Cana Christ's miracle was immediately due to the representation of His Mother in the words, " They have no wine," so conceivably Christ's sacrifice might have been due to her plea that we were all in need of redemption. Apart from other considerations which we shall see later, there is a particular objection against this supposition. Christ's sacrifice, as we know, was entirely in obedience to the mandate of His Father. So far as the evidence of Scripture and Tradition goes, that mandate was independent of Mary's prayers and wishes. We have but to recall the incident of the loss in the Temple, when the Christ-child explained His absence from His parents by the reply that He was about His Father's business.

Finally: Our Lady would have co-operated immediately in redemption in the supposition that her compassion on Calvary constituted, together with the sacrifice of Christ, the total price of redemption. In such a case her compassion, together with Christ's sacrifice, would have been ordained by the Father as the total adequate principle whereby the injury of original sin was to be repaired and grace restored.

Such, then, are some of the ways in which we could conceive Mary in the rôle of immediate co-operator with her Son in the work of redemption. Let us now see what present theological opinion has to tell us.

IMMEDIATE CO-OPERATION: TWO SCHOOLS OF THOUGHT

Generally speaking, there are two schools of thought which, for the sake of reference, we shall designate as the conservative and the advanced school. Supporters of

[3] Epiphanius, *Adv. Collyrid.*, 4, PG 42, 745.

the former are not prepared to admit any immediate co-operation of Our Lady—whether physical or moral—in our redemption. They deny that this opinion has sufficient evidence to support it, either in Scripture or Tradition, and contend that the difficulties which it raises with regard to other dogmas of our faith have not been adequately answered. These difficulties, which are chiefly two, we shall consider later; meantime they can be briefly summarized: (1) Our Lady herself was redeemed, and as such could not have co-operated in redemption; she could not at one and the same time be cause and effect; she could not be redeemer and redeemed. (2) The other difficulty arises from the fact that Christ by His death offered the adequate and essential price of our redemption. Now, if Our Lady's immediate co-operation in that sacrifice is admitted, it would seem to prejudice this accepted teaching of the adequacy of Christ's mediation.

What we have termed as the progressive school of opinion is fully aware of those difficulties, which it endeavours to meet in various ways, influenced largely by the emphasis which several papal pronouncements of recent times have given to Mary's co-operation in the redemption. It maintains that the mind of the Church, as expressed in those pronouncements, implies the immediate moral co-operation of Our Lady in the work of redemption in one or other of the ways which we have already referred to.

An illustration from history may serve at this point to clarify the issue between the two schools. Napoleon gained one of his major military victories at Austerlitz. To an extent the mother of Napoleon can be said to have contributed to that victory and to the glory of the French nation. She gave birth to the general; she reared him through infancy and imparted to him his early training. But does that mean that she was, in any real sense, a co-operator in the victory? Can we say that it was not merely the victory of Napoleon but of Napoleon and his mother? Assuredly not. To apply the analogy: Our Lady contributed to the victory of the Cross by giving us Christ, by her maternal care of Him during infancy, by her co-operation of mind and will with Him at all stages; but all that does not imply any immediate share in the sacrifice of the Cross. This, broadly speaking, represents the point of view of the conservative school.

To return to our illustration: if we imagine the situation in which the mother of Napoleon actually planned the strategy of the battle or persuaded him to engage in battle, or, again, if Napoleon had made it an essential condition of his joining issue with the enemy that this decision have his mother's consent and approval, then the subsequent victory could in some measure be attributed to his mother. This illustrates to some extent the position attributed to Our Lady by those of the progressive school, though it does less than justice to the variety and subtlety of the theories that it illustrates. Indeed, as can readily be surmised from the bibliography on the subject, it cannot come within the compass of a paper like this to do justice to the erudition and resourcefulness of those who champion the theory of Our Lady's immediate co-operation in its many forms. We must confine ourselves to the general thesis of immediate co-operation, indicating the grounds on which it is based and the evidence which is invoked to support it.

As to the sources of the theory of immediate co-operation, it is conceded that its inspiration derives principally from the pronouncements of recent popes. It will be well, therefore, to refer to some of the more important texts which are cited in this connection.

In the *Jucunda Semper* of Leo XIII, issued on 8 September, 1894, the following occurs:

> When (Mary) submitted, as God's handmaid, to undertake the office of mother, and when she offered herself with Him in the Temple, she was already a sharer with Him in His painful expiation on behalf of the human race. . . . There stood by the Cross of Jesus His Mother who, moved by her unbounded charity to accept us as her sons, willingly offered her own Son to the divine Father, dying with Him in her heart, pierced by the sword of sorrow.[4]

The encyclical *Ad Diem Illum* of St. Pius X, issued on 2 February, 1904, has the following:

---

[4] *D.M.*, 413.

Because she excels all in sanctity and in union with Christ, and because she was associated by Christ Himself in His work of saving humanity, she merits for us in equity (*de congruo*) what Christ merited in justice (*de condigno*) and is the chief almoner in the distribution of grace.[5]

Another relevant text occurs in an address of Benedict XV, *Inter Sodalicia*, of 22 March, 1918:

Thus she suffered and all but died with her Son suffering and dying. Thus for the salvation of men she abdicated the rights of a mother towards her Son and, in as far as it was hers to do so, immolated the Son to placate God's justice, so that she herself may justly be said to have redeemed together with Christ the human race.[6]

Pope Pius XI, in his prayer for the close of the Jubilee Year 1935, has the following:

O Mother of pity and mercy, who, when thy most beloved Son was consummating the redemption of the human race on the altar of the Cross, didst stand there suffering with Him and redeeming with Him (*compatiens et coredemptrix*), preserve in us, we beseech thee, and increase in us daily the precious fruits of His redemption and thy compassion.[7]

Finally, we refer to those words of the late Holy Father which occur first in the encyclical *Mystici Corporis Christi*:

She it was who, immune from all sin whether personal or inherited, and ever most closely united with her Son, offered Him on Golgotha to the Eternal Father together with the holocaust of her maternal rights and motherly love, like a new Eve, for all the children of Adam contaminated through his unhappy fall, and thus she who was the Mother of our Head according to the flesh, became by a new title of sorrow and glory the spiritual mother of all His members. . . . She, finally, true Queen of Martyrs, by bearing with courageous and confident heart her immense weight of sorrows, more than all other Christians " filled up those things which are wanting of the sufferings of Christ for His body." May she, therefore, most holy Mother of all the members of Christ . . . use

[5] *D.M.*, 489.   [6] *D.M.*, 556.   [7] *D.M.*, 647.

her intercession with Him, so that from that august Head abundance of grace may flow with steady stream into all the members of His Mystical Body.[8]

Later, in the encyclical *Haurietis Aquas* we find the following:

> For in the eternal will of God the Blessed Virgin Mary has been joined indissolubly to Christ in the accomplishment of the work of man's redemption, in such a way that our salvation has proceeded from the charity of Jesus Christ and His bitter sufferings, together with the love and sorrows of His Mother most intimately associated thereto.[9]

EXAMINATION OF EVIDENCE

Papal Documents

That these and other texts lend themselves to an interpretation which favours the immediate co-operation of Our Lady in the redemption can be readily admitted. *Prima facie* that is the interpretation suggested by the terms " Co-Redemptrix," " Reparatrix " and by such phrases as " she stood with Christ in His painful expiation," " she offered her Son to the divine Justice," " she redeemed us with Christ," etc. It can be conceded that, were the doctrine elsewhere well supported, those texts might well be construed as giving it confirmation and sanction. Without, however, wishing to prejudice opinion on the matter, this can hardly be said to represent the case.

First of all it should be noted that none of the pronouncements cited have an *ex cathedra* force. Then again it must be recognized, in accordance with the laws of hermeneutics, that texts must be interpreted in the light of the context and of the general mind and teaching of the author. And this especially when there is question of an interpretation that represents a new development of doctrine. Can it now be claimed that the intrinsic evidence of the encyclicals establishes beyond doubt the papal advocacy of Our Lady's immediate co-operation in objective redemption? We have

[8] *D.M.*, 713.
[9] CTS, London, section 73.

already cited from the *Jucunda Semper* of Leo XIII a passage which has been employed to support this view. We may recall, however, that the general aim which inspires the Marian encyclicals of Leo XIII is to emphasize the efficacy of Mary's intercession. Her rôle as heavenly intermediary is shown as the consequence of her association with Christ on earth, but there is no clear indication that leads us to interpret this association in terms of immediate co-operation. Her claim to the title of Mediatrix is based on her sanctity and merit which render her intercession more powerful than that of all the angels and saints:

> The recourse we have to Mary in prayer is based on the office which she continuously fulfils in the presence of God of obtaining for us divine grace and in which, by reason of her dignity and merits which render her most acceptable in God's sight, she exercises a power far surpassing that of all the blessed in heaven.[10]

In the *Fidentem Piumque* of the same pope, to which reference has already been made, the same teaching is in evidence; the mediation of Our Lady is distinguished from that of Christ:

> It is certain that the name and function of perfect mediator belongs only to Christ who alone, both God and man, restored the human race to friendship with the Father.

This exclusive mediation, however, allows for the subordinate mediation in which Our Lady, together with the blessed, participates:

> Such are the angels and saints, the prophets and priests of both Testaments; but especially the Blessed Virgin has a claim to the glory of this title.[11]

One cannot, I think, claim that there is here any suggestion to support the doctrine of Our Lady's immediate co-operation. On the contrary the traditional and accepted teaching of Christ's exclusive and unique mediation is repeated. It is offset against the mediation of all secondary agents of redemption, including Our Lady, whose place and function in this connection, however exalted, is by implication of the same

---

[10] *D.M.*, 410.   [11] *D.M.*, 444.

MARY'S RÔLE IN REDEMPTION

kind as that exercised by the saints, and so is entirely distinct
from the mediation of Christ.

St. Pius X in his encyclical *Ad Diem Illum* spoke of Our
Lady as meriting most rightly to be called the Reparatrix of
a lost world. In the same encyclical, however, we read:

> Now surely we do not deny that the distribution of these
> gifts belongs by strict right to Christ personally; after all,
> they have been acquired for us by His death alone, and He is
> in His own right the Mediator between God and men.[12]

Here again the emphasis is on the accepted doctrine of the
exclusive nature of Christ's mediation. Further on there
occurs the passage to which we have earlier referred:

> Because, however, she transcends all others in holiness and
> in the intimacy of her union with Christ, and because she has
> been drawn by Christ into association with the work of human
> salvation, she merits for us congruously, as they say, what
> Christ merited for us condignly, and she is the principal
> minister of the graces to be distributed.[13]

If we interpret those words to mean immediate association
with Christ in the work of redemption, it is difficult to
reconcile them with the principle which has been enunciated
in the same context, namely, that all grace is the exclusive
fruit of Christ's death. Immediate co-operation of Our Lady
in the redemption would mean that grace was not exclusively
due to Christ's death, but to His death and to the sufferings of
His Mother. On the contrary Our Lady's holiness, her union
and association with Christ, which entitle her to merit *de
congruo*, are all the fruit of Christ's death. Mary was redeemed
before she could co-operate in redemption according to the
axiom: *principium meriti non cadit sub merito*.

Benedict XV said:

> Thus she suffered and all but died with her Son suffering
> and dying. Thus for the salvation of men she abdicated the
> rights of a mother towards her Son and, in as far as it was hers

[12] Paul F. Palmer, S.J., *Mary in the Documents of the Church*, London, 1953, 95;
D.M., 488.
[13] Palmer, op. cit., 96. *D.M.* 489.

to do so, immolated the Son to placate God's justice, so that she herself may justly be said to have redeemed together with Christ the human race.[14]

In the same letter we are explicitly reminded that the doctrine here enunciated is that commonly taught by the doctors of the Church. " Etenimvero tradunt communiter ecclesiae doctores B. M. Virginem . . . scil. ita cum Filio patiente et moriente passa est . . . "[15] It would, however, be excessive to claim that the thesis of Our Lady's immediate rôle in redemption has the clear and common support of the Fathers. To cite the words of Father W. J. Burghardt in this connection, which are more of an understatement than otherwise: " As a convincing demonstration of the thesis that Mary co-operated directly and immediately in the objective redemption the extant evidence from the New Eve doctrine of the Fathers is somewhat inadequate."[16]   Lennerz too denies that there is evidence of any kind in patristic tradition and, in addition, refers to a recent study of nineteenth century theologians which demonstrates that none of these held the theory of immediate co-operation.[17]

I shall conclude with the following texts from Pius XI and Pius XII; in the encyclical *Miserentissimus Redemptor* Pius XI wrote:

> . . . she who by giving us Christ the Redeemer, and by rearing Him, and by offering Him at the foot of the Cross as victim for our sins, by such intimate association with Christ, and by her own most singular grace, became and is affectionately known as reparatrix.[18]

The supposition implied in the last words is that there is question of mediation in the distribution of grace, or subjective redemption.   Mary is therefore Reparatrix (1) by

---

[14] Ep. Apost. *Inter Sodalicia*, 22 May, 1918. *D.M.*, 556.
[15] Ibid.
[16] Burghardt, " Mary in Western Thought " in *Mariology*, 1, ed. J. B. Carol, O.F.M., Milwaukee, 1955, 117. Cf. " Mary in Eastern Patristic Thought " in *Mariology*, 2, 1957, 100.
[17] Lennerz, *De Beata Virgine*, ed. 4a, Rome, 1957, 242, 270.
[18] Palmer, op. cit., 98. The quotation continues as follows: " Confident of her intercession with Christ, who alone is Mediator of God and men, and who willed to associate His Mother with Himself as the Advocate of sinners, as the Dispenser and Mediatrix of grace . . . " *D.M.*, 608.

reason of the fact that she gave us the Redeemer, (2) by reason of her association with Christ, (3) by reason of her sanctity. There is nothing here to support immediate co-operation. On the contrary, if her sanctity and her singular grace was a reason for her co-operation, her co-operation obviously presupposed redemption. Once again the axiom *principium meriti non cadit sub merito* is applicable.

And Pius XII in the epilogue of *Mystici Corporis* has the following:

> She (Mary) it was, immune from all sin, personal or in-herited, and ever most closely united with her Son, who offered Him on Golgotha to the eternal Father together with the holocaust of her maternal rights and motherly love, like a new Eve, for all the children of Adam contaminated through his unhappy fall, and thus she, who was the Mother of our Head according to the flesh, became by a new title of sorrow and glory the spiritual Mother of all His members . . . She, finally, true Queen of Martyrs, by bearing with courageous and confident heart her immense weight of sorrows, more than all Christians " filled up those things that are wanting of the sufferings of Christ for His Body, which is the Church." [19]

The mention of the text from St. Paul here implies that the Pope had in mind not Mary's part in objective redemption but in subjective redemption.

Of these, as of other texts, we can say that, were the thesis of Our Lady's immediate co-operation established from other sources, they might well be taken as further vindication of it. But on their own merits what do they imply? One might well expect that, if the intention of the popes was to pro-mulgate a teaching which is admittedly a new development, they would have been more explicit in formulating it. On the contrary, however, we find in the very contexts which treat of the mediation of Our Lady that emphasis is unequivo-cally laid on the doctrine that all grace is the exclusive fruit of Christ's death. Unique indeed as is the co-operation of Our Lady in the redemption of mankind, yet it is of a kind that is shared by other creatures, as is clearly set forth by Pope Leo XIII in *Fidentem Piumque*:

[19] *D.M.*, 713.

Undoubtedly the name and attributes of the absolute
Mediator belong to no other than Christ . . . And yet, as
the Angelic Doctor teaches, " there is no reason why certain
others should not be called in a certain way mediators between
God and man, that is to say in so far as they co-operate by
predisposing and ministering in the union of man with God."
Such are the angels and saints, the prophets and priests of both
Testaments; but especially the Blessed Virgin has a claim to
the glory of this title.[20]

Scripture

If we turn to the Scriptures, we find, as already indicated,
that the evidence in support of Our Lady's immediate part
in redemption is largely based on the text from Genesis:
" I will put enmities between thee and the woman, between
thy seed and her seed. He shall crush thy head and thou shalt
lie in wait for her heel." (Gen. iii:15).

The argument from this text may be formulated as follows:
the words are clearly a prophecy of man's redemption, and
Mary is associated with Christ in that work. Therefore Mary,
together with Christ, is the cause of our redemption.[21] The
argument suffers from over-simplification; it is not that the
text (as we know) is subject to so many and varied interpretations; leaving aside the exegetical differences, and
conceding the full Marian sense of the text, the minor of the
syllogism is not acceptable in so far as it implies that Mother
and Son are one principle of redemption. The text indeed
establishes a state of enmity between the woman and Satan,
but the victory is attributed not to the woman directly but
to her seed, that is, Jesus Christ. It is in virtue of Christ's
victory that Mary was rendered immune from sin and was
immaculately conceived, as was declared in the definition of
Ineffabilis Deus by Pius IX:

We declare, pronounce, and define that the doctrine which
holds that the most Blessed Virgin Mary, in the first instant
of her conception, by a singular grace and privilege granted by

[20] D.M., 444.
[21] Cf. I. A. Aldama, S.J., Sacrae Theologiae Summa, 3, Madrid, 1950, 422.

Almighty God *in view of the merits of Jesus Christ*, the Saviour of
the human race, was preserved free from all stain of original
sin, is a doctrine revealed by God and therefore to be believed
firmly and constantly by all the faithful.[22]

Tradition

To turn to the patristic evidence. From the second century
on Our Lady's part in redemption derives largely from a
series of texts in which the comparison is made between Eve
and Mary, and between Adam and Christ. The texts abound
in the writings of Justin, Irenaeus, Tertullian, Ephraem,
Ambrose, Jerome, and Augustine, and the comparison and
contrast is developed under many aspects. As Christ is the
new Adam, Mary is the new Eve; through Eve came death,
through Mary came life; Eve is the mother of mankind
according to the flesh, Mary is our Mother in the order of
grace; Eve yielded to the suggestion of the serpent and by
her disobedience to God was the cause of sin and death,
Mary accepted the message of the Angel and by her obedience
was the cause of life. The testimony of St. Irenaeus may serve
very well as an example of the general line of thought which
the Fathers have furnished in this connection, for it is
peculiarly rich in the developments which it gives of the
Eve-Mary analogy:

> For as Eve was seduced by the utterance of an angel to flee
> God after disobeying His word, so Mary by the utterance of an
> angel had the glad tidings brought to her that she should bear
> God in obedience to His word. And whereas Eve had disobeyed
> God, Mary was persuaded to obey God, that the Virgin Mary
> might become patroness (advocate) of the virgin Eve. And
> as the human race was sentenced to death by means of a virgin,
> by means of a Virgin is it delivered (*salvatur*). A virgin's
> disobedience is balanced by a Virgin's obedience. For the sin
> of the first-formed was amended by correction from the first-
> born; the guile of the serpent was overcome by the simplicity
> of the dove; and we were set free from those chains by which
> we had been bound to death.[23]

---

[22] *D.M.*, 299.
[23] *Adv. Haer.*, 5, 19, 1, ed. Harvey, Cambridge University Press, 1857, vol. 2, 376.

The text is an example of the principle of *recirculatio*, which is so intimate a part of the mariological thought of St. Irenaeus, and according to which redemption is conceived as the inverse of those processes that brought about the fall. The same principle had been used by Justin in a similar context. And the contrast which we find developed by St. Irenaeus is characteristic of the Eve-Mary analogy, which he, in common with so many others among the Fathers of the Church, employs. A virgin is contrasted with a virgin; the disobedience of the one with the obedience of the other; the one the cause of death, the other, the cause of life.

The analogy makes clear the mind of St. Irenaeus on certain aspects of Our Lady's rôle in redemption. In consenting to become the Mother of God she became the cause of our salvation. By implication her consent had a soteriological character, for was she not informed that her Child was to be called *Jesus*, that is, Saviour?

She has thus in a physical and moral capacity contributed to the work of redemption. She has made possible the conditions in which it is to be realized, and so she is—in the technical sense of the theologians—dispositive cause of redemption. So far the implications of the analogy are beyond doubt; do they extend farther? Do they provide a basis for claiming that Our Lady's consent to the Incarnation is but the initial phase of her redemptive activity which culminated on Calvary, when by her union with the Redeemer she becomes with Him the immediate cause of redemption? It is in the very nature of analogy to leave certain aspects of a problem undefined. And if only because of the difference of opinion on this question, this is obviously one of them. It should, however, be noted that in common with so many others among the Fathers the contrast elaborated by St. Irenaeus is between Eve and Mary, Adam and Christ. It is not between Eve and Adam on the one hand, and Christ and Our Lady on the other. There is nothing in the thought of St. Irenaeus to suggest that Our Lady exerted in regard to Christ an influence that was parallel to that exercised by Eve on Adam, nothing that justifies the claim that Mary and her Son are presented as one total principle of redemption. The relationship between Adam and Christ, between Eve and Mary, engages his thought. The redemptive relationship between Christ and Mary does not. Mary is revealed as the cause of our life because of her consent to become the Mother of the Saviour, and not because of any special rôle in His redeeming sacrifice.

EXAMINATION OF DIFFICULTIES

Thus far we have considered the positive evidence brought forward in favour of Our Lady's immediate part in redemption. What now of the difficulties which it presents? The most fundamental and serious objection arises from the fact that Our Lady herself was redeemed. May I recall the words in which the doctrine of the Immaculate Conception is defined?

> We, by the authority of Jesus Christ Our Lord, of the blessed Apostles Peter and Paul, and by our own, decree, pronounce and define that the doctrine which holds that the Blessed Virgin Mary at the first instant of her conception, by a singular privilege and grace of the omnipotent God, in consideration of the merits of Jesus Christ, the Saviour of mankind, was preserved free from all stain of original sin, has been revealed by God and therefore is to be firmly and constantly believed by all the faithful.[24]

The privilege of the Immaculate Conception, the immunity from sin and the fulness of grace which Our Lady enjoyed, were *in virtue* of the merits of Jesus Christ. They presupposed the redemption. Mary was immaculate because she was redeemed. But if redeemed, how could she, even in a partial and subordinate way, be the cause of her own redemption? Can she be at once cause and effect? Redeemer and redeemed?

The difficulty has been fully recognized by the advocates of Our Lady's immediate co-operation in redemption, and there is no dearth of theories which are proposed to solve it; several of these merit a more thorough and appreciative study than is here possible, if only because of the insight which they give into the unique position which Mary has in Catholic

[24] *D.M.*, 299.

thought. We must be content with the general outline of what they propose. According to one theory, objective redemption has two phases: the sacrifice of Christ in the first instance was ordained to the sanctification of His Mother, in the second Mary's consent combined with it to make one principle effecting the redemption of the rest of mankind. But this distinction meets one difficulty only to raise some others. We recall the teaching of St. Paul in Romans v:12 ff: " As through one man, Adam, death and sin were brought upon all, so by one was the grace of justification made available for all." Neither in St. Paul nor elsewhere is there any indication that the redemption of Christ involved the co-operation of Mary. It would seem, indeed, to be entirely at variance with such expression of his thought as is revealed in the text: " One man commits a fault and it brings condemnation on all: one man makes amends and it brings to all justification, that is, life."

A second difficulty which is involved in the thesis of Our Lady's immediate co-operation in objective redemption, and to which we have already referred more than once in passing, arises from the exclusive nature of Christ's redemption as revealed in Scripture and Catholic Tradition. The Council of Trent repeats the thought of St. Paul (1 Tim. ii:5) when it states:

> If anyone says that this sin of Adam . . . is taken away . . . through a remedy other than the merit of the one Mediator, Our Lord Jesus Christ . . . let him be anathema.[25]

And again:

> The meritorious cause (of justification) is the beloved only-begotten Son of God, Our Lord Jesus Christ, who, when all were enemies (cf. Rom. v:10), by reason of His very great love wherewith He has loved us (cf. Ephes. ii:4), merited justification for us by His own most holy Passion on the wood of the Cross and made satisfaction for us to God the Father.[26]

In the supposition of Our Lady's immediate association with Christ in redemption she is, with Christ, a partial

[25] *Denz.*, 790.   [26] *Denz.*, 799.

cause of redemption; her co-operation is united with Christ's sacrifice as the price of redemption. By the Father's decree both are ordained to the one purpose of redemption, and both are therefore *necessary* for redemption. But if this be so, how can Christ be said to be the one unique and necessary mediator, or how can the grace of justification be attributed exclusively to His Passion and death? Or how can we say that the doctrine of justification has been adequately expressed in the traditional teaching of the Church?

The fact that the co-operation of Mary is necessarily subordinate and dependent, that it in no way adds to the infinite value of Christ's sacrifice, does not affect the position.

The moral value of an act is one thing. Its necessity for the redemption is another. May I use an illustration from psychology? Sensation is, as we know, the effect of a dual principle, the one spiritual, the other material. In itself the spiritual principle ranks of far superior worth to the material principle, but considered with regard to the effect produced they are both equally necessary. The act of sensation is at once dependent on, and can exist only by virtue of both principles. In point of moral worth the act of Christ is infinitely superior to that of His Mother; but if the co-operation of the Mother together with the sacrifice of the Son are ordained by the will of the Father to be the price of redemption, then both are necessary, and redemption is at once the effect of the sacrifice of Christ and His Mother. Mary's co-operation, if immediate, is also necessary; if necessary, it would seem to prejudice the traditional teaching on the exclusive and adequate nature of Christ's mediation.

SUMMARY OF WHOLE POSITION

It only remains to summarize our conclusions. We began with the truth that Jesus Christ is the one, unique, and necessary Mediator between God and man, who by His sacrifice on the Cross offered the all-sufficient and superabundant price of redemption. From this it follows that the mediation of all others, including that of Our Lady, must be understood in a subordinate and dependent sense. The mediation of Our

Lady, however, while subordinate, is of its kind unique.   It
has a double aspect, one in relation to objective redemption,
the other to subjective redemption.   Our concern for the
present has been with the first.   We saw how Mary contributed
to objective redemption by her consent to be the Mother of
the Redeemer, by her caring for the divine Infant, by her
intimate union with the Saviour.   Her mediate co-operation,
as a moral and physical cause, is beyond doubt.   But the question at issue is whether she also co-operated immediately in
regard to objective redemption.   Were her sufferings and
compassion on Calvary redemptive in the sense that they,
together with the sacrifice of Christ, constituted the price of
redemption ordained by the Father?   We have seen some of
the reasons which have been adduced to show that they were.
We have seen the difficulties, notably two, which derive from
the fact of Our Lady's own redemption and from the exclusiveness of Christ's mediation.   We do not and could not, indeed,
claim that the question is closed, but only venture to suggest
that in the present state of theological discussion and investigation the attitude indicated by the evidence is one of
Non Constat.

Mary's Mediation of Graces

By Michael O'Grady, s.j.

IN its wider sense the mediation of Our Lady has two aspects, the one concerning her part in objective redemption by reason of which she is more strictly titled Co-redemptrix, the other concerning her part in subjective redemption in virtue of which she is titled Mediatrix of Grace in the more restricted sense or simply Dispensatrix of Grace. The two aspects are closely inter-related. Theological reasoning sees in the first a reason for deducing the fitness of the second and this insight is supported by the explicit statements of recent popes and by Tradition. Whereas, however, there is much difference of opinion, as we have seen, concerning the function of Our Lady in objective redemption, there is practically no dispute as to her prerogative in the distribution of grace, at least considered in its general terms. It is the commonly accepted teaching throughout the Church today that Our Lady is mediatrix of graces in the sense that all graces are obtained by reason of her intercession. Our object in the present paper is to establish the fact of this truth and to explain as far as we may its nature and scope.

The most explicit evidence we have on this question is furnished by the Magisterium of the Church during the past century. Incidentally, it also indicates the scriptural and traditional sources from which the teaching is deduced. For these reasons our method will reverse the chronological order. We begin with what is clear and explicit and proceed to what is less clear and implicit. We shall use the light of present knowledge to clarify the obscurities in the past teaching. Where, as in the present case, this procedure is possible, it commends itself not only for reasons of clarity and security but also for reasons of brevity. Beginning then with the evidence of the Magisterium we shall proceed to submit the evidence of Tradition from the beginning up to the time when the doctrine was plainly in possession. In a later stage we shall give some consideration to the theological arguments as revealing how the doctrine was evolved from the implicit to the explicit stage of development. Finally, we shall review some particular aspects of the general doctrine in order that the concept which it embodies may be as clear and defined as possible.

MAGISTERIUM

To begin, then, with the evidence of the Magisterium: by the Magisterium is understood the testimony of the Supreme Pontiff and of the bishops under him and with him. It is extraordinary or solemn when proclaimed in *ex cathedra* pronouncements or conciliar definitions, ordinary when otherwise promulgated. Since, as far as the present question is concerned, there has not been any definition of doctrine, we shall be dealing with the evidence of the ordinary and universal Magisterium, and particularly as expressed in the encyclical letters and papal allocutions of the past century. Not indeed that earlier indications of the papal mind are lacking. Already in 1748 Benedict XIV had written: " She is like a heavenly river upon whose flood all graces and gifts are borne to us unhappy mortals." [1] And Pius VII had spoken of her as the " Dispensatrix of all Graces." [2] It was, however, with Pius IX that the doctrine came into that special prominence which it has never since ceased to maintain. In his encyclical *Ubi Primum* he has the following, which takes on a special significance from the fact that it was written at the time of his dramatic flight from Rome:

> The foundation of all our confidence, as you know well, venerable brethren, is found in the Blessed Virgin Mary. For God has committed to Mary the treasury of all good things, in order that everyone may know that through her are obtained every hope, every grace and all salvation. For this is His will, that we obtain everything through Mary. [3]

[1] Bull *Gloriosae Dominae*, 27 Sept., 1748, *D.M.*, 217.
[2] *D.M.*, 235.
[3] Cajetae, 11 February, 1849. Trans. from W. J. Doheny and J. P. Kelly, *Papal Documents on Mary*, Milwaukee, 1954, 3; *D.M.*, 260.

Later, his encyclical *Ineffabilis Deus*, in which he defined the Immaculate Conception, closed with the following words:

> And since she has been appointed by God to be the Queen of heaven and earth, and is seated above all the choirs of angels and saints, and ever stands at the right hand of her only-begotten Son, Jesus Christ Our Lord, she presents our petitions in a most efficacious manner. What she petitions she obtains—her pleas can never be unheard.[4]

We have in these statements the general lines of the teaching on Our Lady's universal mediation of grace. She is revealed as the ground of hope and confidence for the Pope and for the faithful, inasmuch as God has committed to her the treasury of all good things and it is His will that we obtain everything through her. Furthermore, we are told that she exercises her mediation by way of intercession which is singularly efficacious. " What she petitions she obtains—her pleas can never be unheard." [5]

These notions were frequently repeated by Pope Leo XIII in his numerous Marian encyclicals. Of special significance is the following passage from his *Octobri Mense*, which merits to be quoted at length not only as a clear statement of teaching on the mediation but as indicating the sources of his teaching in the mystery of the Incarnation and the Cross and in the Tradition of the Church from the very beginning.

> The Eternal Son of God, about to take upon Himself our nature for the saving and ennobling of man, and about to consummate thus a mystical union between Himself and all mankind, did not accomplish His design without obtaining the free consent of her who was to become His Mother. She was the representative of all mankind, according to the illustrious and learned opinion of St. Thomas, who says that " the Annunciation was effected with the consent of the Virgin standing in the place of humanity." With equal truth may it be also affirmed that, by the will of God, Mary is the intermediary through whom is distributed unto us this immense treasure of God's mercies, " for grace and truth came by Jesus Christ."

---

[4] *D.M.*, 301.
[5] Pius IX, *Ineffabilis Deus*, *D.M.*, 301.

Thus, as no man goes to the Father but by the Son, so no one goes to Christ except through His Mother. . . . Mary is this glorious intermediary. She is the mighty Mother of God. . . . Having chosen her for the Mother of His only-begotten Son, He taught her all a mother's feeling that breathes nothing but pardon and love. Such Christ desired she should be, for He consented to be subject to Mary and to obey her, as a son a mother. As such He proclaimed her from the Cross when He entrusted to her care and love the whole of the race of man in the person of His disciple John. As such does she prove herself by her courage in gathering the heritage of the enormous labours of her Son and in accepting the charge of her maternal duties towards us all. The design of this most gracious mercy, realized by God in Mary and confirmed by the testament of Christ, was comprehended at the beginning and accepted with the utmost joy by the holy Apostles and the earliest believers. It was the belief and teaching of the venerable Fathers of the Church. Christians of every generation received it with one mind; and even when literature and traditon are silent, there is a voice that breaks from every human heart and speaks with all eloquence. No other reason is needed than that of a divine faith which by a most powerful yet sweet impulse moves us towards Mary. [6]

Mary's rôle at the Incarnation is here associated with her rôle as mediatrix. Both are part of the divine plan for our salvation. As by God's will through her the Saviour came, so through her is distributed the treasures of divine mercies. Further, she is shown to be qualified in a special way for her function of mediatrix because of her motherhood of men which was confirmed by Christ's testamentary utterance to John on Calvary. We are also clearly given to understand that this teaching is founded in Tradition and Scripture, and the universal consent in the Church on the matter is evidence that it belongs to the deposit of Revelation.

St. Pius X repeats the testimony of his predecessor. A striking passage in his encyclical *Ad Diem Illum* gives his thought:

[6] *D.M.*, 376, 377, 378.

Moreover, it was not only the glory of the Mother of God " to have presented to the only-begotten God who was to be born of human members " the material by which He was prepared as a victim for the salvation of mankind, but hers also the office of tending and nourishing the victim and at the appointed time of offering Him at the altar. Hence the ever-united life and labours of the Son and the Mother which permit the application to both of the words of the Psalmist: " My life is wasted with grief and my years in sighs." When the supreme hour of the Son came, beside the Cross of Jesus there stood His Mother, not merely occupied in contemplating the cruel spectacle, but rejoicing that her only Son was offered for the salvation of mankind and so entirely participating in His Passion that, if it had been possible, she would have gladly borne all the torments that her Son underwent. From this community of will and suffering between Christ and Mary she merited to become most worthily the reparatrix of the lost world and the dispensatrix of all the gifts that Our Saviour purchased for us by His death and His blood. It cannot, of course, be denied that the dispensing of these treasures is the particular and supreme right of Jesus Christ, for they are the exclusive fruit of His death who by His nature is the Mediator between God and man. Nevertheless, by this union of sorrow and suffering, as we have said, which existed between the Mother and the Son it has been granted to the august Virgin to be the most powerful mediatrix and advocate of the whole world with her divine Son. The source then is Christ . . . but Mary, as St. Bernard justly remarks, is the channel or the neck by which the Body is joined to the Head and by which the Head exerts its power and virtue. " For she is the neck of our Head by which He communicates to His Mystical Body all spiritual gifts." . . . Grace comes from God alone. But since she surpassed all in holiness and union with Christ and has been associated by Christ in the work of redemption, she, as the expression is, merits *de congruo* and is the principal minister in the distribution of grace." [7]

This passage contains a summary of Mariology which enables us to catch a clear if minute view of the place of Our Lady's mediation of grace in the whole redemptive economy. The

[7] *D.M.*, 488, 489.

foundation of this prerogative is seen in the life-long association
of Mother and Son that extended from Nazareth to Calvary.
It was this community of will and suffering that qualified her
to become the reparatrix of the lost world and the dispensatrix of all grace: the distinction, however, is clearly manifested
between *her* rôle and that of Christ. As Christ by His death
and Passion purchased all grace, so to Him by special and
supreme right belongs the distribution of grace; likewise to
Mary by reason of her union with the Redeemer in His suffering and Passion has been granted the privileges of being the
most powerful mediatrix and advocate with her Son. Mother
of the Redeemer, intimately associated with Him throughout
life and particularly at the hour of His death, she merits
de congruo what Christ merits *de condigno*. This, indeed, if
a fitting reward for her unique co-operation, is also of far-
reaching significance in its bearing on Mary's subsequent
function as dispensatrix of all grace. The term merit *de
congruo*—merit in equity—as applied to Our Lady in this
context has been a source of much discussion and of varied
interpretation. For the advocates of Our Lady's immediate
co-operation in redemption it has one meaning; for those who
oppose it, another. In keeping with what we have maintained
in the earlier paper and, as we think, in keeping also with
the context of the terms, we do not understand merit *de
congruo* to imply any immediate co-operation with Christ in
objective redemption. Being herself redeemed by the merits
of Christ's Passion and death she could not in consequence
merit redemption, but, presupposing the merits of Christ,
she was qualified in virtue of them to merit for others the
graces of redemption, not with a merit that was of justice
but of equity.

We may recall here what St. Thomas, later to be followed
by Suarez, taught in regard to Our Lady's part in the Incarnation:

> The Blessed Virgin is said to have merited to bring forth
> the Lord not because she merited that He should become
> incarnate but, by means of the grace which had been given her,

she merited that degree of purity and sanctity in which she
might appropriately be the Mother of God. [8]

Thus Our Lady did not and could not merit the Incarnation,
according to the axiom *principium meriti non cadit sub merito*.
Neither did Our Lady merit redemption, according to the
same axiom, but she did merit as one redeemed—and with
a merit that was of equity and not of justice—that the graces
purchased by Christ should be available to all mankind. In
consequence she is now " the most powerful mediatrix and
advocate with her Son and is the principal minister in the
distribution of grace."

While more recent papal pronouncements have repeated
and confirmed the teaching of Leo XIII and his predecessors
they have not added much to his thought on the subject of
Our Lady's mediation of grace. Of necessity we must confine
ourselves to a few brief extracts.

In the Apostolic Letter *Inter Sodalicia* Benedict XV says:

> Since on this account (i.e. on account of Mary's association
> with the sufferings of her Son) all the graces which we receive
> from the treasury of redemption are granted to us by the hands
> of the Virgin of Sorrows, it is clearly from her that we must
> expect the grace of a holy death, because it is by this gift
> especially that the work of redemption in each individual man
> is effectively and definitively accomplished. [9]

Further emphasis is thrown on the scope and nature of Our
Lady's mediation by a pronouncement of the same Pope in
the process of the canonization of St. Joan of Arc. It was
urged that one of the two cures which were cited as evidence
of St. Joan's sanctity had been wrought at Lourdes and so
should be attributed, not to St. Joan, but to Our Lady. To
this the Pope replied:

> If in every miracle we must recognize the mediation of Mary,
> through whom according to God's will every grace and blessing
> comes to us, it must be admitted that in the case of one of these
> miracles the mediation of the Blessed Virgin manifested itself
> in a special way. We believe that God so disposed the matter

[8] *Summa Theol.*, 3, 2, 11 ad 3.
[9] 22 March, 1918, *D.M.*, 556.

in order to remind the faithful that the remembrance of Mary must never be excluded even when it may seem that a miracle is to be attributed to the intercession or the mediation of one of the Blessed or one of the Saints. This is the lesson which, we think, must be drawn from the fact that Thérèse Bertin obtained her perfect and instantaneous cure at the sanctuary of Lourdes. On the other hand, Our Lord has shown us that, even in that land which has been entrusted to the rule of His holy Mother, He is able to work miracles through the intercession of one of His servants; on the other hand, He has reminded us that in these also we must suppose that there has been an intervention on the part of her whom the Holy Fathers have hailed as the mediatrix of all mediators.[10]

Thus the universal mediation of Our Lady is by the divine disposition of things fundamental. Her intervention is forthcoming even when she is not appealed to herself. Her invocation is implicit in the prayers by which we seek to enlist the help of the angels and the saints in heaven.

In similar strain Pope Pius XI attributes his recovery in health to the intercession of St. Thérèse of Lisieux, but in such a way as to imply also the intervention of Our Lady. In his encyclical *Ingravescentibus Malis* he wrote:

This grace (better health), as we have had occasion to write, we attribute to the special intercession of the Virgin of Lisieux, St. Thérèse of the Child Jesus. But we know likewise that every blessing that comes to us from Almighty God comes through the hands of Our Lady.[11]

We bring this series to a close with citations from the encyclicals of Pope Pius XII, in which Mary's rôle in heaven is linked with her function as Mother of the Redeemer and Mother of the redeemed.

Thus, in his encyclical on " Christian Worship " he says:

Among the holy citizens of heaven the Virgin Mother of God receives honour of a special kind. By reason of her God-given function her life is most closely interwoven with the mysteries of Jesus Christ; and assuredly no one better or more

---

[10] Quoted from *Mary's Part in our Redemption*, G. D. Smith, London, 1954, 164-165. *Documentation Catholique*, 1 (1919), 322.
[11] 29th Sept., 1937, *D.M.*, 662.

closely followed in the footsteps of the Word Incarnate, no
one enjoys greater favour or influence with the Sacred Heart
of the Son of God, and through it with the heavenly Father.
She is holier than Cherubim and Seraphim and enjoys greater
glory than all the heavenly citizens, because she is "full of
grace," because she is the Mother of God, and because by her
blessed child-bearing she gave us the Redeemer. . . . She
became our Mother while the divine Redeemer was offering
the sacrifice of Himself; and therefore by this title too we are
her children: she teaches us all virtue; she gives us her Son
and with Him all the helps we need: for God has willed us to
have everything through Mary.[12]

Again, in the encyclical on the Mystical Body, he says:

She it was who, immune from all sin, personal or inherited,
and ever most closely united with her Son, offered Him on
Golgotha to the Eternal Father, together with the holocaust
of her maternal rights and motherly love, like a new Eve, for
all the children of Adam contaminated through his unhappy
fall, and thus she, who was the Mother of our Head according
to the flesh, became by a new title of sorrow and glory the
spiritual mother of all His members. She too it was who by
her most powerful intercession obtained for the new-born
Church the prodigious Pentecostal outpouring of that Spirit
of the divine Redeemer who had already been given on the
Cross. She, finally, true Queen of Martyrs, by bearing with
courageous and confident heart her immense weight of sorrows,
more than all Christians " filled up those things that are wanting
of the sufferings of Christ for His Body, which is the Church "
(Col. i:24); and upon the Mystical Body of Christ, born of
the broken Heart of the Saviour (cf. Office of the Sacred Heart,
Vespers hymn), she bestowed that same motherly care and
fervent love with which she fostered and nurtured the suckling
infant Jesus in the cradle.[13]

Lastly, in the encyclical *Ad Coeli Reginam* Pius XII says:

Her union with Christ the King raises her to a height of
glory surpassing the excellence of any other creature. He
confers on her the royal prerogative of dispensing largesse

---

[12] *Mediator Dei*, 1947, CTS, London, sect. 181.
[13] *Mystici Corporis Christi*, 1943, CTS, London, sect. 110. *D.M.*, 713.

from the treasury of our divine Saviour's kingdom. Lastly, it is the source of the never-failing power of her motherly intercession with her Son and with God the Father.[14]

LITURGY

A complementary source of evidence as to the mind of the Church is provided by the Liturgy. *Lex orandi est lex credendi*.[15] The prayer of the Church is the expression of her faith. Now, in the liturgies of both the West and the East the belief in the (universal) mediation of Our Lady is abundantly manifested.

For 1400 years[16] the Canon of the Roman Mass has remained substantially unchanged and in it the prayer *Communicantes* clearly expresses belief in Our Lady's mediation. Another prayer which likewise embodies this doctrine is the *Libera nos*. It goes back to the seventh century at least.[17] Besides these two prayers, which represent an unchangeable element in the liturgy of the Mass, we have the feast of Our Lady Mediatrix of all Graces for whose celebration Benedict XV gladly gave permission to all who asked for it.[18] This latter feast has recently been superseded by the feast of Our Lady Queen, which includes and expresses the object of the feast of the mediation as is clear both from the encyclical *Ad Coeli Reginam* and from the lessons in the new office.

There are, too, a considerable number of antiphons and prayers in the Roman Breviary which portray Our Lady as mediatrix.

In the East, in the Byzantine liturgy, we find the following expressive antiphon:

---

[14] *Ad Coeli Reginam*, 11 November, 1954, CTS, London, sect. 29. *D.M.*, 902.
[15] Pius XII, *Mediator Dei*, CTS, London, sect. 50-52.
[16] C. L. Feltoe, "The Saints Commemorated in the Roman Canon," *Journal of Theol. Studies*, 15 (1914), 226 ff; C. Callewaert, *Liturgicae Institutiones*, 1, ed. 4a, 1944, no. 74; M. Righetti, *Storia Liturgica*, 3, 1949, 311; J. A. Jungmann, *The Mass of the Roman Rite*, 1, Benziger, 1950, 55; 2, 171.
[17] M. Righetti, op. cit., 3, 397.
[18] *La Vie diocésaine*, Malines, 10 (1921), 96-106 (reference in du Manoir, *Maria*, 1, Paris, 1949, 553, n. 660); Cardinal Mercier, *La Méditation universelle de la très Sainte Vierge et la vraie dévotion à Marie*, Maison de Marie Médiatrice, Louvain, no date. (Reference in G. D. Smith, *Mary's Part in our Redemption*, London, 1953, 165, n. 2).

Hail Mother of God, Virgin full of grace, refuge and protection
of the human race . . .
Pray Christ, Our God, to give peace to the world.

This intercession of Our Lady with Christ, which is con-
stantly repeated in the Marian formulas, was expressed in
Byzantine art by the theme of the *Deesis* (supplication) in which
Christ was shown between the Virgin and St. John the Baptist
who are interceding with Him for men. There are innumer-
able examples of this in the paintings, mosaics and ikons.[19]
We end this slight outline with an extract from the
Chaldean liturgy in which this prayer is regularly recited to
Our Lady:

> Lord, our God, fit us out with solid and invincible arms,
> through the prayers of the Blessed Mother, the Blessed Virgin
> Mary, and grant us a share of the heavenly bliss along with
> her.[20]

TRADITION

Up to the Eighth Century

Now to Tradition. Naturally, we do not expect to find
the doctrine explicitly formulated in the earlier period of
Tradition. We have only to think of the doctrines of the
Immaculate Conception and the Assumption to appreciate how
obscure and involved the origins of doctrine can be. Thus,
for the first period which we shall consider—that is, up to
the eighth century—the evidence is largely implicit. There
are not lacking texts which belong to this period and which
have something more than implicit evidence but, as investigation has shown their number to be few, we have confined
ourselves entirely to those whose authenticity is beyond doubt.
The most pertinent evidence from the first period derives
from the series of Eve-Mary texts that begin with Justin and
are subsequently found in Irenaeus, Tertullian, Epiphanius,
Ephraem, Ambrose, Augustine, and Peter Chrysologus.

[19] S. Salaville, " Marie dans la liturgie byzantine," *Maria*, 1, 250.
[20] A. M. Massonat, " Maria dans la liturgie chaldéene," *Maria*, 1, 344.

Because of his peculiar position in Tradition as representative of East and West, and because of his more developed use of the Eve-Mary analogy, we take Irenaeus as an example of what Tradition yields in this early stage.

In the *Adversus Haereses* he says:

> Eve . . . having become disobedient was made the cause of death both to herself and the whole human race: so also did Mary . . . by yielding obedience become the cause of salvation both to herself and the whole human race.[21]

In his *Proof of the Apostolic Teaching* which, as he himself tells us, contains a summary of Christian instruction at the time, he said:

> For Adam had necessarily to be restored in Christ that mortality might be absorbed in immortality, and Eve in Mary that a virgin, become the *advocate* of a virgin, should undo and destroy virginal disobedience by virginal obedience.[22]

We may also mention a much discussed passage in which Irenaeus speaks of mankind regenerated in the womb:

> And those who proclaimed Him Emmanuel born of the virgin showed the union of the Word of God with His handiwork, because the Word will become flesh and the Son of God the Son of Man—the Pure One opening purely the pure womb which regenerates men unto God and which He made pure, becoming the same as we are.[23]

One interpretation identifies the virgin with Mary and sees in her regeneration of men unto God the expression of her spiritual motherhood of men. This would have implications for the doctrine of the mediation of grace but the interpretation is open to question. It is possible to identify the virgin with the Church, in which case the text is irrelevant to our purpose.

What now is the bearing of these excerpts on the teaching of Mary's universal intercession? Mary the Virgin is contrasted with the virgin Eve, her obedience with the disobedience of

Eve. She is the cause of life as Eve was the cause of death. This is the substance of what they have to tell us. The term "advocate" (Gr. *prostatēs* or maybe *paraklētos*), patroness, is sometimes cited as significant of Mary's intercession. While philologically this meaning could be admitted, the context does not demand it. No more is required to explain it than the obedience of Mary whereby was undone the disobedience of Eve: this altogether apart from the difficulty of conceiving how exactly Mary could otherwise fulfil the rôle of intercessor on behalf of Eve.

Thus, as far as the texts go, they do not provide of themselves a clue to the mind of Irenaeus on the question of Mary's mediation of grace. Theological speculation at a much later date was to discover a connection between the rôle of Mary, author of life and Mother of the Redeemer, with her rôle as mediatrix of all grace, but the development lay outside the vision of St. Irenaeus. At the same time we should not fail to remember what was the common Christian belief in the Communion of Saints and their intercession.[24] With this in mind it is legitimate to conclude that she who gave us the Author of salvation and life was specially invoked in the prayers of the faithful. In confirmation of this we have the prayer *Sub Tuum Praesidium*, which was in use as far back as the fourth and maybe the third century.[25]

It is also of some importance in this connection to notice that it was in the fourth century that St. Epiphanius, who was also eminently a man of Tradition, had occasion to put devotion to Our Lady in proper perspective. In his work *Concerning Heresies* he is obliged, while on the one hand defending Our Lady's perpetual virginity, to reject the excessive devotion of those who would offer sacrifice to her—and in doing so falls back on the traditional Eve-Mary parallelism.[26]

---

[24] H. Delehaye, *Les Origines du culte des martyrs*, Bruxelles, 1933, 106-109.

[25] *Catalogue of Greek and Latin Papyri in the John Ryland's Library*, Manchester, 3, *Theological and Literary Texts*, edited by C. H. Roberts, Manchester, 1938, no. 470; Ortez de Urbína " Lo Sviluppo della Mariologia nella Patrologia Orientale," *Orientalia Christiana Periodica*, 6 (1940), 51, note 4; O. Stegmüller, " Sub Tuum Praesidium," *Zeitschrift für Katholische Theologie*, 74 (1952), 76 ff.; D. Balboni, " De Prece ' Sub Tuum Praesidium '," *Ephemerides Liturgicae*, 68 (1954), 245 ff.

[26] *PG* 42, 727-730, 735, 739 ff.

What Berthold Altaner calls "the most celebrated en-
comium of antiquity on Our Lord," [27] was pronounced at the
Council of Ephesus and has been attributed to St. Cyril of
Alexandria. It furnishes the following significant testimony:

> Hail then, from us, O holy mystical Trinity, who has
> gathered us all together in this Church of Mary, the Mother
> of God. Hail from us Mary, Mother of God, majestic treasure
> of the whole world, the lamp unquenchable, the crown of
> virginity, the sceptre of orthodoxy, the indestructible temple,
> the dwelling of the Illimitable, Mother and Virgin, through
> whom He is called in the holy Gospels: "Blessed who cometh
> in the name of the Lord." Hail, thou who didst contain Him
> in thy holy virginal womb who cannot be contained; thou
> through whom the Holy Trinity is glorified and adored through-
> out the whole world; through whom heaven rejoices, through
> whom angels and archangels are glad; through whom devils
> are put to flight; through whom the tempter-devil fell from
> heaven; through whom the fallen creature is taken up into
> heaven; through whom all creation, held fast by the madness
> of idolatry, has come to the knowledge of the truth; through
> whom holy baptism has come to believers, and the oil of
> gladness; through whom churches are erected throughout the
> world; through whom the nations are brought to repentance.
> And what more shall I say? Through whom the only-begotten
> Son of God has shone forth, "a light to those who sat in darkness
> and in the shadow of death" (cf. Luke i:97); through whom
> the prophets foretold, through whom the apostles preached
> salvation to the nations; through whom the dead are raised
> and kings reign. [28]

This text speaks for itself of the scope and efficaciousness
of Our Lady's intercession.

From the same century we have the testimony of Severianus
of Gabala (+408) and Basil of Seleucia (+459). Severianus:

> We also have Mary, the Holy Virgin and Mother of God,
> interceding (mesiteuousan) on our behalf. For if any ordinary
> woman has gained the victory, how much more the Mother
> of Christ confounds the enemies of truth. [29]

[27] B. Altaner, Patrologie, ed. 2a, Herder, 1950, 245.
[28] PG 77, 99; Palmer, Mary in the Documents of the Church, London, 1953, 50-51.
[29] Severianus, Homil. de Legislatore, PG 56, 409.

Basil of Seleucia (sometimes attributed to Proclus of Constantinople, +446):

> Hail full of grace ! who dost mediate (*mesiteuousa*) between
> God and man that the dividing-wall of enmity be taken away
> and the things on earth be made at one with the things in
> heaven.[30]

The context in Severianus adds considerably to its import.
In it he recalls how God in the Old Testament overthrew
the enemies of His people by means of a Debora, a Jahel
and other heroic women. He continues:

> In this age there is not lacking to God a Debora, there is
> not lacking to God a Jahel. We also have the holy Virgin
> and Mother of God interceding for us.

While thus Severianus extols the intercessory power of Our
Lady, Basil goes further in suggesting a certain parallelism
between the mediation of Our Lady and that of Christ. One
cannot but call to mind the text of Ephesians (ii:14-18),
where St. Paul speaks of Christ breaking down the middle-wall
and giving us access in one Spirit to the Father, and the text
of Colossians (i, 20), where he affirms that the Father reconciled all things to Himself through Christ: " Both the things
that are on earth and the things that are in heaven."

Eighth Century

In the eighth century for the first time, as it would appear,
the term mediatrix is attributed to Our Lady. She is addressed
by St. Andrew of Crete (+ c. 720): " Hail mediatrix (*mesitis*)
of the law and of grace, the seal of the Old and the New
Testament." [31]

We may bring this first period to a conclusion with the
testimony of St. John Damascene (+ 794), who has been
called by Pope Pius XII " an outstanding herald of the Marian
doctrine of the Assumption." [32]

[30] Basil of Seleucia, *Orat. 39*, PG 85, 444.
[31] *In Nativ. Mariae Orat. 4*, PG 97, 866.
[32] *Munificentissimus Deus*, 1950, D.M., 803.

Now the angels regard me (i.e. Mary), now divine grace dwells in me. I am the source of medicine to those that are sick. I am the perennial fount of healings. I am the rout of demons. I am a city of refuge to those that flee to me. Approach, you peoples, with faith and take in abundance the gifts of grace. Draw nigh you that are least hesitant in faith. " All you that thirst, come to the waters," exhorts Isaias, " and you that have no money come and buy without any price." I cry out to all, announcing good tidings. Whoever thirsts for the curing of ills, for the driving away of vices, for the wiping out of sins, for the clearing away of any troubles whatsoever, for the rest of the heavenly kingdom, let him come to me with faith and take away the most powerful and useful gift of grace ! [33]

TEACHING OF THE SCHOLASTICS

Once we enter the next century the explicit evidence grows as to the universal intercession of Our Lady and its efficacy.

At this stage we can do no more than present a few representative selections from the growing list of those who bear witness to this belief.

St. Anselm (+ 1109), the father of scholasticism, in his well-known prayers invokes Our Lady. Inspired by the conviction of her maternal care of men and her power as Mother of God, he gives expression in his prayers to his belief in her unfailing and all-powerful intercession:

For as everyone, O most blessed, who is turned away from you and disregarded by you must perish, so it is impossible that anyone who is turned towards you and is regarded by you should be lost. . . . For if you, Lady, are His (the Son of God's) Mother, are not your other sons His brothers . . . Hence with what assurance should we hope and with what consolation can we fear whose salvation or damnation depends on the decision of our good Brother and our loving Mother . . . Let (our) good Mother pray and beseech for us, let her demand and petition what is for our good. Let her ask her Son on behalf of her sons, her only-begotten for her adopted

[33] *Homil. 2 in Dormit. B.M.V.*, PG 96, 746.

sons, the Lord for His servants. Let (her) good Son hearken to His Mother on behalf of His brothers, the Only-begotten for those whom He has adopted, the Lord for those whom He has freed.[34]

The doctrine is briefly and explicitly contained in a sermon of Abelard (+1142) on the Assumption of Our Lady:

> She is our mediatrix with her Son, as the Son Himself is (our) Mediator with the Father. The Son could not but listen to His Mother asking on our behalf. Nor could He, who so greatly commends the honour of parents, offend her by any refusal. . . . Hence, if the prayer of the saints is so powerful to appease the wrath of the Supreme Judge, what is to be hoped of the prayer of Mary, in whom sinners must all the more have confidence that she is bound even by a certain obligation in this matter, the more it is agreed by all that she obtained only for sinners the unique honour of her glory, that she should be the Mother of God.[35]

The teaching of St. Bernard (+1153) marks a definite stage in the development of the doctrine. Such phrases of his as " God has willed that we should have nothing that would not pass through the hands of Mary," [36] and again, " This is the will of Him who wished us to have everything through Mary," [37] have become classical in the later exposition of Our Lady's mediation. This teaching is further confirmed and defined in passages such as the following:

> God has placed in Mary the plenitude of every good, in order to have us understand that if there is any trace of hope in us, any trace of grace, any trace of salvation, it flows from her . . . [38]
>
> That stream from heaven flows down through the aqueduct, not indeed representing the fulness of the source (not indeed bringing us the fulness of the source), but rather carrying the trickling flow of grace into our parched hearts, to some in greater abundance and to others in less. The aqueduct indeed

---

[34] *Orat. 7 ad S. Mariam*; cf. *Or. 5* and *6. Op. Om.*, ed. F. S. Schmitt, O.S.B., vol. 3, 22-24, Edinburgh, 1946.
[35] *Serm. 26 in Assumpt. B. Mariae*, PL 178, 544.
[36] *In Vigil. Nativ. Dom. S. 3*, PL 183, 100.
[37] *In Nativ. B. M. Virg. Sermo*, PL 183, 441.   [38] Ibid.

is full, so that others may receive of that fulness, but not the fulness itself . . . [39]

In all our prayers and with all the aspirations of our hearts let us venerate Mary: for such is the will of Him who wished us to have everything through Mary. This He wills, but wills it for us. For, always and in all things caring for the wretched, He calms our fears, arouses our faith, strengthens our hope, banishes our lack of trust, reanimates our faint-heartedness . . . [40]

Our Lady, our mediatrix and our advocate, reconcile us to your Son, commend us to your Son, present us to your Son (*repraesenta*? represent our interests to your Son?).[41]

The influence of St. Bernard on subsequent theologians is too well known to need elaboration. It is to be seen in St. Bernardine of Siena (+1444) whose celebrated analogy has been embodied in the encyclical documents themselves:

No grace comes from heaven to earth but what passes through Mary's hands . . . [42]

Every grace that is granted to this world comes to us in three stages. It is handed down in order from God to Christ, from Christ to the Virgin, and from the Virgin to us. For in the first place the Lord our God is the giver of all grace, as is written in James, chapter 1: "Every best gift and every perfect gift is from above, descending from the Father of lights." And secondly it proceeds from Our Lord Jesus Christ as man. For He, while He lived on earth, merited for us every grace that God from eternity had decreed to give to this world, as is written in John, chapter 1: "Of His fulness have we all received and grace for grace." And in the third place it proceeds from the Blessed Virgin. For as Christ is our Head, the source from which all divine grace flows to the Mystical Body, the Blessed Virgin is the neck through which this current of grace passes into the members of the body. To this Solomon bore witness in the Canticle when he said of Christ: "Thy neck," which is the Blessed Virgin, "is as an ivory tower." Hence Bernard's words: "No grace comes from heaven to earth but what passes through Mary's hands." Rightly therefore

[39] PL 183, 440.
[40] PL 183, 441.
[41] De Adventu Domini Sermo 2, PL 183, 43.
[42] De Nativ. B.V. Sermo 5 in Lennerz, De Beata Virgine, ed. 4a., Rome, 1957, 215.

is she called full of grace from whom all graces flow to the Church militant.[43]

The teaching of St. Bernardine on Our Lady's universal mediation can be seen to be beyond doubt. The fact that his explanation is dubious does not affect the conclusion which he defends.

Francis Suarez (+1619), who is credited with the honour of being the first to create a scientific Mariology, enumerates the various ways in which Our Lady has co-operated in salvation. As she co-operated by her merits on earth, she now co-operates by her most efficacious intercession in heaven:

> (The Blessed Virgin ought to be invoked before all the other saints.) Firstly, because her prayer is of greater worth and efficacy, as we have shown, and, inasmuch as she loves us more (than the other saints) and is more humble, so are her prayers for us more prompt and full of solicitude. Secondly, because her prayer is more universal; for whatever others (i.e. the other saints) obtain by their prayers, they obtain in some manner through the Blessed Virgin, because, as Bernard said, she is the mediatrix with the Mediator, and she is like the neck by which the vital influxes pass from the head to the body. Thus in his 174th letter Bernard urges that whatever we offer to God, we should offer it through Mary. . . . This is the reason why, when we pray to the other saints, we do not use one of them as our intercessor with another, for they are all on the same level of dignity; but we use other saints as intercessors with the Blessed Virgin because she is queen and mistress (of them all). It is in this sense that we recite the Angelic Salutation to the other saints, intending that they should present this salutation to the Blessed Virgin on our behalf. Again, it is for the same reasons that we consider certain saints as our particular advocates for the obtaining of this or that (divine) favour, as is apparent from the practice of the Church. . . . But we regard the Blessed Virgin as our universal advocate for all our needs, for she is more powerful over the whole domain of God's favours, than the other saints are with regard to some particular favour. In this way, finally, it has

---

[43] *De Annunt. B. V. Sermo 6* in Lennerz, op. cit., 216. Cf. St. Ignatius Loyola, *Spiritual Exercises*, sect. 63.

come about that Holy Church invokes the Blessed Virgin in more exalted terms, calling her our Hope, Life, Sweetness, Mother of Mercy etc., and that she prays to her more frequently and more earnestly than to the other saints." [44]

St. Alphonsus Ligouri (+1787), having cited many texts from the saints and earlier writers, asks this question:

What do the saints and writers that have been quoted teach us by texts so strong and so precise? Do they intend to prove that all graces come to us through Mary in this sense only: that she has given us the Author of grace, as our adversary would fain persuade us? Far from it. They, on the contrary, give clearly to understand that every grace given to man in virtue of the merits of Jesus Christ, is conveyed to him by the hands of Mary. This is the conclusion of the venerable Father Suarez of the Society of Jesus. He writes: " It is now the general sentiment of the Church, that the intercession of the Mother of God is useful and necessary." " For the Lord," says St. Bernard, " wishes to grant us nothing without the agency of Mary." Before him, St. Ildephonsus said to the Blessed Virgin: " O glorious Lady, the Lord has confided to you all the gifts He wishes to dispense to His creatures: all the treasures of grace are committed to your care." [45]

GRADUAL UNFOLDING OF THE DOCTRINE

It is unnecessary to prolong further the evidence of the theologians. Suffice it to say that since the seventeenth century the doctrine of Mary's universal mediation is clearly in possession and for some time past the number of those who question it is insignificant.[46] As an illustration, however, of how the germinal evidence of Scripture and early Tradition was evolved into the explicit teaching of the papal pronouncements the theological arguments merit some consideration. Two truths in particular were taken as fundamental in this development.

---

[44] Suarez, De Mysteriis Vitae Christi, Op. Om., Paris, 1877, vol. 19, disp. 23, art. 4, sect. 3, n. 5.

[45] The Glories of Mary, trans. by a Catholic priest, Dublin, 1909, 158-159.

[46] E.g. J. Ude: Ist Maria die Mitterlin aller Gnaden?, Bressanone, Weger, 1928, 118 (reference in Maria, 1, 552); J. Guitton, The Blessed Virgin, London, 1952, 135-139.

The first was that of Mary's association with Christ in the work of objective redemption. It should be mentioned in this connection that this association as the basis of Mary's later prerogative of mediation of grace is entirely independent of the question as to whether it involved her mediate or immediate co-operation in the redemptive sacrifice itself. A recent investigation into the teaching of nineteenth century theologians reveals that there is not a single authority from that period who favours the theory of immediate co-operation, though the vast majority upholds the doctrine of Our Lady's universal mediation.[47]

As René Laurentin points out,[48] Tradition up the eleventh century had been almost entirely concerned with Mary's rôle in the beginning of salvation, namely, in the Incarnation. She has been envisaged as the Mother of the Redeemer but hardly at all from the point of view of her permanent association and co-operation with Him in the redemption of mankind. Henceforth the vision of her place and function became enlarged. The Incarnation was considered not merely in itself but as the beginning of an association with the Redeemer that persisted throughout her life, that was given special significance on Calvary and that had definite implications for Mary's life of glory in heaven. Scripture and early Tradition were explicit on the free deliberate nature of Mary's consent to be the Mother of God. It remained, however, for later speculation to bring into relief the full soteriological character of that acceptance, and to show how closely Mary was identified with the purpose and mission of the Saviour. Meagre as the Gospel evidence is, theological insight did not fail to find certain implications of this union of will and purpose. The mystery of the Purification reveals her association with Christ in the oblation which was to be finally consummated on Calvary. The significance of Simeon's prophecy was not overlooked:

> Behold this child is set for the fall and for the resurrection of many in Israel and for a sign which shall be contradicted,

[47] U. A. S. Leonhard, O.F.M.Cap., *Maria die Gehilfin des Erlösers in der Theologie des 19 Jahrhunderts*, Rome, 1954 (reference in Lennerz, op. cit., 270).
[48] R. Laurentin, *Queen of Heaven*, Dublin, 1956, 57.

and thine own soul a sword shall pierce that out of many hearts thoughts may be revealed (Luke ii:34-35).

Nor again the double significance of Cana, which reveals not only the power of Mary's intercession with her Son but the complete conformity with Him in mind and will. The *Fiat* of Nazareth is echoed in the words of Cana, " Whatsoever He shall say to you, do ye " (John ii:5).

Finally, there was Mary's place on Calvary. The Gospel simply says, " There stood by the cross of Jesus His Mother," but the implications of the words were seen to be profound and far-reaching. As Christ brought to fulfilment the oblation of Himself which He had undertaken with the " Behold I come " at the time of the Incarnation, so is Mary's *fiat* seen in its full significance in the compassion with which she entered into the sufferings of our Saviour on Calvary. But not for her, any more than for Christ, is Calvary seen as the end. It is the beginning of a new rôle which is already adumbrated in the position which she held in the infant Church. Such is the line of thought which leads to the argument which can be formulated thus: Mary was associated in a unique way with her Son in the first phase of redemption which culminates in the sacrifice of Calvary. Now the gifts of God, according to the Apostle, are without repentance, and so it is that the association is prolonged in the life of glory. As she co-operated in the acquisition of grace, so she co-operates in the distribution of grace. She is, in fact, the universal Mediatrix of Grace.

Another form which the argument takes derives from the notion of Our Lady's merit. She merited in equity what Christ merited in justice. Merit implies a certain title to that which is merited. As, therefore, Christ by reason of His condign merit has an absolute right to the distribution of the graces of redemption, so Mary has a title in equity to the distribution of those graces which, with Him and under Him, she purchased.

Another truth which has been widely employed in the development of the doctrine of Our Lady's mediation of grace is that of her spiritual motherhood of mankind. The thought which was furnished by earlier Tradition in this connection is summed up in the statement of St. Peter Chrysologus: " Mary is the Mother of those that live by grace as Eve is the mother of those that die according to nature." [49] It was but another aspect of the motherhood of the Lord and was considered in the early period of Tradition only in connection with the Incarnation. Later Tradition, however, linked it with Mary's compassion on Calvary and with Christ's testamentary utterance from the Cross: " Woman, behold thy son." Rupert of Tuite [50] in the twelfth century was among the first to develop this line of thought which since his time has received considerable favour among theologians and spiritual writers. It is summarized in the dictum: Mary conceived us at Nazareth and brought us forth on Calvary. The bearing of this truth on her rôle as mediatrix is evident. As the function of natural motherhood is not limited to conception and birth, neither is the function of Mary's spiritual motherhood limited to conceiving us and giving us birth by her redemptive co-operation with Christ on earth. Of its nature this function continues to be exercised as long as the need exists to preserve and develop the life of her children. It is exercised in the distribution of all those graces that are essential for their growth in holiness and in fuller likeness to her firstborn, Jesus Christ. Her spiritual motherhood thus involves her prerogative of mediatrix of all grace.

THEOLOGICAL NOTE

It is appropriate at this stage to say something of the dogmatic value of our thesis. There is a difference of opinion concerning the force that attaches to the theological arguments in themselves. This issue, however, is not of importance. The dogmatic value of a truth does not derive from the speculative force of theological arguments, but from the living witness of the Church. It is pertinent to recall the parallel case in the doctrines of the Immaculate Conception and of the bodily Assumption of Our Lady. Even now there is considerable

[49] PL 52, 576.   [50] PL 169, 789 ff.

dispute as to the value of the theological arguments for both these doctrines. But the Church, now by her definition, earlier on by the agreement throughout the Church, made clear that these truths were beyond the region of speculation and were part of the heritage of revealed truth.

Returning to the doctrine of Our Lady's universal mediation of grace, we have seen how the Magisterium, particularly in the last hundred years, has without interruption taught the doctrine of Our Lady's mediation, and that not merely in allocutions and private letters, but in authentic public documents addressed to the whole Church and through the institution of the liturgical feast of Mary, Mediatrix of all Graces.

We have seen that it is the practically unanimous teaching of theologians over the same period.[51] We have seen how it harmonizes with the early Tradition even when it was not explicitly considered. What does all this imply?

It is of interest, at this point, to see the conclusions of theologians at the present time.

Lercher[52] says of the proposition that no grace comes to us except through Mary, that it is safe, common, in keeping with the ordinary universal teaching of the Church and commended by the popes.

Aubron[53]—with whom Lennerz agrees[54]—says that, since the ecclesiastical Magisterium has not defined the doctrine, nor censured the opposing doctrine, it is *juridically* a pious opinion concerning which free discussion is permitted. *Objectively* it seems certain that it is not just some particular opinion, but an integral part of Catholic doctrine.

Druwé[55] states that he does not think that there is any theologian of the present day who would not agree with P. Aubron's conclusion.

The distinction between the objective and the juridical status of a doctrine is of importance. Philosophy is familiar

---

[51] Pius XII, writing in 1942, says of it: " quam tenerrimam salutaremque sententiam theologi omnes modo concorditer tenent." *AAS* 34 (1942), 44.

[52] *Institutiones Theologiae Dogmaticae*, 3, ed. 3a, Innsbruck, 1942, n. 335.

[53] " La Médiation universelle de la Sainte Vierge," *Nouv. Rev. Théol.*, (65) 1938, 35.

[54] *De Beata Virgine*, ed. 3a (1939), 242.

[55] " La Médiation universelle de Marie " in *Maria*, 1, 562.

with the distinction between truth and certitude. The former
has to do with what is objective, what is independent of the
mind, the reality of a proposition in itself; the latter has to
do with the state of mind confronted with the proposition.
Somewhat the same distinction holds with regard to the teaching of the Church in the different stages of its evolution.
The objective truth of a proposition and its relation to
revealed doctrine is one thing. It is to be distinguished from
the clarity and the certitude with which it is held throughout
the Church at this or that particular period of history. Witness
the doctrine of the Immaculate Conception. That doctrine
from the beginning was part of the divinely revealed truth.
However, in the fourteenth century, for example, since the
infallible Magisterium had not intervened on its behalf, it was
a pious opinion that could be and was, in fact, freely disputed.
Such was its juridical status at that time.

The juridical status of the doctrine of the Mediation of all
Graces has certainly not yet been established by any solemn
definition. What of the teaching of the ordinary Magisterium
throughout the world? Has it invested this truth with the
force of a dogma? The opinion of the theologians just cited
indicates that it has not, and we must, at least, leave it an
open question.

Concerning the question of the objective status of the
doctrine, the theologians, as we have seen, are unanimous. The
doctrine of Our Lady's Mediation of All Graces is contained in
the deposit of Faith not explicitly but implicitly. The papal
documents themselves have said this explicitly.[56] It is also
many times implied in so far as they show this activity of
Mary as the prolongation and outcome of her co-operation
with Christ on earth, and of her spiritual motherhood of men.
It is, as we have seen, in harmony with the early teaching of
Tradition, where Mary was spoken of as the New Eve, the
Mother of Life.

For these reasons it seems legitimate to claim that the
doctrine has been formally and implicitly revealed and
consequently that this doctrine might be defined by the
infallible Magisterium as a dogma of Catholic Faith.

[56] Cf. D.M., 378.

PARTICULAR QUESTIONS

Assuming now the general thesis of Our Lady's universal mediation of grace, it remains to see what aspects of it can be further elucidated and defined.

Three questions suggest themselves in this context:

(1) Firstly, what is the nature of the causality implied in Mary's mediation?

(2) Secondly, what is its scope?

(3) Thirdly, what is the relationship of Our Lady's intercession to the intercession of the saints?

With regard to the first question, we cannot fail to notice in the evidence pertaining to our subject the numerous titles that are given to Our Lady and the variety of terms employed to designate her function. She is mediatrix, dispensatrix, treasurer, advocate. She is said to distribute grace, to dispense it, to intercede. While all imply a certain causality, what is its precise nature?

There is not and cannot be any doubt that they imply a moral causality, in the sense that Mary by her intercession procures all graces. Tradition and the Magisterium make this abundantly clear. The question is, whether Mary's function as mediatrix is merely that and nothing more. The weight of theological opinion says so. Some theologians, however, go further and claim that over and above this moral causality of intercession Mary as mediatrix exercises an instrumental and physical causality in the production of grace. Among other reasons they urge especially the description of Our Lady's function as found in some modern documents of the Magisterium. Thus, for instance, St. Pius X gives us the analogy of the neck, which was earlier employed by St. Bernardine, and speaks of the power and virtue which Christ exercises through Mary on the members of His Mystical Body.[57]

We do not propose to subject these theories to any refined analysis or examination. On general principles only they are

[57] D.M., 489.

neither necessary nor acceptable. The analogies employed by
the Pope to illustrate the function of Our Lady do not provide
a sound argument for anything more than the moral causality
of Mary's intercession. To claim that they do is to give them
a force and a meaning beyond the whole weight of the evidence
of the documents elsewhere, and indeed of the Liturgy and
Tradition.

To the weight of extrinsic authority I should add the difficulty of conceiving Our Lady as a physical instrumental cause
in the distribution of grace. A physical cause must be physically
present to its effect, but how can Our Lady as the universal
physical cause of grace be universally present? Moreover,
an instrumental physical cause of its nature contributes
something of its own to the effect. What is it that Mary
contributes to this effect, which is totally in the order of
grace?

Now, as to the scope of Our Lady's intercession: it is
universal both from the point of view of the graces which
she procures and the persons who benefit by them. This is
part of the doctrine itself, as taught by the Magisterium and
by the common consent of theologians. Here a distinction
must be made between Mary's merit and her intercession.
They are not co-extensive. Her merits, like the condign merits
of her Son, are present to God from all eternity and so have
extended to every grace that has ever been granted. But her
intercession could begin only in her lifetime and, in fact,
could not take on a universal character until after the Assumption. Because, to be able to make intercession for all graces,
she must have knowledge of all needs, and that is possible only
in the beatific vision. It is therefore from the moment of
the Assumption that Mary enters into the full perfection of
her rôle as mediatrix.[58] From that time her intercession
extends to all graces: to sanctifying grace, to the infused
virtues, to all actual graces and to external graces.

The fact that the sacraments confer grace *ex opere operato*
is not an argument against this universality. The fruitful
reception of the sacraments demands their valid administration
and the proper dispositions in the recipient. These are the

[58] Cf. Pius XII, *Dum Saeculum*, D.M., 699.

direct and immediate object of Mary's intercession, which thus indirectly reaches to the sacramental graces themselves. Universal in respect of grace, the mediation of Mary is likewise universal in respect of those whom she benefits. By reason of her foreseen congruous merits, her beneficent influence reached to those who lived before her time. Since the Assumption there are none who have not benefited by her intercession.

Now, as regards the third question: the intercession of the saints does not constitute a difficulty against the doctrine of Our Lady's universal mediation. Her intercession is, as it were, the ultimate and necessary step in influencing her Son to distribute grace. It is implied in our invocation of the saints who, observing the divine order of things, present our petitions to Our Lady, who in turn presents them to her Son. The point has already been met by Benedict XV and Pius XI.[59]

Finally, it does not imply any limitation in the scope of Mary's intercession that so many fail to recognize her power and to invoke her help. The truth that Mary intercedes for every grace does not mean that she intercedes only when her help is sought.[60] The marriage feast at Cana is significant here. Unasked, Our Lady made known to her Son the plight of her friends. Symbolic of this maternal solicitude, the petition is also symbolic in its testimony to the unfailing power of her intercession. Who, as Pope Leo XIII reminds us, " sees more clearly in the Eternal Word what troubles oppress us, what are our needs? Who is allowed more power in moving God? Who can compare with her in maternal affection? "[61]

Aptly indeed has Catholic Tradition given her the title: " Omnipotentia Supplex."

[59] Benedict XV; *Documentation Catholique*, 1, 322. Pius XI, *Ingravescentibus Malis*, D.M., 662.
[60] Cf. Leo XIII, *Magnae Dei Matris*, D.M., 391-392.
[61] Leo XIII, *Augustissimae Virginis*, D.M., 453.

Our Lady's Assumption

By Mgr. H. Francis Davis, d.d.

A LONG-STANDING AND UNIVERSAL FAITH

WHATEVER we may say about the relative value of various arguments for the Assumption, the one pre-eminent reason which convinced the Church of the twentieth century that it was part of the revealed truth delivered to her through the apostles and therefore definable was that it had long come to be seen clearly as part of the living faith of the Church. The authority of the Church, which rejoices in the presence of Christ until the consummation of the world, had long given the doctrine its obvious support. For the doctrine that Our Lady, shortly after the end of her life upon earth, was taken up body and soul into heaven has been taught explicitly, and piously accepted by the faithful, since the Middle Ages. It has been preached annually, it has been defended by theologians, it has been a subject for meditation daily during the recital of the Rosary. Converts like John Henry Newman were led to accept it on their entry into the Church as an integral part of Catholic doctrine.

The Assumption has of course for much more than half the history of the Church been the Blessed Virgin's greatest festival. Churches have been dedicated in its honour. I can only illustrate this last point from my own country. There were some forty-five churches dedicated to the Assumption in England during the high Middle Ages, seventeen of which were in the Oxford district. The 15th of August was one of Oxford's red-letter holidays and still figures in the university calendar. In mediaeval Oxford one church had a fraternity of St. Mary formed for the quaint purpose of honouring " God, St. Mary and the festival of the Assumption." Another church, whose founders with remarkable theological insight saw Our Lady's destiny as inseparable from that of her Son, was dedicated to " the Ascension of Our Lord and the

Assumption of Our Lady." Finally, at the request of the Holy Father for the votes of the bishops of the Church a practically unanimous vote was cast for the definability of the doctrine.

If Our Lord's presence through His Holy Spirit means anything for the Church, so long-standing and universal a faith and proclamation could not but indicate that the doctrine was part of the original Revelation. The following words of Our Lord to the apostles apply at least in principle to the Church through the ages: " But the Paraclete, the Holy Ghost, whom the Father will send in my name, he will teach you all things and bring all things to your mind, whatsoever I shall have said to you." (Jo. xv: 26). The same Spirit who inspired the Scriptures and apostolic preaching directs our understanding to the full meaning of what was said in those sources.

Dr. Garbett therefore, when he said that the Church of England " had always honoured the Blessed Virgin as the Mother of Jesus, but could not accept a dogma which had neither scriptural, historical, nor doctrinal foundation," omitted to take note of the fact that four hundred million Catholics, to say nothing of another one hundred and fifty million Orthodox, Nestorians and Monophysites, had for many centuries believed the Assumption on the basis of its doctrinal and scriptural foundations. It was no invention of our century.

WHY SILENCE DURING FIRST FIVE CENTURIES?

On the other hand it has worried theologians that there were so few signs of this living faith in the earliest period of the Church's history. How could the doctrine have been held implicitly for centuries before it came to be expressed? If it were implicit in the Scriptures, why were Christians so slow in realizing it? What suddenly led people to express it for the first time after five centuries? What would a Christian of the fourth century have answered to the question: Was Mary's body taken up incorrupt to her Son in heaven? If they had any explicit knowledge of it, would they not have mentioned it? The silence of six centuries, wrote Dom Capelle in 1950, " does not admit of a favourable interpretation. It does not mean the possibility of traditions of which

we are ignorant, but the non-existence of any tradition." [1]
As a matter of fact Dom Capelle spoke a little too soon.
As will be shortly realized, a document was published for
the first time in 1955,[2] five years after his words, which does
seem to break the silence of those first six centuries, possibly
by a hundred years. A homily of Bishop Theoteknos of Livias
in Palestine appears to have been written within five centuries
of the death of the apostles, and is one of our most valuable
and explicit witnesses to the doctrine. Of course Dom
Capelle's statement still remains in principle true, since it
appears highly probable we shall never bridge the early five
centuries, even though we might come across another such
isolated anticipation of the later clear belief.

WHY AND HOW WAS THE SILENCE BROKEN?

On the other hand why after five centuries do Catholics
suddenly begin to preach and teach the Assumption, which had
been hardly touched upon before? Those who have been
unsympathetic to the doctrine, mainly Protestants, have
stated that it arose from the uncritical acceptance of the
apocryphal accounts of Our Lady's death which arose some
time about the fifth century. Newman put forth a better
reason: up to the fifth century the labours and anxieties
of Christians were mainly consumed in defending the true
nature and full godhead of Jesus Christ. Until that was firmly
established against all attack, the full dignity, glory and
privileges of the Mother could not be profitably discussed.
For, while Mariology in connection with the redemption
goes back to the second century, uninhibited study of the
Mother for herself would only come after she had been
defined as Mother of God. But strictly speaking do we need
reasons for human obtuseness in seeing the full implications
of Scripture? Did not Our Lord blame the disciples on the
way to Emmaus for their slowness of heart in understanding
the things that were written of Him, that the Son of Man
should suffer and so enter into His glory (cf. Lk. xxiv:25-26).

---

[1] Dom Bernard Capelle, "Théologie de l'Assomption," *Nouv. Rev. Théol.*, 72
(1950), 1010.
[2] Cf. bibliography at end of chapter.

Why had so many centuries passed before the Jews understood what had been written about the Messias? How is it that Our Lord was able to blame the Jews for not having sufficiently searched the Scriptures? (cf. Mk. xxii:10; Jo. v:39). Clearly there were truths implied in the Scriptures that the Jews of Our Lord's time had never yet understood; things which they could, and ought to, have understood.

THE PART, FAVOURABLE AND OTHERWISE, OF THE APOCRYPHA

Non-Catholics are always demanding from us historical evidence. If the Assumption were accepted by us as a fact of history rather than as a doctrine of the faith, the theory that it arose from unreliable apocrypha and must be rejected until we can find reputable eye-witnesses' or at least ear-witnesses' accounts would be plausible. But the Assumption, like the Virgin Birth and the Resurrection of Our Lord, is a matter of faith, not of secular history. Neither Assumption nor Virgin Birth can be established on the sort of eye-witnesses acceptable to the historian; and the Resurrection would still be of faith, even if we failed to convince ourselves of the empty tomb and appearances on purely historical grounds.

The apocryphal accounts were not totally devoid of value. Once one makes allowance for the fact that they were sheer inventions devoid of historical value, they should probably be taken as untheological attempts of unhistorically-minded laymen to express the wonders that must have accompanied Our Lady's last moments. There is here an analogy with the apocryphal accounts of Our Lord's childhood or of the apostles' miracles and teaching. In each case there was an unwillingness to regard Our Lord, His Mother or His disciples, respectively, as not favoured with special graces. On the other hand they showed crudeness and childishness in many of the details they invented. In general one could say they seemed in a vague way to realize the sound theological principle that the Mother's predestination was not unlike her Son's. Just as she lived and suffered and died as He did, so the details of her passing from this world were like those of His. Some of these details were obviously borrowed from certain popular stories of Our Lord's last days.

These stories further served the purpose of forming a
background for the homilies which from the sixth century
onwards began to be preached frequently on Our Lady's
Assumption or, as they first called it, her Falling Asleep or
Passing Over. Briefly, they opened people's minds to the
issue, and gave them a useful composition of place for their
thoughts.

On the other hand, however, the apocryphal stories did
much harm to the progress of understanding of the doctrine.
Many of them were so obviously legendary that they got into
bad repute, and got the whole doctrine into bad repute as
well. A number of these stories about the characters in the
Gospel, in their Latin version, were condemned by a decree
of Pope Gelasius. This led many of the Latins to proclaim
a sort of reverent agnosticism, above all the gentleman who
was long to be known to the modern world by the name of
Pseudo-Jerome, from the circumstance that he had pretended
to be St. Jerome, and succeeded for some centuries to win
for himself the latter's authority. We now agree that he was
really Paschasius Radbert. Many people followed him, not
indeed in denying the Assumption outright, but in casting
doubts upon it as not clearly taught by the Church, and anyhow
as being too closely involved in the disrepute of pious legends
that were unauthentic and unhistorical.

THE FAULTY REASONING OF THE AGNOSTICS

These early agnostics made the same mistake that has been
made by modern adversaries of the doctrine. They assumed
that the stories which were used as a background, and even
perhaps as the occasion, of the doctrine, were the real basis
of its acceptance. First of all it is fantastic in the extreme
to take for granted that for centuries some of the most worthy
bishops and theologians should have selected one unhistorical
incident from out of a mass of unhistorical legends without
having any scriptural or doctrinal reasons for doing so. If
they were incapable of resisting the temptation to accept
legends as history, why do the other legends disappear?
What about the details of the angel appearing to Mary, of
the apostles being summoned together, of Christ appearing,

of the Jews attacking the funeral procession and being struck
blind, of the miracles in connection with this, of the procession of angels carrying Our Lady's body to paradise, of its
being placed under the tree of life where the soul was
reunited to it, and of its final being lifted up triumphantly
to heaven? We all know that all these colourful details have
been forgotten, yet the sober fact of Mary's being taken up
body and soul into heaven remains. Even the fact of her death,
which was also included in the legend, remains uncertain.
Most theologians accept it, but it has not been defined, and
is perhaps no more than a highly probable opinion of most
theologians. One fact mentioned in the legend has been
accepted for most centuries of its history not only in the true
Church, but in all the Eastern separated groups, some of
which broke off from the West as far back as the fourth
century. So firmly is the Assumption held among the Eastern
schismatics that not even the definition of the doctrine by
Rome in the twentieth century has been able to shake their
belief in it. No, whatever be the explanation, the fifth and
sixth century apocrypha cannot explain the development and
propagation of this doctrine.

Positively in favour of this conclusion we have the direct
evidence of the earliest homilies and treatises. Though they
often betray an acceptance of the legendary accounts in their
main outlines, to prove the Assumption they have recourse
to Scripture or theology. Perhaps a few writers think there
was an ancient tradition directly and explicitly supporting it,
independently of Scripture. But they do not base their case
on such a conviction.

SCRIPTURE THE ULTIMATE BASIS

It will be found possible to sustain Pius XII's statement in
Munificentissimus Deus that " all these arguments and considerations of the holy Fathers rest on the holy Scriptures
as their ultimate foundation." If this is true we can dispense
with the need for searching for a chain of witnesses reaching
back to the beginning. There are indeed many reasons, such
as the troubled condition of the times and the life-and-death
struggle with christological heresies, why, even though, as we

know, this doctrine is implicitly contained in the revealed facts made known to us through the apostles, Christians of the earliest period should have been too pre-occupied to find it there.

REFLECTED EARLY IN THE LITURGY

It will, however, help us in our theological account of the doctrine to see how Christians eventually became fully and explicitly conscious of it. First of all it became reflected in the Liturgy. There was already a feast in the fifth century called the "Memory of the Mother of God," observed on differing days around Christmas in some Eastern countries, and on 15 August in others. Many think this feast was first observed in Ephesus after the great Council. It was certainly connected with devotion to the ever-Virgin *theotokos*. Once the nature and dignity of the Son were fully established in Ephesus and Chalcedon, the full dignity of the Mother began also to be appreciated. It was, moreover, from that time impossible to go astray about Mary. As Newman said, " He who charges us with making Mary a divinity is thereby denying the divinity of Jesus. Such a man does not know what divinity is."

Some people have long thought, and indeed it now appears established by A. Wenger (see bibliography below) that it was this early feast which developed into the feast of Our Lady's passage to heaven, and therefore of her Falling Asleep. The same feast in time became that of the Assumption. However that may be, it seems probable that the feast came in locally before the Ethiopians, Nestorians and Armenians broke away in that century from the Church; for these Christians keep the feast, as we do, on 15 August. The Falling Asleep, as it was first called, was regulated and officially established throughout the Empire by Emperor Maurice about the year 600.

EARLY FORESHADOWING OF THE DOCTRINE

Before it got into the Liturgy, were there signs of people reasoning their way to it? You have only to study the great modern histories of the dogma of the Assumption to realize that there are quite a number of pointers during the first few centuries. Father Crehan has recently studied [3] one very early Scripture consideration, by which the Ark of the Covenant of the Apocalypse, chapter xi, eventually became associated with Mary's incorruptible flesh from which Christ's flesh was taken. Tertullian, says Father Crehan, had taken this as the type of Christ's pure body, while St. Hippolytus applied it to Mary. " Now the Lord," wrote the latter, " was without sin, being in His human nature from incorruptible wood, that is, from the Virgin, and being sheathed as it were with the pure gold of the Word within and of the Spirit without." [4] Father Crehan shows how in gradual stages this type came to be understood as applying to Mary as the incorruptible Ark of St. John's vision in heaven. Here is but one indication of the ways in which even from the earliest times there was seen in Scripture a connection between Mary and her Son, by which they came to understand a likeness not only in death, but also in resurrection and glory.

THE EARLIEST EXPLICIT WITNESS, THEOTEKNOS

Until 1955 it was often contended that the acceptance of the doctrine in its explicit form followed the official introduction or establishment of the feast throughout the empire in the year 600. In fact it was taken for granted that the first sermon on the subject was one which has come down to us from the seventh century writer under the name of St. Modestus. However, it now appears to be established that Theoteknos, Bishop of Livias in Palestine, preached a long and important homily on the Assumption probably in the second half of the sixth century. Father Galot, who reports on Father Wenger's edition of this work, [5] notes the appropriateness of Palestine for the first signs of explicit devotion towards Our Lady's glorious passage to heaven. Other sources tell us that a century before this the guides to the Holy Places showed an empty tomb of Our Lady, but were

[3] Cf. J. Crehan, in bibliography below.
[4] Fragment of St. Hippolytus, quoted by Theodoret, *Dialogue* 1, *PG* 10, 864-5.
[5] Galot, J., S.J., " Aux Origines de la foi en l'Assomption," *Nouv. Rev. Théol.*, (87) 1955, 631-6.

unable to say for certain whither she had been taken. Timothy, a priest of Jerusalem in the fifth century, had seemed even to say that Mary was taken up without dying.

To go back to Theoteknos, we are amazed that he called his homily not the *Falling Asleep* or the *Passing Over*, as the feast was usually called at this time, but the *Assumption*. Father Wenger thinks that this is an indication of early date. Homilies written in the following few centuries follow the seventh century official title of the feast. There was no hesitation in Theoteknos' sermon about the meaning of the doctrine. A number of times he said explicitly that her body was raised to the heavens with her soul.

Theoteknos spoke as though the doctrine were common-place. Yet external evidence makes it unlikely that the doctrine could long have been accepted as a certainty. His arguments show us how they found the doctrine in the faith already received. He certainly related, though soberly, many details of the apocryphal legend. But he did not support his doctrinal statements on the authority of these legends. On the contrary he supported what he conceived to be fact in the legends by appealing to the faith in Christ and His Mother, as they are revealed to us in Scripture. An example of this is where he defended the credibility of miracles pur-porting to have been worked at Mary's death. " Let not anyone be incredulous, as though it were impossible for the all-holy body of the Mother of God to work this miracle. (Such a thing was possible) because she remained a virgin and knew no corruption." (Theoteknos, *Encomium*, 21).[6] But his support for the miracle-story was merely passing, while his arguments for the Assumption were many and persistent.

Theoteknos began his encomium with the text from Psalm 97: " Sing to the Lord a new canticle: because he hath done wonderful things." The first " wonderful thing " he recalls is the Resurrection of Our Lord and Saviour Jesus Christ. Then, while insisting that Christ did everything for our salvation, he reminded his listeners that Christ afterwards ascended into heaven and took his seat at the right hand of God. Being so exalted, together with the immaculate flesh

---

[6] Full references to the *Encomium*, cf. bibliography.

he took from Mary, he gathered all the saints round the immaculate and pure Virgin.

For Mary, he said, because of her exalted position was to receive more than all the other saints. She was the second Eve, who had undone the evil of the fall, and taken away the curse from all women. " She found what Eve lost. She found what Adam had forfeited through his disobedience " (*Encomium*, 25).

Theoteknos found passages befitting the glories of Mary throughout the Old Testament. He saw the words addressed to the queen of Psalm 44 as addressed to Mary, whose beauty is desired by the heavenly King.

Theoteknos understood, as do all good mariologists, the principle expressed beautifully by Newman, " the glories of Mary for the sake of her Son." [7] The Son cannot forsake His Mother; and the Mother in the mysteries of her life must not be separated from her Son.

> For it was fitting (he said) that the holy one who begot Him should see her Son upon a high throne, raised above all, and should see every knee bend before Him of those above the earth and of those upon the earth, and every tongue confess Him that will come to judge the living and the dead (*Encomium*, 8).

This presence of Mary with her Son must be such as exalts her above other saints and prophets:

> It was fitting . . . that her all-holy body, her God-bearing body, receiver of God, godlike, undefiled, shining with the divine light and full of glory, should be carried by the apostles in company of the angels, and, after being placed for a short while in the earth, should be raised up to heaven in glory with her soul so loved by God (*Encomium*, 9).

Theoteknos recalled the special privileges traditionally accorded to Henoch and Elias of escaping the normal end of human life, and declared that Mary's end must be more privileged than theirs. " How much more then will He glorify in body and soul the one who had been His Mother

[7] Cf. *Discourses to Mixed Congregations*, London, 1902, Discourse 17.

according to the flesh ! In truth he has glorified her, and he will glorify her still " (*Encomium*, 17).

An unusual argument was from the claim upon the Persons of the Trinity based on Mary's holiness and virginity. " For she, the holy one, pleased God the Father. She, the Virgin, pleased the subsistent Word born of the Father from all eternity. She, the Virgin, pleased the life-giving Spirit, the enlightener of all, who fashions all the citizens of heaven " (*Encomium*, 12).

There are many other arguments in his sermon, including one from our Lady's mediatorial position as our ambassadress with her Son in heaven. The arguments are not developed. Most of them are barely stated in outline. Yet there is no ambiguity about what he drew from these arguments, or about the spontaneity with which he connected it with the Scriptures. We should remember that he had no definition of the Church to defend before non-Catholics. He need not have defended the Assumption if he thought it had no basis in Scripture or Tradition. Yet defend it he did, and on at least four occasions was fully explicit about the body being taken up with the soul to heaven (*Encomium*, 9, 10, 15, 36).

EARLY WITNESSES AFTER THE SIXTH CENTURY

In the century after Theoteknos a prayer appeared in the Liturgy which indicated the first official recognition of the doctrine. I refer to the prayer *Veneranda*, which was used by the Church for many centuries. Pius XII quoted it in *Munificentissimus Deus*, reminding us that it was in the Sacramentary sent by Pope Hadrian I to Charlemagne: " O Lord, today we celebrate the festival in which the holy Mother of God died a temporal death; but she who bore Thy divine Son Incarnate, Our Lord, could not be held fast by the bonds of death." Dom Capelle has pointed out the similarity between these words and the words used by St. Peter, in the Acts, of Christ's own Resurrection: " But God raised him up again, releasing him from the pangs of death; it was impossible that death should have the mastery over him." (Acts ii:24, Knox). The prayer *Veneranda* tells us then that she who *de se genuit Incarnatum*, from herself bore the Incarnate One, was, like that Son of hers, freed from the bonds of death. These bonds, as in the case of her Son in the Acts of the Apostles, included the bonds which hold the body to the corruption of the grave.

In the same century as the *Veneranda* lived the writer who has come down under the name of Modestus, until recently thought to be the oldest explicit witness to the Assumption. " Modestus " obviously had not heard of Theoteknos's encomium. " I do not know," he said, " how it happens that on the subject of the Virgin's Falling Asleep, a subject so worthy of veneration, no sermon or Scripture exposition has been left. So we see the faithful people on her feastday hunger for religious instruction, waiting for someone to reveal something of this mystery."[8] So he first told them soberly the apocryphal story, omitting all legendary incidents supposed to have taken place at the burial. What happened to the body? Modestus was silent. He was content to say her virginal body did not know corruption. As for her resurrection and assumption, they took place in the manner known to the Saviour alone.

His theological arguments were not unlike those of Theoteknos. He argued from Psalm 44, about the queen whom the King desired. He argued from the fact that Mary's body was made like to that of her predestined Son in order that His incorruptible body might be taken from it. He argued from her having a rank above all other creatures. He even argued from her mediatorship in heaven in the presence of her Son.

ST. JOHN OF DAMASCUS

A century still later we find St. John of Damascus arguing on similar grounds, though his arguments are more developed. She who retained her *virginity* intact through childbirth is preserved from corruption. Mary, unlike our first parents who lost paradise because of sin, was *sinless*, and so was straightway admitted into paradise. " How can corruption affront the body which received Life? These things are opposed to her and entirely foreign to her God-bearing soul and body." [9]

[8] *Encomium in B. Virgin*, 1, PG 86[2], 3280.
[9] *2 Dorm.*, 3, PG 96, 728; cited by V. A. Mitchel, *The Mariology of Saint John Damascene*, Maryhurst , Mo., 1930, 164.

St. John of Damascus, like Theoteknos and others before him, also argued from Mary's common predestination with her Son. Just as He had come down to her to take His holy flesh, which would be united to the Godhead, from Mary; so she whom He loved beyond measure would be taken up to be with Him in heaven.[10]

THE ARGUMENTS USED IN SUBSEQUENT THEOLOGY

If we were to continue the history of the arguments put forward century by century, we should find that they can be reduced to the following heads:

(1) Mary in her predestination is always associated with her Son.

(2) Immaculate conception and sinlessness imply exemption from corruption in the grave, and so imply immediate resurrection and glory.

(3) Perpetual virginity, as fleshly incorruption, involved exemption from physical corruption after death.

(4) The filial piety of the divine Son implied that He would do this for her, if it were otherwise possible and fitting.

(5) Mary at her death was more exalted in dignity than other creatures will ever be. If, then, other Christians are destined to be bodily with Christ in heaven, this must have applied to Mary straightway after her death.

(6) The doctrine of the Second Eve implies assumption as the final and complete victory of the woman.

(7) The woman of the Apocalypse is already seen in her glory, after being taken by the Eagle.

We said at the beginning that we today accept the doctrine primarily on the basis of the enduring and universal consent of the bishops and faithful over many centuries. We then made an attempt to discover the circumstances and arguments which first enabled Christians to accept explicitly a

[10] 2 Dorm., 14, PG 96, 741.

doctrine which does not appear explicitly either in Scripture or the earliest records of Tradition.

THE VALUE OF THE ARGUMENTS

A scruple might still worry us. These arguments, a person might say, whether from the Immaculate Conception, the integral motherhood, the virginal purity, the prophecy of Genesis, Our Lady's mediatorship or typology—are any of them final, decisive arguments? Are not most of them of that very weak class, arguments from fittingness? Could such arguments give rise to a sound conviction that their conclusions were implicitly revealed in the revelation of their premises?

Some theologians would say that, once the Immaculate Conception is accepted, the Assumption was bound to follow. Undoubtedly the connection is close, as Pius XII recognized. The Scriptures and early Tradition teach most decisively that suffering, death, and corruption in the tomb came not from God's original plan, but from man's revolt against that plan. If once we say that Mary is lifted outside the realm of sin, it seems to follow, as day follows night, that Mary would by rights be exempt from suffering, death, and corruption. Suffering and death were her lot in view of her common predestination with her Son. From corruption she becomes immune for the same reason. This argument, said Pius XII, aroused in Christians a more fervent hope, but he does not say a certainty, that the Assumption would be defined. There are, in fact, some theologians who are not convinced that a return to the state of original justice in Mary must rigidly entail a regaining of all the privileges of that state.

A further difficulty urged against this explanation is that it does not appear to have been used as an argument for the Assumption for many centuries, if only because the doctrine of the Immaculate Conception itself was not yet in un- challenged possession.

What of the arguments from integral motherhood and virginal purity? It would certainly appear to many of us today that no syllogism would suffice to deduce rigidly from these the bodily Assumption.

Again, if we are to argue directly from Scripture texts

what Scripture scholar would risk the assertion that there is a rigid metaphysical link between either the *Protoevangelium*, or any other single Scripture text and Mary's bodily Assumption?

THE INFORMAL REASONING OF SIMPLE FAITHFUL

During the last twenty years many theologians have been led to a closer study of the facts, and they have been forced to the conclusion that our difficulties in understanding how Christians using many of what appear to us individually weak arguments have yet reached a conviction of the truth arise, as was noted in the lecture on the Immaculate Conception, from an unreal and abstract grasp of reasoning in everyday life. I refer to the way in which men, whether in groups or individually, whether naturally or under the Holy Spirit, arrive at a deeper understanding of any truth. For in matters of revealed truth, as in many other matters, the process of growing in one's understanding of the truth one possesses is not confined to either leaders or experts. The Church, in which the Holy Spirit dwells, is not any one group, whether bishops, theologians or laymen. The bishops indeed have the teaching authority, but the faith lives in the minds and hearts of all the faithful.

SUCH AS NEWMAN HAD ENVISAGED IN 1845

Of modern theologians who have written on the Immaculate Conception and the Assumption, C. Dillenschneider and B. Capelle are among those who realize that the key to the way in which the minds of Christians, even with the Holy Spirit, actually reason, is found in what Newman wrote over a hundred years ago on implicit reasoning and development. Men, whether collectively or singly, do not normally grow in understanding through formal, syllogistic argument. This is just a statement of fact, not an attack on logic. People rather argue in a private, spontaneous, elusive way, that they themselves cannot usually analyze clearly or completely. They introduce formal argument only to vindicate their position before others. St. John of Damascus, for instance, and the anonymous mediaeval writer whom we call Pseudo-

Augustine, both introduced numbers of reasons why Mary must have been taken up bodily into heaven, yet they did not reason formally. The nearest formula we could use to reduce their process to form would be to say they used the argument from converging probabilities. One of their reasons alone would as a rule only give rise to probability. As other reasons are added, reasons which point in the same direction, one confirming the weak points of another, there comes a stage when so many converging probabilities pointing to one conclusion generate an absolute conviction. Such was the conviction of Herbert, Bishop of Norwich, at the end of the eleventh century: " Impossible, that the flesh from which the Word was made flesh should corrupt by lasting death . . . Hold, brethren, with full and unshaken faith that she was made immortal in body and soul, and sits at the right hand of God."[11]

The mysterious nature of this personal, spontaneous, informal method of arguing was thus described by Newman in a well-known passage: the mind

> passes on from point to point, gaining one by some indication; another on a probability; then availing itself of an association; then falling back on some received law; next seizing on a testimony; then committing itself to some popular impression, or some inward instinct, or some obscure memory; and thus it makes progress not unlike a clamberer on a steep cliff, who, by quick eye, prompt hand, and firm foot, ascends how he knows not himself, by personal endowments and by practice, rather than by rule, leaving no track behind, and unable to teach another.[12]

In ordinary life it is a precarious ascent and some people fall. Whether one succeeds or not in the order of nature can be judged when the process is over at the court of reason or conscience.

One might object: surely such a system of reasoning is too subjective to be of use when the Church is judging whether a doctrine is part or not of the deposit of faith. Such a process might enable individuals to reach conviction, and the con-

[11] Cf. Dom Bernard Capelle, " Théologie de l'Assomption," *Nouv. Rev. Théol.*, 72 (1950), 1014.
[12] Newman, *Oxford University Sermons*, 3rd edition, 1871, 257.

viction or arguments of one might help to confirm the
conviction, and strengthen the arguments of others, but would
this be a sufficient basis for dogma, where the Church needs
the greatest humanly possible certainty that a doctrine is
revealed before she can define?

THE INFERENCES GUARANTEED BY THE GUIDING SPIRIT OF TRUTH

This objection would be valid if one forgot the protection
and direction of the Holy Spirit. The arguments of a Theoteknos, a St. Andrew of Crete, a Modestus, a St. Germanus
or a St. John of Damascus might not appear easy to articulate
with scientific accuracy. They might fail whether singly or
collectively to convince a Paschasius Radbert or even an
Altaner. But the guiding Holy Spirit will most surely see to it
that the main body of the faithful and all the bishops will not
come to be so won over by the force of the combined considerations to the extent of agreeing that the doctrine is
contained in revelation, unless it really be so contained.
If in such a case the Holy Spirit cannot save the Church from
judging erroneously, of what value to the Church is God's
guiding and protecting Spirit? Nor must we say, as has been
said in caricature, that we renounce reason and substitute
the Church. The Church herself has only reached the conclusion by the reasoning of her children. The Holy Spirit
protects her from thus reaching a false conclusion.

THE PART OF FAITH, GIFTS AND CHRISTIAN PRINCIPLES

In addition we must remember that the Holy Spirit will
see to it that the actual considerations and arguments, together
with the gradually ensuing conviction, will come not as a
result of mere reasoning, but always on the basis of faith and
the gifts of the same Spirit, and always in the light of the
Tradition enshrined in Scripture, and in harmony with the
principles of interpretation which belong properly to the
true Church. Such a principle, mentioned by Newman,
is that of dogma, which persistently maintains that divine
truths can be, and actually are, irrevocably committed to
human language. Then there is the principle of faith, which
accepts as such the truths revealed by the Word. The principle

of theology tells us that since faith is concerned with truth, it is patient of study and deeper understanding by means of inquiry, comparison, and inference. Lastly the principle of grace holds that it is God's intention to share with us the gifts of His godhead.

The Church's life was built on such principles by the grace of the Holy Spirit. In the light of these, with the help of man's natural (and therefore usually informal) processes of reasoning, the simple faithful who cannot argue, as well as the bishops who teach, and the theologians with the help of formal reasoning—all have their share in leading the Church to the full and universal acceptance of a doctrine like the Assumption as being part of the faith once revealed. This is, I think, what Dillenschneider is referring to when he speaks of the part played by the sense of faith, or of the faithful, in the development of mariological doctrine.

THE SENSE OF FAITH IN THE DEVOUT FAITHFUL

May I be pardoned for illustrating the power to persuade possessed by Christian *pietas* when Catholic speaks to Catholic of the convictions of his innermost believing mind with regard to Our Lady by a quotation, no doubt well known to you all, from Newman:

> Mary has no chance place in the divine dispensation; the Word of God did not merely come to her and go from her; He did not pass through her, as He visits us in holy communion. It was no heavenly body which the Eternal Son assumed, fashioned by the angels, and brought down to this lower world: no; He imbibed, He absorbed into His divine Person, her blood and the substance of her flesh; by becoming man of her, He received her lineaments and features, as the appropriate character in which He was to manifest Himself to mankind. The child is like the parent, and we may well suppose that by His likeness to her was manifest her relationship to Him. Her sanctity comes, not only of her being His Mother, but also of His being her Son . . .
>
> It was surely fitting then, it was becoming, that she should be taken up into heaven and not lie in the grave till Christ's second coming, who has passed a life of sanctity and of miracle such as hers. All the works of God are in a beautiful harmony;

they are carried on to the end as they begin . . . I say, it would be a greater miracle if, her life being what it was, her death was like that of other men, than if it were such as to correspond to her life. Who can conceive, my brethren, that God should so repay the debt, which he condescended to owe to His Mother, for the elements of His human body, as to allow the flesh and blood from which it was taken to moulder in the grave? Do the sons of men thus deal with their mothers? Do they nourish and sustain them in their feebleness, and keep them in life while they are able? Or who can conceive that that virginal frame, which never sinned, was to undergo the death of a sinner? Why should she share the curse of Adam, who had no share in his fall? " Dust thou art, and into dust thou shalt return," was the sentence upon sin; she then, who was not a sinner, fitly never saw corruption. She died, then, as we hold, because even our Lord and Saviour died; she died, as she suffered, because she was in this world, because she was in a state of things in which suffering and death are the rule . . . She died, but her death was a mere fact, not an effect; and when it was over, it ceased to be. She died that she might live . . . [13]

---

[13] Newman, *Discourses to Mixed Congregations*, London, 1902, 368-372.

BIBLIOGRAPHY

Apart from books or articles referred to in the above chapter, the following are of special importance :

(a) Two recent works have gathered together painstakingly the main texts in patrology and early theology in favour of the Assumption: M. Jugie, A.A., *La Mort et l'assomption de la Sainte Vierge* (Studi e Testi 114), Vatican City, 1944; C. Balić, O.F.M., *Testimonia de Assumptione B. V. Mariae*, 1, Rome, 1948.

Very valuable evidence discovered since the above works were published will be found in A. Wenger, A.A., *L'Assomption de la T. S. Vierge dans la tradition byzantine du VIe au Xé siècle*, Études et Documents, Paris, 1955 (Institut Français d'Études Byzantines). This includes the work, quoted a number of times in the above chapter, of Theoteknos, Bishop of Livias (*Encomium in Assumptionem B.M.V.*, op. cit., 272-291).

(b) The papal Bull defining the Assumption, *Munificentissimus Deus*, is in *AAS*, 42 (1950), 453-773; also in *Ir. Eccl. Rec.*, 74 (1950), 547-558; also in *Clergy Review*, 34 (1950), 407-420; and, in English, in an *Irish Messenger* pamphlet, 1950.

(c) The petitions preceding the Definition have been published in G. Hentrich and R. G. de Moos (edd.), *Petitiones de Assumptione Corporea B. V. Mariae in Caelum Definienda ad Sanctam Sedem Delatae*, Rome, 1942, 2 vols.

(d) A complete bibliography of the hundreds of works in various languages which appeared 1950-1953 is included in *Echi e commenti della proclamazione del domma dell'Assunzione*, Studia Mariana, Rome, 1954.

(e) Two useful English books are Duhr, J., S.J. (trans. J. M. Fraunces, S.J.), *The Glorious Assumption of the Mother of God*, London, 1950; and Paul Palmer, S.J., *Mary in the Documents of the Church*, London, 1953.

(f) Most of the Irish, English, American, and other English-speaking Catholic reviews had articles on the Assumption in the year 1950.

(g) There are, of course, valuable articles in the *Dict. Théol. Cath.* and in the recent *Catholicisme*, as well as in the currently appearing supplement to the Catholic Encyclopaedia.

Our Lady, Queen of the Universe

BY KEVIN MCNAMARA, D.D.

IN the encyclical letter *Ad Coeli Reginam* of 11 October, 1954 Pope Pius XII proposed and explained to the faithful the doctrine of Mary's Queenship. In addition he established a special feast of the Queenship, to be celebrated annually on 31 May and marked throughout the entire world by the public renewal of the consecration of the human race to the Immaculate Heart of Mary.[1]

In the course of the letter, the Pope emphasized that it was not a new doctrine he was now proposing to the faithful. The Church has in fact held and lived this doctrine down through the ages. Already in the second century the doctrine finds expression in Christian art, which represents Our Lady as Queen on the occasion of the visit of the Magi to do homage to her royal Son.[2] Popular prayers testifying to an unshakable confidence in Mary's royal power have also been a constant feature of Christian life, especially from the fifth century onwards, that is, once the eminent dignity of Mary as Mother of God had been triumphantly vindicated at the Council of Ephesus. For many centuries now the faithful have recited

---

[1] Text of the encyclical in *AAS*, 46 (1954), 625-640; E. tr. by present writer, *Our Lady, Queen of Heaven*, Dublin, CTSI, from which all quotations in this article are taken. I am deeply indebted to the excellent commentary on the teaching of the encyclical, "La Regalità della Madonna: lo stato attuale della questione," by Professor Carlo Colombo of Milan, published in *La Scuola Cattolica*, 82 (Nov.-Dec. 1954), 487-497. The exposition of Pope Pius XII's doctrine on the Queenship given above and the outline of the doctrine's historical development follow, for the most part, the general divisions indicated by this author. The following I have also found particularly helpful: *Marian Studies*, 4 (1953), *Proceedings of the Fourth National Convention of the Mariological Society of America* (general theme: the Queenship of Mary), Washington, 1953; E. Lamirande, O.M.I., "The Universal Queenship of Mary and her Maternity," *Marianum*, 16 (1954), 481-507; F. M. Schmidt, O.F.M.Cap., "The Universal Queenship of Mary," in *Mariology* (Ed. J. B. Carol), 2, Milwaukee, 1957, 493-549; C. Oggioni, "Questioni mariologiche" in *Problemi e orientamenti di teologia dommatica*, 2, Milan, 1957, 407-75; T. U. Mullaney, O.P., "Queen of Mercy," *Am. Eccl. Rev.*, 126 (1952), 412-19, 127 (1952), 31-35. 117-122; and, on the general question of development of Marian doctrine, C. Journet, *Esquisse du développement du dogme marial*, Paris, 1954.

[2] G. Roschini, "Breve commento all' Enciclica," *Marianum*, 16 (1954), 419.

the Litany of Loreto, invoking Mary as Queen under many and varied titles; in the fifth glorious mystery of the Rosary they have honoured her Crowning by her Son as Queen of heaven; in their best-loved hymns they have everywhere sung her praises and entreated her protection; above all they have loved to address her by the title Queen of Mercy. Mary has been traditionally invoked too under royal titles associated with cities, provinces, and nations; and it was in full accord with this tradition that Pope Pius XI, in his radio message on the occasion of the Eucharistic Congress held in Dublin in 1932, invoked Our Lady, Queen of Ireland.

Turning to the official prayer of the Church, we find the same belief enshrined in it. The Church has approved and incorporated in her Liturgy prayers such as the *Salve Regina*, the *Ave Regina Coelorum*, the *Regina Coeli, Laetare*, and in many versicles and antiphons has publicly attributed to Mary the honour and power of a queen. Pope Pius XII quotes some of the most striking of these liturgical testimonies in the encyclical *Ad Coeli Reginam*, having earlier referred to the Liturgy as " a faithful reflection of the teaching handed down by the ancients and entrusted to the apostles."

Despite all this, the fact that the Queenship of Mary should be made the object of formal teaching by the Pope, accompanied by proofs from Scripture and Tradition and supported by theological arguments, did occasion some surprise. That it should have done so is, perhaps, easier to understand when one recalls that, before the encyclical appeared, some of the best manuals of theology contained no reference to the Queenship. Van Noort, for example, surely a *clarum et venerabile nomen*, had nothing to say concerning it; neither had Pohle-Preuss nor Abarzuza, though the latter devotes seven pages to the Kingship of Christ. Thus many had the impression that the invocation of Mary as Queen was a matter of devotion merely, not of doctrine, and bore but a tenuous relationship to theology.

From the early years of his Pontificate, however, Pope Pius XII, in statements relating to the Queenship that became gradually fuller and more explicit, was making it clear that this privilege of Our Lady was an integral part of mariological doctrine, clear in its outlines and supported by solid proofs, and not merely an honorific dignity, with little basis beyond popular piety. It is remarkable, indeed, how often Pope Pius XII has returned to the idea of Mary as Queen, and how extensively he has spoken and written in explanation of it. Some years before the encyclical *Ad Coeli Reginam*, it was already possible for a student of the Pope's Marian teaching to write:

> If we should wish to determine from the documents we have what truth Pius XII has above all illuminated in Our Lady, it seems no mistake to say: the Queenship. To document this affirmation it would be sufficient to point to the solemn act of consecration of the human race . . .
>
> The Queenship of Mary is particularly connected with her Assumption into heaven; and is above all recognized by Pius XII in the consecration of the world to the Immaculate Heart.[3]

The consecration referred to taook place on 31 October, 1942, and had special reference to the requests made by Our Lady at Fatima. As the consecration of the world to the Sacred Heart by Pope Leo XIII had been a public acknowledgement of Christ's dominion and kingship over the human race, so the consecration to the Immaculate Heart was a recognition of Mary's queenly power and a solemn entrusting of the human race to her royal protection. " We consecrate ourselves forever also to thee and thy Immaculate Heart, our Mother and our Queen," runs the formula of consecration, " that thy love and patronage may hasten the triumph of the Kingdom of God." [4] The teaching on the Queenship implied here was repeated and developed in many later pronouncements of the Pope, above all in the famous radio message to Fatima in 1946 on the occasion of the crowning of a statue of Our Lady at Fatima. In this message, later described by the Pope himself as the message of the Royalty of Mary, we find the oft-quoted words which ascribe a fourfold basis to Mary's Queenship:

[3] D. Bertetto, S.D.B., " La Dottrina Mariana di Pio XII," *Salesianum*, 11 (1949), 1-24, cited by E. Carroll, O.Carm., in " Our Lady's Queenship in the Magisterium of the Church," *Marian Studies*, 4 (1953), 61.
[4] *AAS*, 34 (1942), 345.

Jesus is King from all eternity by nature and by right of conquest; through Him, with Him and subordinate to Him, Mary is Queen by grace, by divine relationship, by right of conquest, and by singular election.[5]

Thus the way was well prepared for the encyclical *Ad Coeli Reginam* and for the institution of the feast, for which the Holy See had been so frequently petitioned.

In establishing the feast the Pope desired to accede to these requests. The project was, however, very dear to his own heart also. From the institution of the new feast he expected a further quickening of Marian devotion in the Church, with a consequent outpouring of supernatural blessings. He even expresses the hope that through this feast " a new and blessed era may be born, in which religion shall triumph and Christian peace shall reign." [6]   These spiritual truths are looked for, however, only through the instrumentality of a deeper and more widespread knowledge of the doctrine of Mary's Queenship on the part of the faithful everywhere. Thus the spiritual aim of the encyclical is linked to and dependent on a doctrinal aim, as is clear from the Pope's own words:

We are convinced that many advantages will accrue to the Church if this truth, which is solidly proven, be made more manifest to all and shine forth like a luminous torch from on high.[7]

Clearly, then, the Pope desires that in every way, and particularly through the new feast, the faithful may reach a fuller understanding of the dignity and function of Mary as Queen. Let us therefore turn to the encyclical in order to learn precisely what is the doctrine which is now to be proposed to the Christian faithful throughout the world.

[5] Ibid., 38 (1946), 266.
[6] Ibid., 46 (1954), 638, E. Tr., 18.
[7] Ibid., E. Tr., 17.

A QUEENSHIP OF EXCELLENCE, BUT ALSO OF POWER

According to the teaching of the Pope, Mary is Queen in the first place because of her matchless gifts of divine grace.[8] From the first moment of her existence she enjoys a degree of sanctifying grace which immeasurably surpasses that of the holiest of the saints. Not only the divine life itself, but all its attendant faculties and powers—faith, hope, and charity, the supernatural moral virtues and the gifts of the Holy Spirit —exist in Mary with incomparable perfection. Thus she is placed at the pinnacle of creation, second only to her divine Son. Measured by the standard of her holiness, Mary's dignity is seen to be supreme not only among human persons but also among the angels, and hence she is rightly called Queen of heaven and earth. This is one of the titles of queenship already referred to by Pope Pius XII in the radio message to Fatima: Mary is Queen by grace.

This idea, however, far from exhausts the meaning of the Queenship. For the royal dignity that belongs to Mary in virtue of her Immaculate Conception does not bring with it true queenly power. By grace Mary is Queen in the metaphorical sense only: she is beyond comparison; she is the first lady of the universe, but is not on that account a queen in the true and proper sense, exercising dominion over a perfect society and the individuals who comprise it.

Queenship in the strict sense does, however, belong to Mary. Not that she exercises royal sway in the Kingdom of God independently of the power of her divine Son. A conception that would thus duplicate or divide royal government would destroy the unity that is essential to kingship and would, moreover, be utterly opposed to the Christian teaching concerning the full and absolute supremacy of Christ. Mary's royal power is altogether dependent on the will of her Son who alone, as the encyclical says, " is King in the full, strict, and absolute meaning of the term." [9]   Nevertheless, Mary too exercises royal sway:

[8] Ibid., 635-6, E. Tr., 14-15. Cf. J. C. Fenton, " Our Lady's Queenship and her Immaculate Conception," Am. Eccl. Rev., 133 (Dec., 1955), 401-413.
[9] AAS, 46 (1954), 635, E. Tr., 14.

As Mother of Christ who is God, and as associate in the work of our divine Redeemer in His struggle with His enemies and in His complete victory over them, (Mary) shares in the royal dignity, though in a limited and analogous way.[10]

The Holy Father here assigns to Mary two further titles to queenship, and in what follows he refers to her royal power. In virtue of these titles, therefore, Mary is Queen not only in the wide or metaphorical sense, but as one who exercises true dominion, ruling over her subjects in association with her Son. The two titles are: Mary's divine maternity, already enumerated in the radio message of 1946 under the heading " divine relationship," and, secondly, her co-operation in the redemption, also referred to in the radio message in the terms " right of conquest "—conquest by Mary, together with Christ, of the spiritual kingdom of men's souls.

TITLES TO QUEENSHIP IN STRICT SENSE

Mary is Queen then, the Pope teaches, because she is the Mother of God and Co-redemptress. The Pope takes the two titles in close association, and bases on them a queenship not merely of excellence but of power. He does not openly attribute this queenship of power to Mary on the basis of the divine maternity considered simply in itself, that is to say, as a simple physical relationship of Mother to Son. He views the divine maternity in a wider context, the context of the divine plan of salvation, in which Mary has been predestined not merely to give birth to the Son of God but to accept Him as her Son precisely in His rôle as Redeemer, to enter into His salvific mission and join with Him in offering the sacrifice of redemption. The divine maternity is thus seen as the preparation, anticipation and pledge of the Co-redemption. Mary, as Mother, freely pledges herself to labour and suffer to the extreme limit required by the great public interests of her Son. Her physical relationship of motherhood rests on a spiritual relationship of faith and mutual love. The divine maternity so conceived is assuredly the basis for queenly power in the strict sense on Our Lady's part, according to the teaching of the encyclical.

[10] Ibid.

The Holy Father does not, however, settle a question that has been much discussed among theologians: whether the divine maternity, considered simply as a physical relationship, entitles Mary to queenship in the strict sense. Many theologians have elaborated arguments of a strongly juridical character purporting to prove that Mary, by the very act of giving birth to a Son who from the first moment of His conception is King of men, is necessarily a queen in the strict sense. By an inversion of the ordinary process or inheritance Mary is said to derive queenly dignity and power from the royalty of her Son. Since He possesses overlordship by natural right, by the very fact of His birth from her, to His Mother also must that overlordship be ascribed.[11] The argument fails to carry conviction, mainly because the Kingship of Christ as man is not truly owed to Mary. From Mary Christ derives His human nature, but that nature is kingly not precisely because it comes from her but because it is united to a divine person whose divinity constitutes Him eternal King.[12]

The Holy Father does indeed say that Mary is Queen because her Son is King, but he does not attribute to her strict queenship, and the dominion proper to it, in virtue of this alone. In so far as His words may be taken as referring to the simple relationship of consanguinity, they say nothing that need be taken as going beyond a queenship of honour. It is extremely doubtful, however, if the Pope at any time in the course of the encyclical is thinking of the divine maternity in this restricted way, that is to say, without at least some orientation towards that redemptive mission which she was to fulfil, and which, in fact, she had already consciously begun by consenting to be the Mother of the Redeemer.

One thing is absolutely clear, however. Divine maternity and co-redemption taken together entitle Mary to royal

[11] This argument, with slight variations, is proposed by e.g. Christopher de Vega, S.J. (d. 1672), Bartholomew de los Rios (d. 1652) and, in modern times, by Cardinal Lepicier. For references consult A. Luis, C.SS.R., "Immaculata Beatae Mariae Virginis Conceptio ejusque Regia Dignitas," in *Virgo Immaculata, Acta Congressus Mariologici-Mariani Romae Anno 1954 Celebrati*, 12, Rome, 1956, esp. 60 ff.; W. F. Hill, S.S., "Our Lady's Queenship in the Middle Ages and Modern Times," *Marian Studies*, 4 (1953), 161 ff.

[12] Cf. G. D. Smith, *Mary's Part in our Redemption*, London, 1954, 136 f.

dominion over the souls of men. Following on the passage I have already quoted, in which the Pope refers to these two titles, he writes :

> For by this association of hers with Christ she has attained that splendid pre-eminence which raises her above all creatures; from this association with Christ springs that royal power by which she can dispense the treasures of the divine Redeemer's Kingdom; and, finally, from this association with Christ derives the inexhaustible efficacy of her maternal intercession with her Son and the Father. [13]

Here we are shown two aspects of Mary's queenly power: on the one hand her mediation of graces, on the other her powerful influence over her divine Son, deriving from her motherhood.

DOMINION OVER MEN BY GRACE

A little later in the encyclical the Pope returns to Mary's rôle as mediatrix: " The Blessed Virgin," he writes, " has been given a share in that power by which her Son and our Redeemer is rightly said to rule the minds and wills of men." [14] Mary is Queen of all hearts, ruling them by the gentle and persuasive action of divine grace, always in dependence on her royal Consort and Son. The Pope goes on to explain this action of Our Lady :

> For if the Word, through the human nature which He has assumed, works miracles and gives grace; if He makes use of the sacraments and of His saints as instruments for the salvation of souls, why should He not use the rôle and work of His most holy Mother, to impart to us the fruits of redemption. [15]

It is part of the Catholic faith that God did so use His Mother, that He has given to her the privilege of distributing all graces. In this way she leads men to Christ who is Himself the common good of the Kingdom of Heaven, the end that we are all seeking. Thereby Mary performs the proper function of a ruler.

[13] *AAS*, 46 (1954), 635, E. Tr., 14.
[14] Ibid., 636, E. Tr., 15.
[15] Ibid.

The question discussed by Father O'Grady in his paper on the mediation of graces is very closely related, obviously, to the point we are discussing.[16] Though the theory, put aside by Father O'Grady, fails also to commend itself to the present writer, Mary's queenly power considered as mediation of graces may possibly include a physical intermediacy. Should this view ever be established, it would certainly add a new immediacy, a further personal quality to Mary's rule by grace over the hearts of men. However, it seems much more in keeping with Mary's rôle in the economy of salvation, with her spiritual maternity in particular, that the graces we owe to her should pass to us directly from the human nature of Christ rather than by her physical intermediacy. It was her function and privilege to give us Christ, our Saviour and Head, and to co-operate with Him in the winning of redemption. It seems neither necessary nor fitting that she should now take up a new rôle as physical channel between the Head and members of the Mystical Body. What remains to her in the period after the winning of redemption is, it seems, an indirect dispensation of graces through moral causality, and this function is certainly sufficient to assure to her true dominion by grace over the souls of men.

The Pope, of course, does not go into this question in discussing Mary's queenly power as mediatrix. The central point is that Mary leads us to Christ by enriching us with His grace, however these riches are bestowed. What the Pope does emphasize is that this queenly power of Mary is predominantly maternal; it is a point that is stressed right through the encyclical, but particularly in the section we are now discussing. Mary's concern for the human race is the concern of a mother for her children. It is because they are her children that she seeks to lead them to eternal life, even if they themselves are utterly remiss in their filial duties towards her. She brought them forth on Calvary through her part in the sacrifice of redemption; now she brings them forth anew individually by placing at their disposal the grace of Baptism. And having in this way given life to them, she watches over that life at every moment, providing for its increase, safeguarding it

[16] Cf. p. 185 supra.

against ever-present dangers, making the road easy towards its recovery should it be lost through the waywardness of her children. Her inspirations are ever inviting souls to draw closer to her Son, the first-born of all her children, according to whose image she constantly strives to form all the others. And all the time Mary, as Mother of the entire Mystical Body—and not merely of the individuals who compose it— is watchful over the larger issues in the Church: purity of doctrine, the holiness of the hierarchy and of all priests, the extraordinary vocation of the saints, the forms of religious life in the Church, the powerful spiritual and apostolic movements that are ever infusing new strength into Christian life and preparing fresh conquests for the Kingdom of God.

In all these ways Mary exercises an influence that is at once maternal and royal, combining the love of a mother with the power of a queen. The queenly dignity of the Blessed Virgin, properly understood, cannot obscure in the least her office and rôle as Mother, for the two are intimately connected. The Queenship in fact is best regarded as an aspect of Mary's maternal office: by considering Mary as Queen we see more fully what a truly noble, powerful and loving Mother she is. Here St. Thérèse of Lisieux, whose teaching on many points theologians consider it worth their while to study, has a phrase that sums up much in a few words. Mary, she says, is "more Mother than Queen." [17]   Or, if we prefer to avoid even the appearance of opposition between the two rôles, we may say that Mary is perfect Mother, and all the more Mother for being also Queen.[18]

MATERNAL AND QUEENLY INFLUENCE WITH HER SON

The second aspect of Mary's queenly power mentioned by the Pope is her infallibly efficacious intercession with her divine Son and the eternal Father. In order to watch over and provide for her children, Mary becomes a suppliant at the throne of the King of Mercy, and her prayers are all-powerful. "Having been constituted by the Lord Queen of

[17] *Novissima Verba*, Dublin, 1953, 112.
[18] Cf. Lamirande, art. cit., 486 ff.

heaven and earth," writes Pius IX in a famous passage,[19] reproduced by Pope Pius XII in *Ad Coeli Reginam*, " she stands at the right hand of her only-begotten Son, Our Lord Jesus Christ, where she makes powerful intercession for us with a Mother's prayers, obtains what she asks and cannot be refused." This maternal influence of Mary over her Son is a truly queenly prerogative.   To the queen belongs the privilege of presenting to the king the petitions of his subjects, drawing attention to their needs, obtaining pardon for their faults, and, in innumerable ways, supplying for their inadequacies.   " What is thy petition, Esther," asks King Assuerus of his queen, " that it may be granted thee? And what wilt thou have done ?   Although thou ask the half of my kingdom thou shalt have it."   And Esther answers: " If I have found favour in thy sight, O King, and if it please thee, give me my life for which I ask, and my people for which I request." [20]   The king is swayed by the prayers of Esther; how much more perfectly does Christ respond to the wishes of His Queen and Mother.   The more fully united the queen is to her king in mind and heart and will; the more perfect that partnership whereby their separate personalities combine to form a single harmonious principle of government—so much the more pervasive and effective will be the influence of the queen.   Between Christ and His Blessed Mother this union of hearts is perfect.   There is nothing to compare with it on earth, no standard in our experience by which we can truly measure it.   Moral identity of will, absolute unity of interests and unique bonds of mutual love set Mary's influence with her Son in a class apart, and ensure for it unfailing efficacy.

This queenly dominion of Mary does not, of course, constitute a distinct activity from that mediation of graces which we were discussing a few moments ago—if we prescind, that is, from the controverted question of physical mediation. If Mary's mediation of graces is, as seems most probable, of an exclusively moral order, if it is completed by intercession alone, then it is precisely and solely as Queen over the heart of her Son that she exercises maternal sway over the hearts

[19] *Ineffabilis Deus, Acta Pii IX*, 1, 618; cf. *Documentos Marianos*, Madrid, 1954, n. 301.
[20] Esther vii:2-3.

of her spiritual children. For her, to ask is to obtain, and therefore to accomplish her will, to rule men's hearts by that grace which is the object of her prayers. In this context we must rid our minds of all the imperfections, delays, detours and hesitations which we normally associate with advocacy and intercession. Here we are in the sphere of perfect mutual understanding, of a delicately tuned mutual responsiveness, of execution following immediately on the decision of the will. Mary desires, asks, obtains; Christ listens, responds, effectively commands—all in one movement as it were, so that Mary's wish is already an efficacious decision. Thus Mary's queenly influence over her Son, and her royal dominion over her spiritual children by grace, are but two aspects of a single activity. They are distinct aspects, however, and by keeping the distinction in view we acquire a fuller understanding of Mary's queenly rôle. Again it should be noted that the second aspect of Mary's power as Queen, that by which she commands the favour of the King, is also maternal, so that here too Mary's Queenship fills out our understanding of her motherhood.

INFLUENCE OF MARY'S VIRTUES

To these two aspects of Mary's queenly power mentioned by the Pope in the encyclical we may add another, not explicitly noted by him but nonetheless contained indirectly in what he says of Mary's excellence. Mary's supernatural perfection of soul and body is in itself a source of influence over the hearts of men. From this point of view she exercises over them the attraction of an ideal that is loved, admired, and imitated. Here we touch on the theme that originally inspired many of the invocations of the Litany of Loreto: Queen of Apostles, Queen of Martyrs, Queen of Confessors, Queen of Virgins, etc. Mary is the model for all these classes of saints. In an eminent or superior way she contains in her Immaculate Heart the separate vocations, perfections, and graces of them all. She is the perfect realization of each distinct ideal, and an unfailing source of inspiration for those who follow it. We may say, therefore, that Mary, in addition to being Queen by what she *does*, is already, though in the metaphorical sense only, Queen by what she *is*.[21]

SIGNIFICANCE OF *Ad Cœli Reginam*

We have now reviewed the teaching of the encyclical concerning the meaning of Mary's Queenship, its doctrinal foundations, the manner in which it is exercised. This is the teaching that is to be presented to the faithful as *certain* doctrine in the Church. The encyclical is not an infallible pronouncement, defining the Queenship infallibly. Nevertheless, the encyclical makes it impossible for anyone to maintain in the future that the true queenship of Mary is merely a probable theological opinion. All must now accept it as an integral part of the Church's mariological teaching.[22]

In the designs of the Holy Spirit it has been left to the present age to see this doctrine formally proposed by the Magisterium and explained in masterly fashion for acceptance by all the faithful. Should we wish to find reasons, according to our limited human wisdom, why this doctrine should be made a centre of attention in the Church of the present time, I do not think we should have far to seek. One thing at least is immediately obvious. Today, not merely individuals but the entire world is in imminent danger of disaster and destruction. How appropriate, therefore, to direct attention to one whose empire is the entire universe, who reigns in the hearts of men everywhere, implanting in them the rule of grace, order, and love; who is the Queen of Peace and the comforter of the afflicted; whose rule extends to the mightiest forces of nature, some of which now threaten to elude the control of men or are in danger of being wilfully set in motion for the world's destruction. At Fatima, of which I have already made mention in connexion with the Queenship, Our Lady gave proof of this supreme dominion of hers over the forces of the physical universe; the miracle of the Sun, whatever its precise nature, was an exercise of Mary's queenly power, a sign to the human

[21] Cf. Colombo, art. cit., 494 f.
[22] Cf. ibid., 488 f.

race that if the world has recourse to her in prayer and penance it will have nothing to fear from those immense, mysterious forces which today menace the entire globe.

SCRIPTURAL AND PATRISTIC BASIS FOR THE QUEENSHIP

To return to matters more directly theological, something further must now be said concerning the basis for Mary's Queenship in the sources of Revelation: Scripture and Tradition. We have already seen how a true and proper queenship belongs to Mary because of her divine motherhood and co-redemption. These doctrines are themselves revealed, and in the harmonious deposit of Marian truths revealed by Christ the Queenship has the closest connections and affinities with them. What I now propose to do briefly is to indicate the scriptural passages which were the immediate starting-point and stimulus of the Church's initial reflections on Mary's Queenship, and to show how these reflections developed through a number of stages down through the centuries. For we may say concerning the Queenship what Pius XII stated in the Bull defining the Assumption: " The proofs and considerations of the Holy Fathers and theologians are based on the sacred writings as their ultimate foundations." [23]

Nowhere in the Scriptures is Mary expressly described as Queen. Nevertheless, the Church, aided by the light of the Holy Spirit, has been able to reach the doctrine of the Queenship by penetrating beneath the immediately obvious meaning of certain phrases and events in the New Testament. [24]

In the encyclical the Pope refers to two passages in Scripture. One is the salutation of Elizabeth to Mary: " Mother of the Lord ";[25] the other is the message of the Angel Gabriel, declaring the royal dignity of the Son to whom Mary was to give birth: " He shall be called the Son of the Most High, and the Lord God will give to Him the throne of David His

---

[23] *Munificentissimus Deus*, *AAS*, 42 (1950), 770; English translation in Paul Palmer, S.J., *Mary in the Documents of the Church*, London, 1953, 101 ff.

[24] On the scriptural foundations of the Queenship cf. E. J. Smith, O.F.M., " The Scriptural Basis for Mary's Queenship," *Marian Studies*, 4 (1953), 109-115; Schmidt, art. cit., 520-24.

[25] Lk. i:43.

father, and He shall reign in the house of Jacob forever, and of His Kingdom there shall be no end." [26] The words of Elizabeth, " Mater Domini," appear to provide the true beginning of the process of development. The word *Dominus* (Greek *Kyrios*) in this passage, as in the New Testament generally, connotes divinity and royalty, according to many modern scholars;[27] if this be true, Elizabeth salutes Mary as Mother of God, Mother of the King. Certainly the Fathers and early writers find in the words " Mater Domini " a warrant for glorifying Mary, thus setting in motion a line of development which will lead to the clear acknowledgement of her Queenship.[28] The " Mater Domini " soon became " Domina ": this title is attributed to Mary in a text apparently belonging to Origen, in the general sense of Mistress, noble Lady.[29]

Gradually the idea becomes more definite and significant; the majesty and power of the Son reflect ever greater glory on the Mother, and " Domina " comes to mean Sovereign Lady —an idea that is already on the threshold of Queenship.[30] By the time of the Council of Ephesus the title " Sovereign Lady," " Domina," is beginning to be reserved for Mary by Christians.[31]

Parallel with this line of development runs another, stemming from the Annunciation account and other scriptural testimonies to the Kingship of Christ. Mary is described as mother of the King, by St. Ephraem for example (d. 373),[32] and by his contemporary Gregory of Nazianzus, who speaks

[26] Lk. i:32.

[27] See esp. L. Cerfaux, "Le Titre *Kyrios* et la dignite royale de Jésus," *Rev. Sc. Phil. et Théol.*, 11 (1922), 40-71; 12 (1923), 125-53.

[28] Cf. M. J. Donnelly, S.J., " The Queenship of Mary during the Patristic Period," *Marian Studies*, 4 (1953), 86-88. Cf. H. Barré, C.S.Sp., " La Royauté de Marie pendant les neuf premiers siècles," *Rech. de Sc. Relig.*, 29 (1939), 129-162, 303-34.

[29] In this text Elizabeth addresses Mary: " Cur me igitur prior salutas? Numquid ego sum quae salvatorem pario? Oportebat me ad te venire: tu enim super omnes mulieres benedicta: tu *Mater Domini* mei: tu *mea domina.*" *Fragmenta Origenis ex Macarii Chrysocephali Orationibus in Lucam*, PG 13, 1902, cited by Donnelly, art. cit., 87,

[30] St. Ephraem of Syria (d. 373) is the outstanding witness to this development; cf. *Hymni de B. Maria*, 16, 6 (Ed. Lamy, 2,590) and *Hymni de Ecclesia et Virginitate.* 15, 4, Lamy 4, 532. Cf. M. J. Donnelly, art. cit., 87.

[31] Barré, art. cit., 143 ff.

[32] *Hymni de B. Maria*, 19, 12, Lamy, 2, 624.

of the " Mother of the King of the entire universe." [33] From " Mother of the King " to " Queen " the transition is relatively easy, and it appears for the first time, as far as surviving evidence goes, in the fourth century, again in the writings of St. Ephraem:

> Imperial maid and mistress (he addresses Mary), *Queen*, sovereign lady, take me under thy protection, guard me lest Satan, the author of destruction, rise up against me, lest the accursed enemy triumph over me.[34]

Another factor must be mentioned in the history of the doctrine in these early centuries. In the fourth century St. Jerome declares that in Syriac the name Mary means mistress—" Domina." [35] The interpretation is by no means certain; yet it was accepted and became a commonplace in later teaching on the Queenship. Innumerable writers refer to the name Mary when discussing the queenly dignity of the Mother of God: the etymological explanation of St. Jerome becomes a centre around which the faith of the Church in Mary's Queenship crystallizes and takes shape. Whether Jerome was right matters little from our point of view here; what matters is the belief of the Church which comes to light in the context of his statement.[36]

Mother of the Lord, Mother of the King, Sovereign Lady, Queen, Mary whose name signifies dominion—these are so many stages or sign-posts in the early history of the Queenship.

LIGHT ON QUEENSHIP FROM OTHER PRIVILEGES

In the fourth and fifth centuries a new factor comes into play: the gradual emergence of Our Lady's title *theotokos*, and its triumphant vindication at the Council of Ephesus. This gave a great impetus to Marian devotion and the development of Marian doctrine, and inevitably impressed on the minds of the faithful Mary's surpassing dignity, excellence and power. The titles " Mater Domini " and " Mater Regis "

---

[33] *Poemata Dogmatica*, 18, 58, PG 37, 485.
[34] *Or. ad S. Dei Matrem, Opera Omnia* (Ed. Assemani), 2, Rome, 1747, 546.
[35] *Liber de Nominibus Hebraicis*, PL 23, 842.
[36] Cf. Donnelly, art. cit., 90.

now gradually yield place to " Mater Dei." The divine maternity assumes a predominant place in the ideas of the faithful
concerning Mary, encompassing and transcending the more
ancient titles of nobility and rank. In this way Mary's Queenship, in common with her other privileges, comes to be
attached directly to her divine maternity, thus assuming its
proper place and testifying to its *raison d'être* in God's designs
concerning her. Mary is Queen because she is the Mother
of God: hence her rank, her dignity, her power.[37]

With the divine maternity of Mary her perfect sanctity too
emerges in clearer light, and once again the result is a fuller
understanding in the Church of Mary's pre-eminence and
dignity. And then, in the sixth and seventh centuries, explicit
belief in the Assumption everywhere makes its appearance,
and Mary, in body and in soul, is resplendent with the glory
of the risen Saviour. And this glory is seen in close connection
with her sanctity, for it is regarded as the reward of her
perfect imitation of her Son and her intimate union with
Him in the work of redemption.[38] This theme was later to
find artistic expression all over Europe in paintings and
sculpture depicting the crowning of Mary by her Son.[39]

By the end of the patristic period the doctrine of the
Queenship is clearly established: a queenship especially of
excellence and grace, but also a queenship of power, of
intercession, protection, and patronage.

These ideas are greatly developed in the Middle Ages.
The mediation of graces assumes great prominence. Mary
is Queen principally through her influence over her Son and
the guidance of her children towards salvation.[40] The
Salve Regina and other antiphons clearly express these ideas,
and Mary is invoked as Queen of Mercy, whose prayers are
all-powerful.[41] In the fifteenth century this teaching appears
clearly in a Papal document, the Apostolic letter *Cum Praeexcelsa* of Sixtus IV, in which Mary is spoken of as " a Queen
who makes intercession without ceasing before her Son

[37] Loc. cit., 85, 91 f., 105.
[38] Cf. Colombo, art. cit., 492.
[39] Cf. Roschini, art. cit., 420 ff.
[40] Colombo, loc. cit.
[41] Cf. W. F. Hill, art. cit., 136 ff.

to whom she gave birth." [42] The *universal* character of Mary's mediation is not yet truly recognised, however: though she is seen as universal Queen, this rôle is not at this time attributed to her mediation of all graces to all men, but rather to her pre-eminence above all.[43]

Only in the modern period, roughly from the seventeenth century onwards, is the truly universal character of Mary's spiritual dominion clearly recognised. The doctrine of Mary's Co-redemption was the source of this final illumination. Once it was appreciated that Mary had played an integral part in the work of redemption, whereby all men were enabled to enjoy the friendship of God, it was readily concluded that her mediation of graces likewise extended to all men, without exception. In other words, by " right of conquest," Mary received a universal queenly power.[44] At this point, as in so many others in this brief review of traditional teaching on the Queenship, we are back again at the encyclical: it will now be abundantly clear that the doctrine of the Pope is solidly based on the twin sources of Revelation: Scripture and Tradition.

MARY'S QUEENSHIP IN RELATION TO THE KINGSHIP OF CHRIST

Theological discussion of Mary's Queenship has found in the encyclical a new stimulus. While giving invaluable guidance on all the main issues, the Pope has refrained from deciding a number of points that have been a matter of debate among theologians for some time. I have already mentioned the problem of the precise way in which the divine maternity contains the Queenship. I should like to conclude by mentioning another point of dispute among theologians. The question has been asked whether Mary shares in the three powers proper to kingship: legislative power, judicial, and executive. A number of writers on the Queenship, following de Gruyter, O.P., who published an important book on the Queenship in 1934,[45] have answered in the affirmative. Since Mary's

---

[42] *Cum Praeexcelsa* (28 Feb., 1476), F. Cavallera, *Thesaurus Doctrinae Catholicae*, n. 803.
[43] Colombo, loc. cit.
[44] Ibid.
[45] L. de Gruyter, *De B. Maria Regina*, Buscoduci-Torino, 1934.

is a truly royal power, they argue, and since, moreover, her
Queenship is to be understood in the light of the Kingship
of Christ, we should accord to her that threefold power over
souls and the entire universe which Pope Pius XI attributes
to Christ in the encyclical on the Kingship, *Quas Primas*.
Mary is truly law-giver, judge and executive authority in the
Kingdom of Christ.[46]

Against this conception a majority of theologians of the
Queenship have reacted, some of them very vigorously,
Congar for example, Nicolas, Luis, and Barré. In the tren-
chant phrase of Congar this, they say, is to make Mary not
a true queen but " a king of the female sex." [47] Mary, they
point out, is not in reality a queen ruling in the place of a
king, but rather a Queen who rules at the side of the King,
in intimate association with the government which He alone
formally exercises. Such is the authentic idea of queenship,
they point out: the true queen is she whom the king has made
the companion of his life, the repository of his confidences,
the object of his unique affection; she is the advocate of his
people before his throne, and exercises over them in turn
a winning and persuasive influence in the interests of good
order and obedience to the king. It does not pertain to her to
give laws, to execute commands, to judge her subjects.[48]

What must chiefly be borne in mind in considering this
problem is that Mary's Queenship is to be interpreted in the
first place not in the light of natural queenship or kingship,
even in their most authentic form, but rather in the light of
divine Revelation, of traditional ideas concerning Mary's
royal power. Only when safe guiding lines have been thus
established should one have recourse to natural queenship to
fill out the ideas contained in revelation.[49]

Acting on this principle, we find that Tradition seems to
lend little support to the conception of a formal exercise of

[46] Cf. Carroll, art. cit., 33 for a summary of the opinion of these writers.

[47] *Rev. Sc. Phil. et Théol.*, 25 (1936), 762. Cf. M. J. Nicolas, O.P., " La Vierge
Reine," *Rev. Thom.*, 45 (1939), 1-29, 207-231; A. Luis, *La Realeza de Maria*, Madrid,
1942; Barré, " Marie Reine du Monde," *B.S.F.E.M.*, 3 (1937), 20-91.

[48] This view is defended by T. U. Mullaney, " Queen of Mercy," Part 3, *Am. Eccl.
Rev.*, 127 (Aug. 1952), 118 ff; cf. Carroll, art. cit., 33 f.

[49] Cf. Colombo, art. cit., 494.

legislative, judicial, and executive powers by the Mother of God. All the emphasis is on a power of patronage and intercession, on the influence exerted over the heart of Christ by her who is at once His Mother and willing associate in the acquisition and government of His Kingdom.[50] There is here adequate basis for the suggestion of Congar and others that much may be learned about Mary's Queenship if we reflect on the function of an earthly queen at the side of her royal consort. Such a queen, by her gracious presence, her proven fidelity and her unfailing love, exerts a vast influence over the king and his entire kingdom; so too does Mary, but to an altogether supreme degree and with a perfection proper to her alone. Bearing in mind what we have already seen concerning the ideal harmony of mind and will between Mary and her Son, we may say, indeed, that, in a sense, she shares in the legislative power of Christ's Kingdom. Her will in truth is law, for it distributes all grace to men, and grace, as St. Thomas assures us, is the supreme and characteristic law of the new covenant,[51] leading men to the attainment of their common good. In this rather special sense Mary may be said to exercise the power of a law-giver. In a somewhat similar way she has a share in the execution of the will of the King, since she concerns herself with all the means and influences by which the increase of the Kingdom of God is brought about: the preaching of revealed truth, for example, the administration of the sacraments, the offering of the sacrifice of the Mass, the sufficiency of the clergy, the fight against evil spirits, the ministry of the good angels. In regard to judicial power, it is clear that it does not pertain to a mother to judge her children; yet, here too, Mary's influence is powerfully active, inasmuch as she seeks to prepare souls to appear worthily before the seat of her Son's justice, thus ensuring that her maternal pleadings for them at the moment of judgement will not be rendered useless by the obstacle of a will forever fixed in sin.[52]

[50] Cf. Donnelly, art. cit., 106; Hill, art. cit., 136 ff., 143, 157, 158 f.
[51] 1-2, 106, 1.
[52] Cf. P. R. Bernard, O.P., Le Mystère de Marie, 4th ed., Paris, 1954, 328.

QUEEN AND MOTHER

When all this has been said, however, one is left wondering what purpose is served by approaching the Queenship from the point of view of the threefold power. A certain forcing of terms is undoubtedly involved in fitting Mary's royal power into these categories, while the reality and extent of that power is sufficiently safeguarded by such concepts as mediation of all graces, *Omnipotentia Supplex*, Queen of Mercy, etc. Besides, the maternal quality of Mary's Queenship is in danger of being obscured by the somewhat rigid and juridical concepts of the threefold power. The specific lineaments of the Queenship are blurred, and Mary tends to appear as a kind of Christ-King on a reduced scale, a " smaller edition," so to speak of the original royal power. This consideration is sufficient in itself, it seems to me, to make us wary of the approach to the Queenship suggested by de Gruyter. For all that we have seen is calculated to impress on us that Mary's Queenship is, from first to last, maternal. As such it does not appear remote or awe-inspiring; rather is it brought near to us, awakening in men's hearts feelings of confidence, gratitude and love, such as they have always associated with the name of mother, and have immeasurably greater reason for associating with one whose services to them in the past, and power to help them in the future, are in absolute truth, on a royal scale.

Our Lady and the Church

By Noel Dermot O'Donoghue, o.d.c.

TWENTY years ago the title of this lecture would have seemed strange and puzzling, suggesting a devotional rather than a theological study. It will seem puzzling even today to those who have not kept in touch with what is called " scientific mariology," the Church's meditation about Mary. For some years now this meditation has united with the Church's meditation on its own nature, and the theme of Mary and the Church has come to be much talked about and much written about. Some idea of the extent of this talking and writing may be had from two facts, the fact that the famous *Société Française d'Études Mariales* devoted three of its yearly meetings to the sole consideration of this topic and the fact that the International Mariological Congress to be held in Lourdes in September of this year is taking *Maria et Ecclesia* for its theme. A glance at the topics treated at these congresses or at the bibliography—already " dated "—prepared by Father Laurentin for the 1951 and 1953 congresses of the *Société Française* will show that the theme branches off in several directions and that it would be foolish to deal with all these ramifications in a single talk. I have, therefore, decided to limit myself to one main topic, that of Mary as *type* or *prototype* of the Church.

MARY AS *TYPE* OF THE CHURCH

The expression *Maria typus Ecclesiae* seems to have been first used by St. Ambrose, but the notion that it expresses has earlier origins and is found in Tertullian and in St. Peter Chrysologus.[1] Later writers sometimes substitute the words *forma* and *figura* for *typus*, and there were other synonyms

---

[1] Cf. Barré, 63, Coathelem, 33. Full bibliographical information will be found in the Bibliographical Note at the end.

as well, but without any variation in the idea underlying the terminology. This idea had its origins in the fact that the Church, to use Semmelroth's phrase, was " rediscovering her own features in Mary's countenance." [2] It does not require much reflection to see that the Church is at once virgin and mother, the virgin-spouse of Christ and the mother of the faithful. Mary is obviously the perfect type or ideal of virginal maternity. The Church receives the word of God which grows within it. In Mary the Word was made flesh, after having been first conceived in faith—*prius concepit mente quam corpore.* These and other parallels could be summed up in the phrase, *Maria typus Ecclesiae.*

What exactly did these fathers and early theologians mean by *typus*? Was it simply a blanket term covering the various resemblances or parallels between Mary and the Church? It was a blanket term certainly, and perhaps in the minds of some writers it was no more than this. But it must be remembered that the word had already, before ever it was used to link Mary and the Church, a fairly definite meaning and belonged to a particular mental world. Newman contrasts this world with the classical world in which abstract ideas are dressed up in personal attributes. " So on monuments done in the classical style we see virtues, vices, rivers, renown, death and the like turned into human figures of men and women." Scripture, says Newman, deals with types rather than personifications.[3] The distinction cannot of course be pressed to the limit, but it is useful for our purpose. For these early writers who thought in the scriptural style Mary did not simply personify the Church in the way that, say, Pallas Athene personified the Republic of Athens. The relation was rather that of Adam to Christ or the manna to the true bread from heaven. It was a relationship which could only be understood within the whole mystery or economy of salvation and God's dealings with man. It was seen as part of Mary's vocation that she should prefigure the Church, living in the individual

<hr/>

[2] " . . . ein Wiederfinden der eigenen Wesenszüge in der marianischen Gestalt," *Urbild der Kirche,* 33.

[3] " Letter to E. B. Pusey " in *Difficulties of Anglicans,* 2, London, 1892, 59. The text appears also in *The New Eve,* a collection of the Cardinal's writings on Our Lady, published by the Newman Bookshop, Oxford, p. 32.

mode the mysteries which the Church would live in the
community mode. The Fathers and early Latin theologians
expressed this by saying that Mary prefigured *in specie* what
the Church would accomplish *in genere*, in the way that, for
example, the city of Jerusalem prefigured the whole human
race.[4] It is perhaps worth remarking that the *species-genus*
couple is not used here in the scholastic sense; neither is
there question primarily of the relation of a special or privileged case to the group of which it is a member; there is
question rather of two modes of existing and acting, the
individual mode and the community or collective mode.
Mary has lived personally, individually what the Church lives
socially, communally. This simple statement has very much
in it, as we shall see.

PARALLEL RÔLES OF MARY AND THE CHURCH

So far I have been trying to analyze what might be called
the *form* of the idea of *typus* as it appears in the phrase, *Maria
typus Ecclesiae*. To say that Mary is the type of the Church
means that there are certain resemblances which justify the
statement that Mary has lived what the Church is living, has
done and suffered what the Church is doing and suffering.
Now it is obvious that these resemblances may be few or many,
and that more of them may be discovered as time goes on and
as the Church comes to know herself better and to know
Mary better. We are in fact dealing with an idea in which
there is large room for growth. In fact this growth has taken
place and is still taking place. I have no intention of tracing
all the stages of this growth even summarily, but I would like
to say a few words about some of its principal aspects or
manifestations.

One of the earliest parallels between Mary and the Church
—it goes back to Justin and Irenaeus—was that which arose
from relating each of them separately to Eve. Curiously

---

[4] This terminology, which with its derivatives, *speciatim-generatim* and *specialiter-generaliter*, was widely used up to the 12th century (cf. Barré, 121 ff.), goes back to the *Rules of Typology* of Tychonius, a 4th century African exegete (*PL* 18, 33-46).
Cf. Barré, 120 f.

these early writers gave much attention to the Eve-Church and Eve-Mary parallels and hardly concerned themselves at all with establishing the Mary-Church relation; this latter seems to have emerged as a rather unexpected consequence of the others.[5] The Church is the New Eve born of the New Adam as the blood and water gushed from his side; Mary is the New Eve whose obedience at the Annunciation restores the order broken by the disobedience of the First Eve. It is clear that the facts that relate Eve and Mary are not always coincident with those that relate Eve and the Church; nevertheless this relating of Mary and the Church through Eve brings us face to face with the mystery in which these three feminine figures are united—the mystery of corruption and incorruption, of virginity and motherhood, of birth and death. The Church is made up of the children of Eve, yet they are born again within it, born of the Church, born of Mary. As Father Laurentin puts it:

> From these three scriptural figures, these three feminine figures, there emerges a general idea of the transfiguration of humanity saved by God and of its co-operation in effecting its own salvation.[6]

Perhaps what is most clear in the whole matter is the idea that the Church though linked by nature to Eve must find its model and ideal not in Eve but in Mary; she must become another Mary, not another Eve.[7]

The Eve parallels gave rise to another basis of comparison between Mary and the Church, that of marriage or espousals. The Church is the spouse of Christ, the new Adam. This is stated unequivocally by St. Paul in that famous passage in Ephesians where the simple moral precept that wives must obey their husbands leads him on to talk about that mighty mystery which the union of man and woman symbolizes, the

[5] Cf. Coathelem, 122: ". . . à travers tout le courant traditionnel il existe un parellelisme Marie-Église, d'abord implicite dans le thème des deux nouvelles Eve, puis s'affirmant expressément et se développent pour son propre compte."

[6] *Queen of Heaven* (E. Tr. of *Court Traité de théologie mariale*), Dublin, 1956, 42. With many contemporary mariologists Fr. Laurentin makes much of the rôle of woman as the receiver and keeper-conserver of God's gift. Cf. Henry, 43 ff.

[7] This is without prejudice to the tradition that Eve is in fact among the justified and a member of the Church.

love of Christ for the bridal Church for which He had delivered Himself up on the Cross and the love of the bridal Church, holy and spotless, for her bridegroom.[8] The Church did not have to discover this truth about herself; it was there from the beginning. Not so the conception of Mary as *Sponsa Verbi*. At first Mary is seen as the bridal chamber in which took place the marriage of the divine and human natures; she is also the model of the Christian virgin who is Christ's spouse. These conceptions are definitely patristic but they cannot be identified with the concept of Mary as *Sponsa Verbi* insofar as it has ecclesial significance. Nevertheless the conception of Mary as the personal, special unique spouse of the Word is well rooted in Tradition, and is solidly established by the twelfth century although it never became then or later a major Marian theme.

> Mary is as the spouse the first realization and the pattern of the espousal of every soul which comes to believe. She is the pattern of the universal Church for, in the words of Paschasius Radbertus, the evangelist Matthew sets her forth as a spouse to prefigure in the species, Mary, what is yet to be in the genus, the universal Church. [9]

The relationship of bride and bridegroom is, in part at least, a relationship of *faith*, and it is clear that in her faith Mary is a type and model of the Church.[10] In the matter of faith Semmelroth's phrase is particularly well verified; the Church was rediscovering one of her own features in the countenance of Mary. It was in her faith that Mary was blessed, as Elizabeth saw under the inspiration of the Holy Spirit, and this faith stood the test of Calvary when even that of Peter failed; Mary is indeed the faithful spouse and the Church may well take her as model. Nevertheless there is more in the spousal relationship than faith. Faith is an essential condition certainly, but the relationship is in itself a relationship of love, of love

---

[8] Ephes. v:22-32. Cf. 2 Cor. xi:2.

[9] Flanagan, 98. The foregoing account of the conception of Mary as spouse of Christ is based entirely on Dr. Flanagan's thesis. Cf. D. Flanagan, "Mary and the Church," 235 ff.

[10] "When we examine the patristic and later tradition on the Church as the bride of Christ it emerges . . . that the Church was the bride of Christ because she was espoused to him in faith." Flanagan, 157.

communicated and fruitful. If the Church is the spouse of Christ she must see herself as the lover of Christ; it was therefore natural that the great scriptural love-song, the Canticle of Canticles, should be understood in terms of Christ and the Church. From the twelfth century onwards the Canticle began in fact to be applied to Christ and Mary, Mary being regarded as at once spouse and mother. Since it is the love of bride and bridegroom that is predominantly stressed in the Canticle, Mary and the Church were thereby related as the beloved of Christ.

Mary is more obviously Mother of Christ than *Sponsa Verbi*; indeed it is in her maternity that she is first compared with Eve, the mother of the living.[11] Mary is not only the Mother of Christ but of the whole Mystical Body of Christ. The faithful soul is the daughter of Mary and the daughter of the Church. Maternity implies an encompassing care and attention, the giving of nourishment and shelter, action that is tender and very gentle, for that which is being brought forth is weak and fragile. To paternity belongs origin and generation, to the mother co-operation and mediation. This idea has been most wonderfully expressed by the Creator in woman, better expressed than through a thousand abstract formulations. And it would seem that in the divine intention the Church was to learn motherhood from Mary, perfect woman and perfect mother. The Church was to be a mighty organization, hierarchical, full of honour and dignity, having its laws and penalties and strength to enforce them. But the Church was also to be *Ecclesia Mater*, patient, gentle, tender, full of understanding for her wayward children, and the image of Mary has been there before her always to remind her of all this.

Tradition testifies to another likeness between the motherhood of Mary and the motherhood of the Church. The Church is not only the mother of the individual soul born at Baptism *ex utero Ecclesiae*; she is also the mother of Christ, for Baptism is also the birth of Christ *in* the Christian soul. This mothering of Christ is continued in the other sacraments, since the

---

[11] Lécuyer, 32.

giving or augmenting of grace is the renewal or growth of
the soul's life which is Christ. The Eucharist may be said
to involve a double work of motherhood; not only does it
give an increase of Christ the life of the soul, but it is itself
Christ in His Real Presence. In both cases the Church is
mother: she administers the sacrament whereby Christ is
increased in the soul, and she brings forth, as it were, the
sacramental presence and lovingly surrounds it with tokens
of tenderness.

This maternal rôle of the Church is especially connected
with the name of St. Bede the Venerable who coined the
striking and daring phrase, *Dei Genitrix Ecclesia*.[12] He finds
a scriptural basis for the conception in Matthew xii:50, where
Our Lord speaks of the true believer as His mother and sister
and brother. The Church is the mother of the Mystical Body
as Mary is the Mother of the Head of the Mystical Body.
This conception is not confined to Bede,[13] but it does not
seem to have been much developed, probably because it
comes up against the difficulty (pointed out by Father
Lécuyer)[14] that the Church in fact *is* the Mystical Body.
Perhaps the best formula is that of Alan of Lille: " sicut enim
Ecclesia Dei mater est Christi in membris per gratiam, sic
Virgo mater Christi per humanam naturam." [15]   There is,
however, another formula of Bede's which is worth quoting:
" semper Ecclesia, dracone adversante, Christum parit." [16]
The phrase *dracone adversante* indicates what seems the most
solid scriptural basis for the whole doctrine. A very strong and
constant tradition sees the woman with child of Apocalypse xii
as the Church, and there can be hardly any doubt but that the
Child who shall rule the gentiles with a rod of iron is Christ.

Here then are the main elements in the content of the idea,
Maria typus Ecclesiae. In Mary's faith, Mary's love, Mary's
motherhood the Church finds itself prefigured. Somehow
Mary and the Church reflect each other, explain each other

---

[12] *In Matt*. ii, *PL* 92, 13d. For the patristic texts cf. Barré, 73 ff.
[13] It is more particularly associated with Isaac of Stella; cf. Barré, 75. The reference is *In Assump*., 1, *PL* 194, 1729 c.
[14] P. 34.
[15] Cf. Barré, 75. The reference is *In Cant*., 1, *PL* 210, 60ab.
[16] *In Apoc*. ii, 12, *PL* 93, 165d and 166. *Apud* Barré, 74.

and complete each other. Mary has lived as an individual person what the Church is living as a community of persons. Perhaps I may recall here what I said earlier, that this rôle of *typus* is seen as part of Mary's vocation; in the divine plan she prefigures the Church. The relation is factual, objective. It is not something imagined or superimposed by theologians; it is ordained by God.

DEFINITION OF *CHURCH*

It may be well at this point to say something about the definition of *Church*. Do we mean the Church to include Mary? Do we restrict the term to the Church militant? Are we relating Mary to the Mystical Body with Christ at its head? Do we prescind from the hierarchical aspect of the Church? These are some of the questions on which theologians are seeking to reach agreement in their discussions of Mary and the Church. In one of his communications to the *Société Française d'Études Mariales* Father Nicolas, in relating Mary and the Church, not only includes the hierarchical side of the Church but places Mary too within the Church, and in fact goes so far as to make the angels part of the Church.

The question of the definition of the Church is a very large one since it involves, in fact *is*, a discussion of the exact nature or essence of the Church.[17] I beg, therefore, to be excused from discussing it even in summary fashion. I cannot, however, avoid discussing the question whether Mary as type of the Church is to be regarded as within the Church or distinct from it, and I hope to throw some light on this in the philosophical part of the paper. It is true that " the definition of names is the beginning of discussion "; otherwise we may be using words in different senses. But it is hardly necessary to give a nominal or partial definition of something with which we are all familiar in the concrete, and I do not think there would be agreement on an adequate definition.

[17] Cf. Ch. Journet, *Théologie de l'Église*, Paris, 1958, ch. 11.

MARY AND THE CHURCH "ONE MYSTERY"

So far I have been dealing with the theme, *Maria typus Ecclesiae*, as it has been handed on to us by Tradition and elaborated by the early theologians of the scholastic age. It was a very minor theme even within Mariology, and it does not seem to have affected Ecclesiology significantly at all. It is only quite recently that the theme has become a major one—the subject of articles, books and conferences. This literature on the general topic of Mary and the Church is so profuse that it is well to keep strictly to our theme and to confine ourselves to the main developments of that theme.

It is worth noting that contemporary mariologists succeed in making the " type " conception into a major theme simply by bringing together all that has been said by Tradition on the subject without adding anything really new. This is of course a common and legitimate theological device, but it must be noted that it sometimes gives more size to a doctrine than it ever had in Tradition. The first chapter of Father Rahner's book, *Marie und die Kirche*, is a good example of this. No statement is made that is not based on patristic evidence, neither is there any forcing of texts, yet the picture that finally emerges is fuller and larger than anything envisaged by any particular writer in the past. The same may be said of most contemporary treatments of the theme. It may in fact be said that it was only quite recently, in our own day, that the conception of Mary as type of the Church has attained currency and, so to speak, maturity. The theme has found favour in Germany especially, and a new terminology has grown up through the writings of what might be called the German School—Mary is the *Urbild*, *Vorbild*, *Inbegriff* of the Church (we may translate *Urbild* as " prototype " and *Vorbild* as " figure " or " prefiguration," but it is difficult to suggest a translation of *Inbegriff*. It is no less difficult to translate this term into French; the translator of Father Rahner's book suggests " représentation-contenant-la-totalité de "). The main purpose of the new terminology seems to be to emphasize almost to the point of identification the correspondence of type and anti-type.

Why has the type-conception been developed in Germany rather than elsewhere?   Probably the main reason is that Scheeben's influence is strongest there.   Now Scheeben's Mariology rests on the conception of Mary as not merely Mother of Christ but, primarily and anteriorly, spouse of the Word.   We have seen that the idea of Mary *Sponsa Verbi* is found in Tradition; Scheeben was the first, however, to put the idea at the centre of Mariology and to work it out, as he likes to say, scientifically.   It is not enough, he contends, to speak of Mary as Mother of Christ.   The *Logos* is greater than Mary and she has been taken up into the embrace of the *Logos* is an embrace which is " a figure of the Hypostatic Union of Christ's human nature with God ":[18]

> Scheeben makes it quite clear that there is found in the motherhood of Mary all that is found in the motherhood of a merely human son.   But he goes on to emphasize powerfully that the Person for whom Mary performs this office is a pre-existent divine Person . . . who makes her His Mother, who accepts her as His Mother, and who gives Himself to her as her Son.   It is this emphasis on the divine initiative springing from the stress he has already laid on the divinity of the Person who is the Son, that leads Scheeben on to the concept of " divine bride " which he applies to the Mother of God.[19]

It is clear that this conception of Mary's vocation opens the way to a closer correspondence of Mary and the Church. As long as the Church is seen as spouse of Christ and Mary as Mother of Christ there is always a contrast within the resemblances; the conception of Mary's " bridal motherhood " breaks down this contrast and allows large scope to the language of identity.   This language is not meant to imply that Mary and the Church are one reality, but that they are somehow one *mystery*.

This identification has what seems a very solid scriptural basis in the famous twelfth chapter of the Apocalypse:

[18] *Mariology* (E. Tr.), St. Louis, 1948, 1, 163 f.
[19] D. Flanagan, " Scheeben and the Basic Principle of Mariology," 370 f.

And a great sign appeared in heaven. A woman clothed with the sun, and the moon under her feet, and on her head a crown of twelve stars. And being with child she cried travailing in birth: and was in pain to be delivered . . . And she brought forth a man, who was to rule all nations with a rod of iron. And there was another sign in heaven. And behold a great red dragon having seven heads and ten horns and on his heads seven diadems . . . And that great dragon was cast out, that old serpent, who is called the devil and Satan who seduceth the whole world.[20]

This vision seems to be at the centre of the Apocalypse, the last book of the Scriptures. The passage has of course been much interpreted and the greater number of commentators over the last fifty years understand the woman to be the Community of the Just of the Old and New Covenants. According to these authors the passage can be applied to Mary only in an accommodated sense. On the other hand many commentators see a direct reference to Mary in the passage, and among these there is a group who hold that the sacred writer describes simultaneously Mary and the Church under the figure of the woman. Father Le Frois, whose account I have been following, accepts this latter view and sums it up as follows:

St. John, under the figure of the woman in Apoc. xii, *portrays Mary as the Church*. In his mind they are identified as a totality: an individual which impersonates a collective, and a collective which is embodied in a concrete person. It is not enough to say: the woman is Mary, but portrayed as the archetype of the Church. Nor is it enough to say: the woman is the Church, but portrayed in the features of Mary . . . One must say: St. John under the figure of the woman depicts Mary as the perfect realization of the Church. The supreme task of the Virgin-mother is perpetuated in the gigantic work of the Church to regenerate all men in Christ. The mother of Christ is one. In truth the intimate relation of Mary and the Church, set forth so frequently in recent years from a number

[20] *Apoc.* xii:1. The verses are quoted in the order: 1, 2, 5, 3, 9. Newman remarks appositely that such a meeting of man, woman and serpent has not been found in Scripture since the opening book. Loc. cit., *supra*.

of aspects, has its scriptural basis in the twelfth chapter of the Apocalypse.[21]

We are now in a position to understand how some writers have come to use the language of identity in speaking of Mary and the Church. There is no question of a numerical or absolute identity but of an identity of mystery, of vocation. As Father Müller puts it:

> The mystery of Mary and the mystery of the Church are one, so much so that one can be defined through the other.[22]

It must be noted that this language of identity is used chiefly by German mariologists. But the writers of what might be called the " German School " are enthusiastically committed to the theme that Mary and the Church are one mystery. Müller, Rahner, Schückler, Semmelroth may be mentioned as representatives of this school which has its source in Scheeben. These writers claim that they are simply interpreting Tradition, bringing forward clearly what is already enshrined in phrases such as *Maria typus Ecclesiae, Maria sponsa Christi, Ecclesia sponsa Christi, Dei Genitrix Ecclesia*.

What do these writers mean by saying that Mary and the Church are one mystery? Perhaps the best general answer to this question is to be found in the sub-title of Father Rahner's book on Mary and the Church: *Ten Meditations on the Spiritual Life*. For these writers meditation on the Marian mystery becomes of its nature meditation on the mystery of the Church. Mary is the Mother of God; the Church in which Christ is born daily is also mother of God. Now the more we enter into the mystery of the divine motherhood of Mary, into all that it involved of glory and sorrow, the better we understand the Church, its constitution, its history, its sacraments. " The Church advances over the dark roads of time and the

---

[21] P. 202. This is a repetition almost of what Fr. Müller had already said (*Ecclesia . . . 228*), but Fr. Le Frois's endorsement is important since it comes at the end of a minute exegetical study of Apocalypse xii. Müller in turn is echoing Scheeben: " The features of the vision are borrowed from Mary; Mary is not taken merely as an ordinary example or even as a prototype of the Church, but as a prototype that is organically united to the Church and radically concerns and represents it, and also works both in it and through it." *Mariology*, vol. 1, 15.

[22] *L'Unité . . . 36.* Cf. Rahner, ch. 9, Schückler, 140.

centuries, as long ago Mary went up from Nazareth to Bethlehem, carrying within her the Eternal Word." [23] The various
aspects of Mary's mediation are also realized in the Church
which constantly renews Calvary and is a mediator of grace
in the sacraments.[24]   At the Annunciation Mary's *fiat* is
given, to use the traditional phrase, *loco totius generis humanae*;
that *fiat* and all the suffering it entails is constantly being made
by the Church, and each soul is invited to make it for itself,
for Christ is not born within us without pain.   It is claimed
that this kind of meditation on Mary is far more profitable
than seeing her as the model of all the virtues, since in
revelation we see her in her mysteries not in the exercise
of various virtues.[25]   It is obvious that this approach opens up
a wide field for we can bring this type of meditation to bear
on all the Marian mysteries.   It must be added, however,
that in this meditation the German School keeps closely in
touch with Tradition, and asserts nothing which has not been
asserted equivalently already; what is new is the accumulation
of assertions and the scientific working out of the theme after
the manner of Scheeben.[26]

TOWARDS A MORE PRECISE TERMINOLOGY

I hope I shall not be misunderstood if at this point I confess
that I find the language and conceptions with which we have
been concerned somewhat disconcerting. The whole matter
of Mary's relation to the Church is undoubtedly attractive and
even stimulating, and there is very much to admire in the
writing on the subject. Yet the mental distress persists and
in reading the literature on the subject I have been on the
alert for any expression of this distress on the part of others.
I found it in one author only, Father Bonnefoy, O.F.M., one

---

[23] Rahner, 53.
[24] Semmelroth, 90 ff.
[25] Schückler, 92 ff.
[26] " Eine vom Rationalismus geleitete Marienfrömmigkeit verehrt die Gestalt
Mariens fast nur noch als Vorbild für menschliches Tun. Man ergeht sich in marianischen Tugendschilderungen, für die man keine andere Grundlage hat als das
allgemeine Gesetz, das, weil diese Tugenden zum Heiligen gehören, Maria als die
Heiligste sie auch gehabt haben muss." Semmelroth, 35.

of the contributors to the third and final congress devoted to our subject by the *Société Française d'Études Mariales*. He ends his contribution with the following words:

> May I be permitted to recommend for theological work the employment of a technical language. Many of our problems: spiritual maternity, mediation, co-redemption, queenship of the most Blessed Virgin, would advance more quickly towards a solution if we treated them not as poets but as metaphysicians.[27]

This is a rather strong statement, but it helps to explain the uneasiness caused in some minds by the type of thinking that is done on our subject. There seems to be profusion of imagery and poverty of thought; careful analysis of concepts advances only a short distance before appeal is made to mystery or to one of these phrases which confuse rather than enlighten. It is the scholastic in us that is distressed, for we are in the world of appearance and symbol rather than in the world of concept and demonstration. It is not an accident that the doctrine we have been considering seems to have gone underground, as it were, in the thirteenth century. That is, as far as we know, for nobody has done (or at least published) any research on the treatment of our theme by the great scholastics, and it is doubtful whether there is any great treasure to discover there. Dr. Flanagan has gone over the ground on a cognate subject and found very little. As far as I know St. Thomas has little or nothing to say about our theme.[28] Not that the theme was lost or the parallelism of Mary and the Church called in question; there were still writers who used it and who thought in terms of types and symbols. Yet the theme did not flourish in the atmosphere of high scholasticism, and it is the poorer for this.

But perhaps the theme does not admit of treatment in scholastic terms? Is there not an essential difference between symbolic thinking and rational thinking? This is not so, for

[27] P. 73.
[28] The commentary on Psalm 44 is sometimes cited to show that St. Thomas had a clear perception of the relation of Mary and the Church. It is true that the saint applied some verses of the Psalm both to Mary *and* to the Church but he keeps the applications quite distinct.

theological doctrines which at first were worked out in the atmosphere of symbolic thinking were later given metaphysical shape by the great scholastics; for example, the theology of the Mass, or sacramental theology. And indeed this must be so, for in giving metaphysical shape to a doctrine all we are doing is expressing it in terms of those first concepts which are implicit in all coherent and solidly grounded thinking. It is not my intention here to attempt to do this for the theme of *Maria typus Ecclesiae*, but I hope to be able to give some indications of the way in which it might be done.

We can begin with a term which is already in use by writers to describe Mary's relation to the Church: she is the *exemplar* of the Church. Now an exemplar idea always implies an architect or artist who does or makes something in accordance with the idea. In this case God is the architect and that which is being made to the form of the exemplar is the Church. In other words the relation of Mary to the Church is no longer static but dynamic; the Church is in movement towards Mary as that which the Church must become. Again, Mary is exercising an influence on the Church, the influence which philosophers term final causality.[29]   For many people the word " cause " means something that influences another by means of action. This is a good description of one type of causality, what is usually called efficient causality. Now final causality is just as important as efficient causality, indeed it is more important, since it governs efficient causality, and yet the final cause does not in any way *act* on the effect. Thus the idea or plan of a church in the mind of the architect does not *do* any of the actual work of building, yet it *influences* and determines everything. To say then that Mary bears a relationship of final causality to the Church is to give her a rôle of the greatest importance, and this is true even though we recognize that she is not in any sense an *ultimate* final cause;[30] it implies that her influence

[29] On exemplarity and finality see De Raeymaeker, *Philosophy of Being*, St. Louis, Mo. and London, 1954 (E. Tr.), chapter 10. Cf. St. Thomas, *D. de Veritate*, 3, art. 1 and 2; Q. D. de Potentia, 51.

[30] Obviously there can be no question of considering Mary to be an *ultimate* or *first* cause in any order of causality. Neither am I advancing the thesis that the Church is in any sense *for* Mary, nor do I wish to defend any kind of identity or

is felt or present at all times everywhere, for it is towards her the Church is growing as the seed and sapling is growing towards the tree. This way of looking at it gives movement and freedom to our theme; we are no longer dealing with a lifeless parallelism as of two paintings on a wall; we are watching the growth of an organism towards its perfection.

I do not intend to try to develop fully this conception of Mary as final cause of the Church, but there are some obvious difficulties that I would like to consider briefly. It may be said, for instance, that Mary is not simply an exemplar idea but a living person, and cannot then be seen as a final cause. The answer to this is that the existence of a thing does not destroy its idea; a thing may exist and yet serve as a model for something else coming into existence as, for instance, the human body may serve as a model for the sculptor. The same idea may be embodied in different ways, attaining existence according to different modes of existing; for example, the rule of a religious order may be written in a book or may be expressed in the life of an individual religious or in the life of a community of religious; the idea is the same though it exists in different ways. To say that Mary is the final cause of the Church is to say that the idea or conception which has attained perfect and personal realization or existence in Mary is attaining existence in the Church in an inter-personal or community way.

Between the final cause and its effect there is a very strong bond. The effect is striving to attain to the perfection of its final cause and the cause is drawing the effect towards it; the proper operation of the final cause is this *drawing* or *attraction*. The medieval phiosophers spoke of the *pondus naturae* by which each thing gravitated as it were towards its

coincidence of Mary and the Church. My thesis is that Mary is the exemplar of the Church, exercising on it a real influence in the order of final causality, in due subordination to more ultimate influences in the same order. This does not exhaust Mary's rôle in relation to the Church—as Mother of the Church she has clearly an influence also in the order of efficient causality—but it provides, as I see it, the best statement in real or ontological terms of the conception with which I have been concerned: *Maria typus ecclesiae*. Some may prefer to speak of exemplarity, but the exemplar as such does not really influence the exemplatum; if it does, then there is real causality, and it does not matter whether we speak of exemplar causality or final causality. The main thing is that the *typus*-concept should come to life in real terms.

proper end and purpose. This is Dante's " love that moves the sun and the other stars." In rational beings this tendency is intelligent and free, yet there is nonetheless attraction and response. To say that Mary is related to the Church as final cause is to say that Mary exercises a profound attraction on the Church to which the latter responds intelligently and freely. In other words it sees Mary as the beloved of the Church, she in whom the Church finds realized her deepest desires and strivings. The lover seeks the beloved because in her he is somehow perfected, he discovers his full being at some level. He is not so much seeking the beloved as seeking his own fulfilment through possession of or union with the beloved.[31] So it is that the Church seeks Mary, with this difference that Mary not only makes the Church's perfection possible but in a sense *is* this perfection. In loving her the Church is loving its own perfection; devotion to her corresponds to a deep ontological need, and it will increase as this need is better understood.

In order to carry the discussion further it is necessary to introduce another philosophical concept—that of personality. The classical definition of person states that a person is " an individual substance of a rational nature." Now rationality immediately takes the individual substance beyond its individuality, for rationality necessarily implies an object.

Mary and the Church are distinct entities with different modes of existing. Mary is a person, the Church is a community or society of persons. Nevertheless they have personality in common, and it is by analyzing this that we can see how and where they meet. Mary is a person, that is, primarily, a being who knows and loves, and who therefore exists in relation to that which she knows and loves.[32] Now Mary's knowing and loving, that by which her personality realizes itself *actually*, has one sole adequate object, Jesus

---

[31] This is not egoism but the escape from egoism. " When I love another directly . . . I discover a new existence, I am present to a new and transcendent revelation of that value I love in myself. And by that very fact I cure myself of the exclusiveness, the poverty, the solitude that are my lot and my curse, when, through egoism, I constitute myself the centre of the universe and the absolute." R. O. Johann, *The Meaning of Love*, Maryland, 1955, 43.

[32] Cf. the scholastic axiom: " omne ens est propter suam operationem."

Christ. Her whole personality expresses itself in a supreme activity of knowing and loving Him in whom dwells all the fulness of the Godhead corporeally.[33] During her life on earth she attained through contemplation and suffering an immense capacity for this activity; at the Assumption this capacity was fully actualized and it involved her whole being, body and soul. She was and is nothing apart from this knowledge and love, at once particular, immense and personal. The mysteries of her life and vocation are but modes or expressions of this activity.

The Church is a community of persons each of which is called to the knowledge and love of Christ. Each soul is thus in truth the spouse of Christ. Each soul is destined to know Christ in its own way, for each soul is unique. A deep sense of the uniqueness of the individual person is one of the most precious acquisitions of modern philosophy; both scholastic and existentialist are united in emphasizing it. The community of persons which is the Church achieves an immense and varied knowledge and love of Christ, for, in the words of St. John of the Cross, " Christ is like an abundant mine with many recesses containing treasures, of which, for all that men try to fathom them, the end is never reached; rather in each recess men continue to find new veins of new riches on all sides." [34] It is this total achievement of knowledge and love that is the whole purpose of the Church, which is therefore most accurately described as the Bride of Christ.[35] This achievement is much more than the sum of the individual achievements, since each can possess what all possess.[36] For whereas in the material order possessions engender division and isolation, since what is possessed by one man cannot be possessed by another, in the spiritual order possessions unite, so that the individual soul while retaining its incommunicable personality knows and loves Christ with the

---

[33] Coloss. ii:9. This love is, of course, also love of the Father and the Holy Ghost.

[34] *Spiritual Canticle*, Stanza 36, Peers, *Complete Works of St. John of the Cross*, 2, London, 1934, 169.

[35] Cf. Ch. Journet, *Théologie de L'Église*, 400: " Enfin l'apôtre ayant comme fondu l'un dans l'autre les deux significations de corps et d'épouse (Eph. v:28-9) on dira que l'Église est l'Épouse du Christ."

[36] Cf. Johann, op. cit., 30: " Each creature is a unique value, yet communing in its uniqueness with every other creature in *the* Unique Value."

love of the whole community, of the whole Church.   The soul loves Christ within the Church and through the Church. Love is at once giving and receiving, and that which the soul receives from Christ is a love of all men, of the whole Church; the love of Christ is by no means a personal and private affair. Its true nature and proper dimensions may not be fully appreciated by the individual soul, but it is by nature and in its dimensions an act in which the individual is not only himself but the whole Church, and it is in being the Church, Bride of Christ, that the soul is truly itself.

Mary is the model of the knowledge and love of Christ, the prototype of the perfect spouse. She alone has grasped, as far as creature can, the immeasurable riches of the Word made flesh; she alone loves Christ as He thirsts and demands to be loved by created love.   It is to this fulness of comprehension that the Church, and the individual soul within the Church, aspires.   And the Church achieves this not by emulating Mary but by striving towards such purity of faith, hope, and love that it attains, *attingit*, to Mary, and so possesses her love and knowledge in possessing her very self as *membrum principalissimum et praestantissimum*.[37]   In a sense Mary is within the Church continuing its act of loving knowledge to the very limit of creaturely possibility.   In a sense the Church is within Mary, for hers is the greater knowledge and love exploring further the unsearchable riches of Christ.   Above all Mary and the Church are united in loving.   Between the two loves there is no division; there is not only continuing but constant intercommunication, constant dialogue, constant mutual rejoicing.   For it is Christ and only Christ that each knows and loves.

The Church in seeking Mary seeks its own proper perfection, for in Mary that perfection is mirrored and transcended, yet not transcended for the Church possesses Mary.   The proper perfection of the Church consists not in thus loving Mary but in loving Christ by thus loving Mary.   The love by which it aspires towards its final cause and proper perfection is the same as that by which it rests in its final object and perfection, Jesus Christ.

[37] Cf. Barré, 89 ff., for the use of this description in Tradition.

It is not difficult to translate the language of type and symbol into the metaphysical terminology I have been using. In fact I have been using both kinds of language all along. Mary is the prototype of the Church in that she is the perfect lover, true model of the other Bride of Christ. She is the *Inbegriff* of the Church in that all the treasures of love which the Church seeks for herself are already present in Mary. Mary and the Church are identical in that their sole and adequate object is one, Jesus Christ. This unity in the object is very striking and very perfect, yet it allows diversity in the subjects; in fact it allows for a flexible and nuanced conception of the exact relation of Mary and the Church. The motherhood of Mary and the motherhood of the Church are realizations at different levels of a most wonderful and tender mode of love, for Christ was mothered not because he desired or needed a mother but because he desired to be loved in that most marvellous way.

PRACTICAL APPLICATION

It remains to say a word on the practical or spiritual application of our theme. I have already mentioned Father Rahner's book—*Marie et L'Église* is its French title. This is a series of meditations on various aspects of our theme. For example in the chapter on " Mary at the Baptismal Font " the author brings out the implications of our birth from Mary and the Church:

> If our spiritual life is so often joyless and lukewarm, the reason is that we have no longer sufficient awareness of its sacramental baptismal source . . . At the origin of this grace there is also Mary, for at Baptism Christ is born of our hearts.[38]

This sample will perhaps show how the theme of Mary and the Church may be brought to bear practically on the individual life. There is here, it seems, a very rich vein that is only now being explored. I should like, however, to

[38] P. 75.

conclude with a more general consideration, arising out of
what I have been saying a moment ago. For many people
nowadays there is consciously or unconsciously a tension
between private prayer and common prayer. Clearly there
is something wrong with the man whose prayer speaks only
of his own spiritual and physical needs; I do not mean the
hermit, for the hermit may, and as a rule is, conscious of
his insertion in the Church. I mean the mediocre person,
who minds his own business in spiritual matters, who loves
God out of his solitary heart and whose devotion to Mary is
that of the only child to its mother—of course, such a person,
does not usually think himself mediocre, and he may follow
a very pious routine. But he is mediocre, for his heart has
not opened out to the Church and his fellows; he does not
feel himself the greatest of sinners among sinners glorying
only in repentance; he does not suffer with the weak and
persecuted; he does not rejoice in the Church's triumphs
and festivals; above all he does not love Christ from out of
the burning heart of the bridal Church. This is not always
corrected by immersing ourselves in the Liturgy, for this may
be merely an escape from the personal encounter with God.

Now our theme suggests one way in which this tension
may be eased, in which the personal and social elements of
religion may be properly balanced. The more the image and
idea of Mary and the image and idea of the Church become
united in the single idea of the *Sponsa Christi* the more does
the individual feel, in his contact with the Church, the
presence of a gentle and comforting personality, even in
matters legislative and administrative, and the more does he
feel, in his communication with Mary, that universal charity
that radiates throughout the whole Church from her Immaculate Heart. His love of Christ is *through* the heart of Mary
and *from out of* the heart of the bridal Church—*ad Jesum per
Mariam et cum Ecclesia.*

BIBLIOGRAPHICAL NOTE

1. For the patristic background I have consulted the following books and articles and am entirely in debt to their authors for all I have said:

H. Coathelem, S.J., *La Parallélisme entre la Sainte Vierge et l'Église dans la tradition latine jusqu' à la fin du XIIIe siècle*, Rome, 1954. This doctoral thesis was presented to the Faculty of Theology of the Gregorian University in 1939. Its publication came about through the growth of interest in the subject over the last decade.

A. Müller, " L'unité de l'Église et de la Sainte Vierge chez les Pères des IVe et Ve siècles," *Bulletin de la Société Française d'Études Mariales*, Paris, 1951, 27-38. This is, the author tells us (p. 27) " simply a résumé " of a larger work entitled *Ecclesia-Maria. Die Einheit Marias und der Kirche*, Freiburg (Switz.), 1951. This larger work I have not been able to consult. Fr. Müller's researches are confined to the first five centuries.

H. Barré, C.S.Sp., " Marie et l'Église du Vénérable Bède à Saint Albert le Grand," *B.S.F.d'E.M.*, 1951, 59-143. This is a considerable and painstaking piece of basic research in which the evidence is sifted under various heads. Pages 63 to 72 deal with our theme.

D. Flanagan, *Mary, Spouse of the Second Divine Person—the Usage and Meaning of a Marian Term in Tradition, with special reference to the Mariology of Matthias J. Scheeben* (cited as Flanagan). This doctrinal thesis was presented last year to the Maynooth Faculty of Theology. It is the only work of scholarship I know of that has been done on the theme of Mary spouse of Christ, and it is the only examination of the Post-Albertine literature on any topic akin to our theme. It is a valuable monograph and one hopes it will be published in full. Meanwhile one may consult Dr. Flanagan's articles, " Mary and the Church," *Ir. Eccl. Rec.*, 90 (October 1958), 231-45; " Scheeben and the Basic Principle of Mariology," *Ir. Theol. Quart.*, 25 (October 1958), 367-81. I am much indebted to Dr. Flanagan for help in preparing this paper.

2. For the views of what I have called the " German School " I have consulted, as well as Fr. Müller's article mentioned above, the following:

O. Semmelroth, S.J., *Urbild der Kirche, Organischer Aufbau des Mariangeheimnis*, Würzburg, 1954, 186 pp. The few quotations I have given from this work hardly indicate its excellence. Fr. Semmelroth's intellectual parentage is clear from the many references to Scheeben and to Scheeben's follower and successor, Feckes.

G. Schückler, *Maria im Geheimnis der Kirche: zur Mariologie der Kirchenväter*, Köln, 1955. A brilliant study, at once scholarly and original. The author keeps close to the patristic texts all the way.

H. Rahner, S.J., *Maria und die Kirche*, Innsbruck, 1951. A very skilful weaving of the patristic texts to form a series of profound and suggestive meditations on Mary and the Church. This book has been translated into French under the title: *Marie et l'Église*, Paris, 1955.

3. On the scriptural side I have confined myself to the principal text: Apocalypse xii. An article by Fr. Braun, O.P., in the 1952 *B.S.F.d'E.M.* entitled " Marie et l'Église, d'après l'Écriture " provides a good (and very stimulating) summary account of the scriptural background of the general theme of Mary and the Church. The most complete and up-to-date work on the crucial text, Apoc. xii, is that of Fr. B. J. Le Frois, S.V.D., *The Woman Clothed with the Sun*, Rome, 1954, pp. 280. A full bibliography is given.

4. In general, the three issues of the *B.S.F.d'E.M.* devoted to our subject have been of the greatest assistance. From the point of view of the precise theme of *Maria typus Ecclesiae* the following articles, besides those quoted above, are important:

J. Lécuyer, C.S.Sp., " Marie et l'Église comme Mère et Épouse du Christ," 1952, 23-41. Cf. especially the last section, pp. 36 ff., where Fr. Lécuyer, from a different point of view, arrives at conclusions similar to those I have put forward in the latter part of my paper.
A. M. Henry, O.P., " Virginité de l'Église, virginité de Marie," 1953, 29-49. Cf. especially pp. 41 ff., where the author treats of " la mission de la femme."

Fr. J. Bonnefoy, O.F.M., " Marie dans l'Église ou la primauté de la Sainte Vierge," 1953, 51-73. Fr. Bonnefoy is the only author I have found to attempt to express our theme in metaphysical terms. He uses the concepts of final causality and exemplarity (he seems to assume a distinction between the two which he does not explain) as well as efficient causality. His treatment of the thesis that Mary is the purpose of everything—the *negotium saeculorum*—is especially noteworthy (pp. 62 ff.).

J. M. Nicolas, O.P., " Marie et l'Église dans le plan divin," 1953, 159-69. As the title indicates this article considers the general theme of Mary and the Church from the point of view of finality. Fr. Nicolas does not take the philosophical side of the analysis very far. It is worth remarking that the article aims at drawing together the threads of all the previous discussions: it would seem then that the concept of finality is central in the whole discussion, even though it was not much used.

For a full bibliography of the general theme of Mary and the Church cf. the 1951 and 1953 numbers of the *B.S.F.d'E.M.* A critical estimate of some of the contemporary writing on the subject will be found in the Roman Servite review *Marianum*, 47 (1953), by G. Philips (fasc. 4, 436-511). The best and most comprehensive treatment in English of the general theme is the article entitled " Mary and the Church " by Cyril Vollert, S.J., in vol. 2 of the American *Mariology* (Ed. J. B. Carol), Milwaukee, 1958. The author does not concern himself much with the topic of *Maria typus ecclesiae*. (See, however, p. 560).

INDEX OF SUBJECTS

INDEX OF PERSONS